Women in Qing China

Women in Qing China

Bret Hinsch

ROWMAN & LITTLEFIELD
Lanham • Boulder • New York • London

Published by Rowman & Littlefield
An imprint of The Rowman & Littlefield Publishing Group, Inc.
4501 Forbes Boulevard, Suite 200, Lanham, Maryland 20706
www.rowman.com

86-90 Paul Street, London EC2A 4NE

Copyright © 2022 by The Rowman & Littlefield Publishing Group, Inc.

All rights reserved. No part of this book may be reproduced in any form or by any electronic or mechanical means, including information storage and retrieval systems, without written permission from the publisher, except by a reviewer who may quote passages in a review.

British Library Cataloguing in Publication Information Available

Library of Congress Cataloging-in-Publication Data
Names: Hinsch, Bret, author.
Title: Women in Qing China / Bret Hinsch.
Description: Lanham : Rowman & Littlefield, [2022] | Series: Asian voices | Includes bibliographical references and index.
Identifiers: LCCN 2021053326 (print) | LCCN 2021053327 (ebook) | ISBN 9781538166390 (cloth) | ISBN 9781538166406 (paperback) | ISBN 9781538166413 (epub)
Subjects: LCSH: Women—China—History. | Women—China—Social conditions. | China—Social life and customs—History. | China—History—Qing dynasty, 1644-1912.
Classification: LCC DS754 .H646 2022 (print) | LCC DS754 (ebook) | DDC 305.40951—dc23/eng/20211202
LC record available at https://lccn.loc.gov/2021053326
LC ebook record available at https://lccn.loc.gov/2021053327

I must ask why women
Must yield to men?
Heaven should forbid this!

—Gu Zhenli[1]

Contents

Introduction		ix
1	Family	1
2	Marriage	21
3	Government	33
4	Wealth	49
5	Education	65
6	Virtue	89
7	Image	111
8	The Late Qing	123
Conclusion		135
Glossary		141
Notes		147
Bibliography		165
Index		191

Introduction

Historians love turning points, as they make a narrative of past events seem more dramatic and consequential. Because of this foible, they often describe the history of China as a series of dramatic transitions. Several shifts stand out as particularly significant. In antiquity, Qin Shihuang united China and established the emperor system to rule this vast domain. Much later, the transition between the Tang and Song dynasties around the tenth century stands out as another major turning point. The Japanese historian Naitō Konan declared that titanic shifts in economy, social structure, and governance at that time mark the beginnings of China's modern history. The Ming and Qing dynasties are often identified as a third major turning point. In the late imperial era, China became more prosperous, populous, and expansive than ever before. This book examines the circumstances that women faced during this final period of imperial China's major transformations.

In the field of Chinese women's history, the late imperial era stands out for what feminist scholars refer to as declension—an overall decline in women's status and opportunities.[1] From the Yuan dynasty onward, women's inheritance rights contracted. Emperors and officials constructed administrative systems intended to insulate empresses from affairs of state. And women's freedom of movement continued to decline. In fact, most women preferred to stay at home because their crippled bound feet made walking excruciatingly painful. Housebound women could not participate in most types of labor, decreasing their economic potential. Most confined themselves to domestic chores and home industries such as spinning and weaving.

Historians hold different views on when the general decline in female status began. Until recently, many scholars identified the Song dynasty as the start of this regression. They assumed that the emergence of Neo-Confucian ethics initiated increased restrictions on female autonomy. In recent years, revisionists have challenged this interpretation, arguing that the conquest dynasties of Jin and Yuan that succeeded the Northern Song saw the beginnings of significant regression in women's status. They contend that certain aspects of steppe culture, together with the general cruelty of these authoritarian regimes, diminished female autonomy. Regardless of which of these views is correct, female status had already undergone a major decline long before the Qing dynasty. The outcome of long-term trends that began much earlier conditioned the general circumstances of Qing women.

Historians have divided and subdivided the late imperial era into shorter periods, each with distinctive features. Most fundamentally, they distinguish the basic features of the two dynasties that constitute this era. Although the term "late imperial" brings together the Ming and Qing dynasties, these eras differed in many ways. During the Ming, ordinary people had new opportunities to make money and elevate their position in society, yet they also suffered under a long succession of unusually cruel and inept rulers. In contrast, the Qing emperors were generally capable and diligent. The Manchu Empire was also much larger and more diverse than the previous dynasty. The Ming and Qing can each be further subdivided into discrete periods marked by distinctive characteristics. Most obviously, the early and late Ming dynasty differ in some fundamental ways. While the early Ming was authoritarian, autarchic, and culturally orthodox, during the latter part of the dynasty the government ruled with a far lighter touch, unleashing economic and cultural effervescence.

Historians divide the Qing dynasty into several distinct eras. When the Manchus conquered China in the seventeenth century, at first they lacked stable institutions. A systematic administrative framework emerged during the High Qing, the era from about 1680 to 1820. During the dynasty's highpoint, a succession of three outstanding emperors ruled China for more than a century—Kangxi, Yongzheng, and Qianlong. Like hereditary monarchs elsewhere, most Chinese emperors were mediocre or worse, so such a long period of competent rule seems almost miraculous. A population boom attested to the impact of this long stretch of good government. In 1700 China's population stood at about 150 million, but by 1850 it had ballooned to 430 million.[2] The economy expanded in tandem, and both trade and manufacturing became increasingly sophisticated. Farmers employed agricultural techniques that raised their productivity to unprecedented levels.[3] Education became more widespread, for both men and women. And the state financed impressive cultural projects, including massive compendia intended to sum up and preserve the quintessence of Chinese learning.

The situation deteriorated during the late Qing, which ran from the 1860s until the end of the dynasty. At that time, protracted population growth gave rise to severe economic troubles.[4] Some regions, particularly in the southeast, had become so overpopulated that farmers lacked sufficient land. Even though the fields yielded rich harvests, many rural families suffered food shortfalls or outright destitution. A series of crises sent the weakened state into terminal decline. In 1842, the First Opium War ended with China's defeat by Great Britain. Many historians single out this event as a catastrophic blow so intense that the nation has yet to fully recover to this day. Prior to incursions by Western powers, Chinese had traditionally regarded themselves as the world's only fully civilized people, living in the precise center of the realm they called Heaven and Earth. When a relatively small English force crushed the Chinese military, perceptive members of China's elite realized that they were being forced into a subordinate position in a world system dominated by distant powers. Foreigners had no interest in China's ancient classics or refined poetry. They put much greater value on practical matters, such as science, technology, industry, and weapons. When Chinese judged themselves by

Figure 0.1. Manchu Woman
Wikimedia Commons | Wellcome Images

these foreign criteria, they began to perceive their country as alarmingly backward (figure 0.1).

As the dynasty tottered, rebellions broke out in many places. Most calamitously, rebels centered in the lower and middle Yangtze valley proclaimed their intention to overthrow the Qing dynasty and replace it with a utopian state called the Taiping Heavenly Kingdom. Inspired by a mishmash of Chinese and Christian beliefs, at first the insurgents were surprisingly successful. The Taiping army captured Nanjing, former capital of the Ming dynasty, and established a government that ruled the surrounding region. Rebels battled government troops from 1850 to 1864, one of the bloodiest wars in world history. During the ensuing battles, famines, and plagues, somewhere between twenty and thirty million people died. To put that number in perspective, about six million people died during the Napoleonic Wars. Although the Qing eventually quelled the rebellion, the dynasty had been fatally weakened. The court and officialdom spent the remaining decades of the dynasty struggling to maintain order and trying to cope with the unprecedented challenges posed by aggressive foreign powers.

Of course, the history of the Qing consists of far more than humiliations, shocks, and turning points.[5] The dynasty is particularly notable for the ethnicity of its rulers, which affected China in many ways. The Qing was the last, and perhaps most successful, of the conquest dynasties that ruled over Chinese for a large portion of imperial history. Although the ruling elite called themselves Manchu, in fact they did not constitute a unitary people. Manchu was a constructed identity encompassing Jurchen nomads and their allies from various cultures. Some Manchus were even descended from Han Chinese. Rather than seeing the Manchus as a race, historians consider them a political grouping created specifically to conquer and occupy China.

The Manchus centered on a tribal clan called Aisin-Gioro. Under a succession of gifted chieftains, this clan attracted support from surrounding peoples and appropriated useful Chinese ideas and organizational techniques. The Aisin-Gioro began using Mongol script to write the Manchu language, which they used to build up effective administrative and military institutions. In the early seventeenth century, Manchu leaders initiated an organizational scheme known as the banner system. Eventually there were eight banners, each named after the color of an identifying emblem. Each banner functioned as a military, economic, and residential unit. This innovative system allowed the Manchus to transform their entire society into an effective war machine.

The Manchus rapidly advanced their government system by assimilating Chinese bureaucratic techniques and ideology. Many capable Chinese felt deeply disappointed with the decayed Ming government, and some went north to serve the Manchus. However, the Manchus did not simply superimpose a Chinese superstructure on their own society. Manchu chieftains had to deal with many other peoples besides the Chinese, such as Mongols and Tibetans. Manchu rulers used different institutions and procedures to manage relations with each ethnic group, giving rise to a complex political system under which they took on multiple identities and managed each part of their growing realm in different ways. These flexible arrangements set down the blueprint for the subsequent multiethnic Qing Empire.

In the mid-seventeenth century, a combination of political malfeasance, epidemics, crop failures, and other disasters caused the Ming system to fail. The Chinese rebel Li Zicheng captured Beijing and proclaimed it the capital of a new dynasty he called Shun. Although Li styled himself an emperor, in fact he was simply a bandit, and his horde of followers were only interested in rape and plunder. When they raided central China in search of loot, Ming forces defeated them. However, rebels killed the father of the Chinese general Wu Sangui, causing this important military leader to lose faith in the Ming. Wu led his troops to occupy Beijing and handed the capital city over to the Manchus, as he considered them best positioned to restore order and institute a new dynasty. In 1644 the Manchu Shunzhi emperor ascended the throne in Beijing. Although previous Manchu rulers had styled themselves emperors of a Chinese-style dynasty called Qing ("pure"), Shunzhi (r. 1643–1661) was the first Manchu to reign from within China. Thereafter, the conquest of north China came easily, as local leaders welcomed a competent government that could put an end to the pandemonium.

The Manchus ordered their male Chinese subjects to shave their foreheads and bind their hair into a long queue, a traditional symbol of submission in Jurchen society. They also ordered Han women to unbind their feet, as the Manchus lacked this custom and found it repellent. Both edicts provoked fury, taking the Manchus by surprise. They immediately rescinded the prohibition of footbinding but continued to insist that men adopt the unfamiliar new hairstyle. In consequence, some surrendered areas rose up in revolt.

Conquering south China was far more difficult than pacifying the north. Ming forces took a stand at the prosperous city of Yangzhou, where the two sides fought a bitter battle. Manchu soldiers were angered by this show of defiance, so when the city finally fell, they took out their wrath on the civilian population. They raped and murdered an untold number of the city's residents, an event that came to be known as the Yangzhou Massacre. An eyewitness who recorded this terrible event emphasized how Qing forces brutalized women in particular.

> Some women came up, and two among them called out to me.... They were partially naked and they stood in mud so deep that it reached their calves. One was embracing a girl, whom a soldier lashed and threw into the mud before driving her away. One soldier hoisted a sword and led the way, another leveled his spear and drove us from behind, and a third moved back and forth in the middle to make sure no one got away. Several dozen people were herded together like cattle or goats. Any who lagged behind were flogged or killed outright. The women were bound together at their necks with a heavy rope—strung one to another like pearls. Stumbling with each step, they were covered with mud. Babies lay everywhere on the ground.[6]

The carnage at Yangzhou was not unique. The Manchus massacred hundreds of thousands of civilians in other southern cities as well.

These atrocities shaped the initial Chinese reaction to the Qing. Writers composed poems and stories about the fall of Yangzhou, often focusing on the victimization of women. A poem by the scholar Gu Yanwu (1613–1682) described a pathetic scene of Chinese women being sent off to an unknown fate among nomadic conquerors.[7]

> Three hundred boats headed north,
> Every single one filled with fair ladies.
> Wu beauties, hugging camels,
> Enter the northern pass to ringing fife music.

Wu Jiaji (1618–1684) described women being killed for resisting rape. Rather than pitying them as passive victims, he praised them as righteous martyrs who sacrificed themselves to defend their chastity.[8]

> The husband had already died,
> What more could the wife hope for?
> She gave her brains to the walls,
> Her heart and lungs, she gave to the enemy.
> He did not balk at eviscerating and decapitating her—
> He had to make the onlookers shudder and cower like cows and sheep.

Literature portrayed the Manchus as rapacious barbarians, poisoning popular Chinese attitudes toward their new masters.

Although the Manchus quickly occupied north China, the conquest of the rest of China took four decades. Manchu forces had to overcome a succession of Ming emperors and pretenders, loyalists, warlords, and bandits. During this long period of conquest, the Manchus focused on consolidating their hold over China. When the Shunzhi emperor suddenly died of smallpox at age twenty-three, the Qing had yet to institute a comprehensive system of administration.

It was up to the Kangxi emperor (r. 1661–1722) to establish the enduring institutions of the Qing. Kangxi was intelligent, curious, cultured, and talented in many ways. Most importantly, he was not only a martial emperor who personally led successful military campaigns but also distinguished himself as a diligent and competent administrator. At the beginning of the dynasty, Manchu authorities treated the Chinese as a conquered people, but Kangxi decided to embrace the political legacy of his subjects. He established the Qing system of government atop a framework of traditional Chinese administrative practices. Although the Manchu Empire included vast regions inhabited by various peoples, China was the undisputed core of the realm. In adopting time-tested Chinese institutions, Kangxi stabilized the dynasty and won support from his Han subjects.

Manchu authorities sought to minimize the size of government to reduce the burden on ordinary people. Tax rates were low and officials relatively few. To rule with such a light touch, the state relied on local elites to help maintain order. The Qing won the Chinese gentry's support by granting them opportunities and privileges. Whereas some Ming emperors had seized large landholdings, the Qing respected the property rights of the wealthy. They gave the gentry legal authority over their bondservants and tenants. And civil service examinations brought talented men from wealthy landowning families into government service. These measures forged a de facto alliance between the throne and local community leaders. In addition, lineages, guilds, charities, and religious groups aided the state by performing many basic services. Until the nineteenth century, this minimalistic model of administration worked extremely well. Compared to the chaos and misrule of the Ming dynasty, the Qing stands out for its relatively effective institutions.

Kangxi's reign lasted sixty-one years, the longest of any emperor in Chinese history. When he ascended the throne, the new dynasty's prospects seemed doubtful. By the time of his death, China was at peace and thriving. His successor Yongzheng (r. 1722–1735) may have lacked his father's brilliance, but he was diligent and realistic. He expressed himself bluntly and surrounded himself with similarly plainspoken advisers. The Yongzheng emperor furthered Kangxi's project of refining the administrative system.

Yongzheng was succeeded by the Qianlong emperor (r. 1735–1796). Qianlong's reign could have been even longer than that of his illustrious grandfather, but he abdicated after sixty-one years as a show of filial respect. Like his predecessors, Qianlong believed that the government should not demand too much from the populace. He kept taxes low and avoided excessive meddling in the economy. Overall, Qianlong believed that wealth should remain in the hands of the people instead of being handed over to government officials, as they would likely squander it.

Besides distinguishing himself as a talented administrator, Qianlong excelled in other pursuits as well. He was both a warrior and a keen aesthete. Qianlong expanded the realm considerably by conquering a large region to the west of China proper that he named Xinjiang (New Dominion). He also assembled perhaps the most remarkable art collection of any emperor since the Song dynasty.

The three successive reigns of Kangxi, Yongzheng, and Qianlong constitute the High Qing, the dynasty's golden age. Economic policy at this time differed from previous dynasties.[9] Government officials generally refrained from interfering with commerce, leaving merchants and craftsmen with more leeway to manage their own affairs. To fill the void of the retreating state, guilds regulated wages and prices. Moreover, unlike previous eras, almost all land was under private ownership. The expanding commercial economy integrated agriculture with the market forces. Cash crops proliferated, and immense amounts of cotton, sugar, tea, and tobacco were transported between provinces.

The successes of the High Qing gave ordinary people confidence. They had more children, expanding the population to an unprecedented level. Unlike Europe, which was rapidly urbanizing, most of China's population growth took place in the countryside. The growing demand for farmland lured large numbers of Han migrants into sparsely populated regions. They surged into frontier regions in every direction: Taiwan, Yunnan, Xinjiang, and the northeast. They also moved up into the mountains, where they adopted new ways of life appropriate to the spare environment. These massive movements of people led to interethnic rivalries and conflicts but also spread Chinese civilization farther than ever before.

In terms of culture, the Qing initially repudiated the excesses of the late Ming. The end of the previous dynasty had seen brilliant cultural effervescence but also shameless hedonism and nihilism. Louche literature circulated freely, some of it blatantly erotic. Early Qing officials and scholars reacted by encouraging dignified propriety. The Manchus detested erotic literature, and in 1714 the government banned pornographic fiction. Ming freethinking had also nurtured critical opinions, and the Qing state sought to repress these unsettling ideas by reasserting Neo-Confucianism orthodoxy. As creative thought fell into disfavor, educated men turned to less controversial topics of discourse. Whereas Ming thinkers had enjoyed speculating about abstract topics such as metaphysics, the intellectual elite of the Qing preferred practical issues such as administration and family management.

Ming merchants had fueled the rise of middlebrow culture, and their Qing counterparts continued to demand similar types of novels, performances, and artworks. The scope of literacy expanded notably during this time, giving commercial fiction a larger audience. Storytelling and stage plays made popular culture easily accessible, even to the illiterate. Even educated literati imbibed these influences and wrote popular fiction. Popular literature and performances were more than just entertainment. For many people, commercial printed fiction and oral performances served as the main ways that they learned about the world. Women absorbed ideas about normative female behavior in this manner.

Academic learning also underwent notable innovations. During the heyday of the Qing, scholars undertook critical investigations of classical writings, rejecting airy speculations in favor of hard empiricism. Scholars affiliated with the so-called Han Learning (Hanxue) movement researched highly technical fields such as philology, epigraphy, and orthography. They endeavored to purge the Confucian classics of accumulated copying errors, forgeries, and interpolations to recover the unblemished wisdom of the ancients. These investigations led scholars to criticize Song dynasty Neo-Confucian thinkers, particularly the revered Zhu Xi (1130–1200). Successive governments had made Zhu's opinions canonical, and everyone studying for the civil service exams had to memorize his interpretations of the classics. Scholars affiliated with Han Learning read key texts in ways that contravened many of Zhu Xi's explanations. Interpreting the classics differently had important implications. Because these texts constituted the foundation of intellectual discourse, widespread revisionism in classical studies allowed new ideas to emerge.

Qing scholars also sought to collect and classify vast bodies of knowledge into accessible compendia. The Kangxi emperor assembled a group of lexicographers to compile a comprehensive dictionary of the Chinese language. Given the vast number of characters that had been invented since the Bronze Age, this was an audacious project. After five years of painstaking research, they published the *Kangxi Dictionary* (*Kangxi zidian*). With entries on 47,035 Chinese characters, it was by far the most inclusive dictionary that had ever been created. Subsequently, Qianlong undertook another stunningly ambitious academic project. He ordered a large group of scholars to review all known books and manuscripts and publish the most significant ones in a massive compilation. The committee selected and edited 3,450 books, which were then copied using a standard format. They published seven sets of *Complete Library in Four Sections* (*Siku quanshu*), each consisting of 36,000 volumes. These unprecedented academic projects helped organize the vast corpus of Chinese learning.

The monarchs who succeeded Qianlong may not have been incompetent, but they lacked vision and drive. The Jiaqing (r. 1796–1820) and Daoguang (r. 1820–1850) emperors dithered and hesitated to make important decisions. Under their weak leadership, government morale fell, corruption rose, and administration languished. Population increases continued to reduce the average size of peasant plots, giving rise to widespread destitution and fomenting discontent. These troubled circumstances led adherents of a religious sect called White Lotus to rebel, plunging the realm into chaos. Although the state quelled the rebellion, the Qing never completely recovered from this shock. To make matters worse, currency instability and insufficient precious metal for coinage hit the economy hard, causing a lengthy economic depression. Because the Qing took a minimalist approach to governance, these difficult challenges overwhelmed the bureaucratic apparatus.

The Qing also faced a formidable new threat from abroad. European powers had long chafed under a highly regulated system of imports and exports that restricted trade. The British were particularly incensed by Chinese suppression of opium imports, as this drug was mostly grown in their Indian possessions. Whereas Europeans had traditionally been awed by China's size and strength, during the nineteenth century they recognized a clear shift in the balance of power. By 1840 China's per capita GDP was only about one-fifth that of Great Britain.[10]

Although China's leaders remained blithely confident in their innate superiority, foreign powers perceived their growing advantage and attacked. The First Opium War (also called the First Anglo-Chinese War), which began in 1839, forced Chinese to confront a modern Western army and navy for the first time. This experience came as a shock. Previously Qing forces had repeatedly vanquished numerous opponents in every corner of their vast realm. This time, however, a compact European force readily overcame China's military. The humiliating Treaty of Nanjing of 1842 ceded Hong Kong to Great Britain and opened Chinese ports to foreign traders. This war marked the beginning of a long series of threats and incursions by Western powers. Europeans repeatedly pummeled China to gain more privileges, exacerbating the growing sense of failure and crisis.

A second shock hit China soon after, almost bringing down the dynasty. In the 1850s, a school teacher named Hong Xiuquan (1813–1864) read a pamphlet written by a Christian missionary. He started having religious visions and came to believe that he was the younger brother of Jesus Christ. Hong mixed Christian dogma with a hodgepodge of traditional beliefs and declared the advent of the Kingdom of Heavenly Peace (Taiping Tianguo). He shared his revelations with others and attracted a group of believers from society's margins. When famine struck, Hong took the opportunity to lead an uprising with the intention of toppling the Qing and replacing it with a theocracy.

The Taiping rebels captured Nanjing, the former southern capital of the Ming dynasty, and turned it into their religion's holy city. They burned down the temples of rival religions and forced residents to attend sermons and pray together. The rebel government reorganized each occupation and service into centralized organizations headed by regime officials, disrupting the economy. They also tried to reform gender relations. Authorities prohibited footbinding and prostitution, encouraged women to come out of seclusion, and even allowed them to serve in government. The Qing army cooperated with local militias to bring down the Taiping rebels. After a lengthy conflict, they succeeded in suppressing the fifteen-year rebellion. However, this cruel war laid waste to much of south China. Afterward the southern economy recovered only gradually. This enormous military campaign was also massively expensive. The government issued large quantities of paper currency to defray expenses, setting off rampant inflation.

After the Meiji Restoration of 1868, Japanese rapidly forged an industrial society with modern institutions, allowing them to field a formidable army. Although China fixated on the threat posed by European powers, the greatest shock eventually came from an emboldened Japan. Conflict over Korea culminated in the Sino-Japanese War of 1894. To China's shock and horror, the Japanese army easily defeated Qing forces. Chinese had always dismissed the Japanese as insignificant barbarians on the edge of the civilized world, so they found this defeat unbearably humiliating. This war exposed the terminal weakness of the Qing Empire, and the populace reacted with fury. Reformists sought to create a constitutional monarchy while revolutionaries agitated to overthrow the dynasty. In 1911 an army uprising incited revolts across the country. Faced with pervasive opposition, the Qing dynasty collapsed, to be replaced with a republic.

In large part, the building blocks that constituted the lives of Qing dynasty women were the outcome of centuries or even millennia of developments.[11] Many foundational ideas about married life, kinship, and work had emerged long before the Qing dynasty began. Basic work roles became associated with gender as early as the Neolithic period. Soon after China's unification, monogamy became the standard conjugal bond. Early writers set down many other fundamental gender norms that guided people's thinking until the end of imperial history.

Historical precedents regarding gender roles often seemed unclear or even contradictory, confronting people with a range of options. For example, the ancient rites depicted marriage as a solemn bond that a couple took to honor the ancestors and produce descendants. Yet some late Ming dynasty writers considered a companionate marriage grounded in shared sentiments (*qing*) the ideal union.[12] Both visions of married life had some appeal to the people of the Qing. Which were they supposed to choose—ritual propriety or emotional fulfilment? The answers to these sorts of questions were never obvious.

When taking in the grand sweep of Chinese women's history, a major disjunction stands out. Beginning around the Jin and Yuan dynasties, women's status clearly declined.[13] At that time, Neo-Confucianism became the most important ideology, providing theoretical justification for restricting female autonomy. Thereafter women had fewer inheritance rights. Remarried widows lost their dowries. Chastity became an increasingly important virtue. And footbinding eventually became so common that a woman with normal feet would find it almost impossible to marry well. By the beginning of the Qing, these earlier developments constituted the background of women's lives.

Most of these restrictive ideas had a long history, making them seem orthodox and authoritative. Yet people did not always accept this legacy uncritically.[14] Many traditional values conflicted, prompting discussions about which took priority. Even some men questioned the assumption that the sexes are innately unequal. However, the significance of these critiques should not be exaggerated. They had limited scope and exerted little impact on the behavior of average people. Imperial China never gave rise to anything akin to modern feminism. Women also related to Chinese gender norms in different ways depending on their cultural orientation. For example, Taiwan's aboriginal tribes may have been living under Qing rule, but their attitudes toward marriage, family, and work were often extremely different from those of the island's Han residents.[15] Within the diverse Qing Empire, women of various ethnicities faced a range of restraints and opportunities.

When the Qing began, scholars debated the reasons for the collapse of the previous dynasty. Although the Ming had faced considerable administrative and military challenges, early Qing thinkers attributed its decay to a precipitous fall in morals. This assessment inspired a reaction against the extravagance of late Ming culture.[16] To avoid the mistakes of the past, Qing thinkers reasserted conservative Neo-Confucian values, which included severe rules regarding women's behavior. The state apparatus enthusiastically promoted conservative female virtues and literati wrote at length about women's ethics.

Confucianism grew out of a recognition that the norms of social relations inevitably restrict human agency. Confucian thinkers realized that absolute freedom of the individual is an impossibility. To thrive, people must conform to the expectations of those around them. However, they also recognized that each individual can exercise a degree of creativity when deciding how to carry out the obligations that accompany key social roles.[17] Given the space for personal action, some historians have recently put more emphasis on the agency of Chinese women. They argue that women often managed to exercise considerable autonomy, in spite of the restrictions they faced.[18] A savvy woman could act thoughtfully and strategically, either conforming to expectations or transgressing them according to particular circumstances.[19] Sometimes she might act out the roles of ideal wife and daughter-in-law to gain approval. At other times she could behave jealously to force her husband to do her bidding. This sort of pragmatic strategizing often appears in literature written by women. Female poets also employed anger, sarcasm, and assertiveness to broaden their personal agency.[20]

Recovering female agency gives a more positive view of the lives of Qing women. They may have faced many restrictions and expectations, but this did not doom them to a meaningless existence. Even when women were confined to the home, they still had ways to socialize, teach, learn, work, and use their talents and creativity. The female realm may have been highly constrained, but it was nevertheless a dynamic place where numerous important activities took place. In fact, the domestic world of women and children made up an estimated two-thirds of the population, so in terms of sheer numbers, the supposedly hidden world of women in fact constituted mainstream life.[21] Men moving about outside the home were in the minority.

Women's history is grounded in recognition of the importance of gender in human interactions.[22] Women and men often did not relate to one another as equals. Their gender identity gave them different degrees of power. However, people continuously renegotiate gradations of dominance and deference, so gendered relationships are never simplistic or absolute.[23] This book is dedicated to exploring the most important aspects of women's circumstances during a key era of Chinese history. The Qing was not only the final phase of the imperial era, but it also saw the culmination of the ideas and values that had defined more than two millennia of imperial history. The traumatic decay and fall of the Qing constitute the backdrop of everything in China that has happened thereafter. In many respects, Chinese today are still responding to events that occurred in the nineteenth century. Even though the Qing has disappeared, it remains an integral part of today's China.

The book reveals the details of women's lives by exploring their activities within the contexts of the major realms of female endeavor. A discussion of family structure describes women's domestic context. Next, a chapter on marriage explores the nature of conjugal life. This is followed by a discussion of women's roles in the Qing government, in particular the controversial rule of the Empress Dowager Cixi. A chapter on wealth explains women's dowries, inheritance, property rights, and occupations. Then there is a description of women's education, as well as the writings and other cultured activities of literate women. There is also an overview of religion as a medium that allowed women to learn abstract concepts. This is followed by a discussion of the complex theme of female virtue, in particular the cult of widow chastity that reached a peak at this time. A chapter on female image discusses how women and womanhood were perceived in the abstract. Finally, there is an account of the myriad social, economic, political, and cultural changes during the late Qing and the new vision of women that began to emerge in reaction. A conclusion sums up and emphasizes some of the key themes from the book. Social scientists refer to this sort of comprehensive approach, which attributes intentionality and meaning to a wide range of behavior, as thick description.[24] By examining many types of Qing women from myriad perspectives and pondering their motivations and goals, it is possible to reclaim some of the central features of women's history during the final phase of China's imperial era.

1

Family

Chinese traditionally emphasized the importance of names, as they expressed a person's identity. A man often had several names and used each in a different context. These reflected a particular characteristic, stated his rank within the family hierarchy, or were thought to bring good luck. When he encountered setbacks, he might change his name, hoping to reverse his fortune. But while families were attentive to male nomenclature, they showed much less interest in the names of daughters.[1] Some women lacked a given name. Others had a name but did not use it. Even princesses in the imperial palace were not addressed by name. People referred to all of them as "eldest daughter" (*daniu*), a custom that surely gave rise to endless confusion.

Within the family, women were usually addressed by kinship terms such as "daughter" or "sister." Written records often referred to an unmarried woman as the "daughter of" her father rather than stating her own name. After a woman married, people addressed her as her husband's wife or son's mother. In other words, society did not treat a woman as an individual deserving a name of her own but as a member of her family. Kinship roles constituted her identity. Given this mindset, any discussion of Chinese women's history must be firmly grounded in family organization.[2]

Due to the Qing principle of limited government, officials trusted families to manage their own affairs. Authorities ensured that marriages and family life conformed to basic standards of decent conduct. They prohibited bigamy and incest to uphold the moral order. Otherwise, they preferred not to intervene unless a family's elders were clearly incapable of handling a major problem on their own.[3]

The government also took steps to bolster the hierarchies that underpinned the ideal social structure. Parents had legal authority to arrange their children's marriages.[4] And as in previous dynasties, people of base (*jian*) status, such as prostitutes, could not marry ordinary people from a good (*liang*) family.[5] This provision prevented awkward social mixing. Being a multiethnic empire, the Qing state also paid close attention to ethnicity. Instead of promoting ethnic mixing, as in some previous conquest dynasties, the Qing prohibited certain types of intermarriage. Han Chinese could not legally marry people from very different backgrounds, such as Mongols or Miao.[6] The state also demanded that Manchus adhere to high standards of family conduct to protect their collective reputation. Unlike their Han peers, the law prohibited Manchu bannermen from committing adultery.[7]

Qing families did not conform to a single model. People constructed families differently depending on the resources at their disposal and the challenges they faced. Most fundamentally, the rich and poor had distinct forms of domestic life.[8] Wealthy families tended to be larger, as the rich could afford to raise more children. Extended kin also sometimes resided together if they had sufficient resources.[9] In contrast, poor families tended to be small. Most consisted of people related by the two most basic kinship bonds: parent and child, wife and husband. When a poor family became too large, members divided into nuclear families that were less expensive to maintain.

The gentry had a distinctive mode of family organization. To claim superiority, they often made a show of embracing Confucian virtues.[10] They were intimately familiar with these ideals because of their high level of education. While studying for the civil service examinations, men from gentry families engaged intensively with the ancient classics and conservative Song dynasty Neo-Confucian glosses. This training turned most of them into reflexive advocates of orthodox ethics. The most important ethical ideals, such as filiality, involved family life, so the gentry tended to have conservative views of kinship relations. Ancient teachings held that the ideal family consists of several generations residing under one roof. Although this arrangement was difficult to sustain in practice, it remained an aspirational goal that influenced the thinking and behavior of the elite.

Because people valued family so highly, they frequently tried to extend its scope by creating fictive kinship bonds with useful friends and contacts.[11] Two men might declare themselves sworn brothers, and women on good terms could speak of themselves as sisters. People constantly exchanged gifts and favors to draw closer to others. Sometimes they declared these relationships akin to family ties.

At a minimum, the model family consisted of parents, children, and perhaps a grandparent.[12] More than two-thirds of families had between three and seven members. Most commonly there were four to six people, with five the most common number. The average family had one or two children. Sons tended to reside with their parents long after they reached adulthood, as they could not legally divide up family land and establish separate households until both their father and mother had died.

A family had a designated patriarch who exercised authority over its members. The law obligated everyone in the family to obey the elder. A family's head was usually male. However, under certain circumstances, Qing law allowed a woman to act as family elder (*zunzhang*).[13] Most often, female elders were widows. Filial piety required her children to obey her, giving her control over family assets. Although a widow did not inherit her husband's land, her sons and grandsons could not sell it without her permission.

Marriages tended to be arranged far in advance, and women usually wed at a young age.[14] The families of bride and groom usually finalized the engagement and exchanged betrothal gifts before the couple had reached fourteen years of age. The wedding would take place two to ten years later. The minimum legal age of marriage was sixteen for boys and fourteen for girls.[15] One study of 17,174 women found that 87.6 percent married between the ages of thirteen and nineteen. Marriage at age seventeen and eighteen was most common for women. Almost all had married by the time they turned twenty. Men married slightly later, most frequently at age twenty to twenty-two, so a wife was usually several years younger than her husband.[16] The average age of marriage varied somewhat by region. For example, people in Shaanxi typically wed a few years younger than average. Marriage ages also fluctuated over the course of the dynasty. Toward the end of the Qing, conditions became increasingly unstable and many people experienced financial hardship. It took them longer to save up the sum needed for a wedding, pushing up the average age of marriage.

Seen within the context of world history, the early marriage age of the Qing does not seem unusual. Although teenage marriage is now uncommon in developed countries, it was the norm during the imperial era and in most premodern societies worldwide. The marriage age in contemporary societies is generally much higher than before. Moreover, the age of marriage in premodern Europe was unusually high by world standards, so it cannot be taken as the norm. In fact, historic Chinese marriage ages were close to the global average for premodern societies.[17]

Wealth influenced fertility, as women in higher-status families tended to marry younger and bear children sooner. According to a study of genealogies of women from different backgrounds in the late Ming and early

Qing era, gentry women bore their first child about two years earlier on average than women from lower backgrounds.[18]

Table 1.1. Age of Mothers in Tongcheng, Anhui, at the Birth of Their First Child

gentry	20.96
near-gentry	21.96
nongentry	22.95

Husbands were older than wives at the time of the wedding, so they were also older than new mothers when their first son was born.[19]

Table 1.2. Age of Fathers in Tongcheng, Anhui, at the Birth of Their First Child

gentry	21.96
near-gentry	24.95
nongentry	27.94

Because the family constituted the fundamental building block of society, parents usually did not allow their children to choose their spouses, particularly in elite families. Elders arranged marriages to benefit the entire kin group, not those directly involved.[20] People had different priorities regarding the choice of marriage partners. Neo-Confucian thinkers put a high value on family harmony, so they emphasized the compatibility of spouses. However, family elders usually sought tangible benefits from the marriages of their children. The gentry sought to marry their children with someone from an equally respectable family to publicly affirm their social status.[21] They wanted to ally their family with in-laws of high standing or learning. Prestigious affines could also be useful. Many prominent men were very close to their maternal relatives, and the two sides helped one another to further their civil service careers, educations, and cultural endeavors.

Families also hoped that a marriage would bring an infusion of cash, and they sought the highest possible dowry or betrothal gift. Merchants in particular stressed financial considerations. During the engagement process, the two families negotiated a written marriage contract that set down the details of the union, particularly financial matters. The contract stipulated the value of betrothal gifts to be presented by the groom's family to that of the bride and the dowry that the bride would bring into the groom's home.[22]

A study of the marriages of 286 men with the esteemed *jinshi* examination degree shows how families with the highest educational qualifications

Table 1.3. Family Background of Wives of *Jinshi* Degree Holders

low examination rank	33.57%
low office	15.73%
middle examination rank	2.45%
middle office	7.70%
high examination rank	0.7%
high office	2.10%

and greatest career potential chose their spouses.[23] Surprisingly, most of these men took wives from families with much lower qualifications.

The most eligible men usually married women from families outside the officialdom or from families whose men had held low office or had a minor examination degree. This disparity can be explained by the paucity of men who served in high office or had a *jinshi* degree. People preferred a spouse from a local family for the sake of convenience and compatibility, and a highly qualified man would be unlikely to find a wife from a comparable background in his own locale. For this reason, men with the brightest prospects usually married down. At the very least, by making a match with a prominent local family, a degree holder could win useful contacts that might help his family dominate the community around his hometown, an important goal for the Qing elite.

The tight bonds between many fathers and daughters also encouraged families to seek local matches. Writers often described a daughter as a "pearl in the palm" (*zhang zhong zhu*).[24] This image surfaced in medieval literature and originally referred to anyone whom a writer treasured, but by the Qing it referred specifically to a beloved daughter. Many men had affectionate relationships with their daughters. A doting father often sought to marry his daughter to a man living nearby, ideally an acquaintance or distant kinsman. This ensured that she would be treated well, and he could also see her regularly.

Because marriage connections were so important to a family's success, people spent substantial sums on weddings.[25] The classical rites portrayed weddings as solemn occasions that did not require a large expenditure. However, the commercial economy of the late imperial era fostered materialism, and this mentality affected wedding customs. Wealthy families used a wedding to demonstrate their high status by flaunting their wealth. They put out large sums for the dowry, clothing, luggage, travel, shipping costs, and matchmaker's fee. Even though ancient ritual texts did not mention the wedding banquet, people considered a large feast essential to finalize a union. These banquets could be extremely lavish. Even poor laborers spent as much as they could to mark this important occasion.

Ordinary families had less to gain from marriage than the elite, so they had lower expectations. Many peasant men preferred a bride from a family of somewhat lower status, as she was more likely to be an obedient wife and daughter-in-law. At the bottom of society, poor families often treated their children as chattel and simply sold them into marriage. Surviving marriage contracts document many instances of spouses being sold.[26] These arrangements took many forms. Most commonly, parents would sell off a son or daughter. In some cases, an uncle would sell his niece or a master would sell a servant. Most people sold into marriage were extremely young, usually below age sixteen, so they could not resist. The commoditization of young people emerged in response to worsening economic conditions. Population growth, downward mobility, and natural disasters put many families under great financial stress.[27] They had to make money however they could, using any assets at hand, so they sometimes sold off their daughters.[28]

The Qing Empire was large and diverse, so even though authorities set down standard rules for marriage, actual practices varied considerably by region and ethnicity.[29] Although Han made up the majority of the populace, the Qing state included many other ethnic groups as well, particularly along the margins of the empire. Each had distinctive kinship customs, so many marriages diverged from the mainstream model.

Manchu family organization differed from Chinese norms in certain respects. At the beginning of the Qing, the Manchus decided to maintain their distinct kinship relations and family ethics. They knew that previous conquerors had assimilated after settling in China, and they wanted to avoid losing ethnic solidarity. The Jurchens put little value on virginity but prized wifely fidelity. Young women traditionally had considerable sexual freedom before marriage, but wives were expected to be absolutely faithful to their husbands.[30] Moreover, a wife's commitment to the marriage extended beyond her husband's death. Like many other nomadic peoples, the Jurchens practiced levirate, requiring a widow to marry one of her deceased husband's kinsmen.[31] Having paid out an expensive betrothal gift, a family considered the wife to have been purchased, and they did not want to lose her labor and reproductive capacity.

Many other northern nomadic people also practiced levirate, including the Mongols, so this custom became very common during the Yuan dynasty.[32] The Ming government sought to purge China of Mongol influence, and the Ming code prohibited levirate. Even so, the practice did not disappear. In fact, levirate remained fairly common during the Ming.[33] Ethnic Han had realized the utility of levirate marriage, so even though Chinese traditionally considered it a type of incest, some widows nevertheless entered into these unions. Levirate continued into the Qing. The state theoretically mandated monogamy, yet officials turned a blind eye to Manchu men who took a brother's widow as a second wife.[34] Government functionaries may have encouraged chastity among the Han, but they never expected Manchu widows to decline remarriage.

Ethnic Han also engaged in marriage arrangements that departed from official standards. Sometimes a groom agreed to move into the home of his bride's parents. This sort of matrilocal marriage altered the relations between wife and husband.[35] In most societies, patrilocal residence is the norm. This practice separates wives from their blood kin, leaving them with no natural allies in the home. In contrast, matrilocal residence empowers a wife. She has her family's support and exercises more control over household resources.

Matrilocal marriage usually occurred when the bride's parents had no son.[36] According to kinship rules, such a family would be extinguished when the parents died. To ensure the family's continuity, they could marry their daughter to a man willing to be akin to an adoptive son. The first son born to a matrilineal couple would take the mother's surname, ensuring the survival of her family line. Subsequent sons might be given the father's surname. Matrilocal marriage dated back to antiquity, and in some eras of Chinese history it seems to have been fairly common.[37] Even so, people considered matrilocal marriage embarrassing and unorthodox. Both law and custom discouraged the practice, and lineage elders would likely object. Nevertheless, many families resorted to this expedient measure for lack of a better alternative.[38]

Usually only a poor man would be willing to accept a matrilocal marriage, as living with his wife's family carried some stigma. But if he was willing to swallow his pride, he could enjoy rapid upward mobility. Even some men from respectable backgrounds consented to this sort of arrangement, albeit for different reasons.[39] It was common for a man marrying into a literati family to live in the home of his father-in-law for the first few years after the wedding, particularly if the groom came from a lower background than the bride. Living with a higher-status family gave the new husband opportunities to study, gain cultural capital, and forge useful connections with the local elite. The bride's father used this arrangement to elevate his daughter's new husband and increase his chances for success.

In some regions, people undertook a very different form of unorthodox marriage. Sometimes two families would finalize their children's engagement while the couple was still very young. The future bride then moved in with her fiancé's family, who would raise her until the age of marriage. Then they would hold a wedding and the marriage would officially commence.[40] This arrangement first appeared during the Song dynasty and became common in south China during the Ming and Qing, particularly in Guangdong, Fujian, and Taiwan. These marriages usually took place among people at the bottom of society. Some child fiancées were orphans.

In other cases, a family was unwilling to raise a daughter or too poor to feed her, so they sent her away to be raised by her future in-laws. Money was usually the main motivation for child engagement. The girl's family could collect the brideprice immediately, and they would be saved the expense of raising her. As for the groom's side, this custom ensured that their son would have a suitable bride when he came of age. His family also benefitted from the bride's labor as soon as possible. Moreover, a girl raised by her in-laws would likely be docile and fit in to their family.

This arrangement, sometimes referred to as minor marriage, was particularly popular in Taiwan, where there was an unusual shortage of potential brides. Men outnumbered women in many border regions, but the sex ratio in Taiwan was particularly skewed.[41] In 1649, when the island was still under Dutch control, there were only 838 women among a Han population of 11,339. Although there are no statistics for the number of women residing on the island during the Qing era, writers commented on the paucity of Han women. Manchu authorities considered Taiwan a haven for Ming loyalists, so they discouraged migration to the island. To keep the population down, they prohibited women from relocating to Taiwan. Women who made it across the straits did so in violation of the law. In any case, few women wanted to make the trip. Not only was it illegal for a woman to move there, but frontier life was hard and precarious. Most early Han migrants were pioneers. A man could not marry until he established himself, and success took time. Many migrants never accumulated sufficient resources to bring over a wife from the mainland. Due to the skewed sex ratio, Taiwanese families had trouble finding suitable brides for their sons. They were willing to raise their future daughter-in-law to guarantee that their son would eventually have a wife.[42] In many cases, sisters married their children to one another to ensure that their sons could wed, so many Taiwanese ended up marrying their first cousins.

The Guangdong Delta region had another distinctive custom. Adolescent girls in many villages would spend time in a local girls' house prior to marriage.[43] They worked and ate with their families, so the building was usually empty during the day. But after they completed their chores, they went to the girl's house. There they spent their evenings chatting, singing, playing games, and telling stories. Instead of sleeping at home, girls spent their nights there with their peers. This custom allowed each age cohort of girls to build strong ties with one another, stabilizing village life.

Some families in the same region practiced delayed transfer marriage that anthropologists call natalocal residence.[44] After the wedding, the newlyweds spent three days in the groom's home. Then the wife returned home to live with her family for three more years. During that time, she would usually only visit her husband on festive occasions such as major holidays or family celebrations. They did not begin to reside with their husbands until age twenty or older. This arrangement emerged during the late Qing in tandem with mechanized sericulture. People considered young women particularly adept at silk manufacture, so brides lived at home and worked in a factory for three years before moving in with their husbands and devoting themselves to domestic tasks. Three years of factory work allowed a young wife to bring in income at the beginning of the marriage, putting the couple on a firmer financial footing. It may also have functioned as a form of birth control, as Guangdong had become highly overpopulated by the late Qing.

Families in Guangdong and elsewhere also sometimes conducted posthumous marriages.[45] This arrangement had been undertaken periodically since high antiquity, though its popularity varied over time.[46] During the Qing era, some families still found posthumous marriage appealing. If a son or daughter died young, their parents might arrange with the family of another dead child to conduct a wedding ceremony to unite their deceased children. Spirit marriage responded to the ideology of Chinese kinship, as only marriage allowed a person to become a full member of the system of descent. This custom was also believed to appease the dead. People feared that restless ghosts could cause serious problems for the living, such as ruining the harvest. They believed that marrying dead children to one another would help prevent them from haunting the living.

When a bride married, she usually moved in with her husband's family. There she found herself at the mercy of potentially hostile strangers. The stereotype of the cruel mother-in-law had some grounding in fact. A mother feared that her son would shift his loyalty toward his wife, stealing her most valuable ally in the family. She might mistreat and belittle her daughter-in-law to keep from being challenged.

Despite the threat of a hostile mother-in-law, some wives managed to create arrangements that gained them allies and increased their power. A shrewd wife could demand absolute loyalty from her children, excluding their father and paternal grandmother from their affections. By doing so, she created a circle of supporters that anthropologists call a "uterine family."[47] As her loyal sons matured and gained authority, she would gain a higher status in the home. However, when a son married and brought in a wife, his mother would be tempted to take on the role of abusive mother-in-law to try to preserve her uterine family, and the process would be repeated.

A wife sometimes became intimate with other women living in her husband's home. In large households, numerous women lived in close proximity, and female residents occasionally entered into physical relationships.[48] Educated people considered forthright discussions of sexuality embarrassing, so there is almost no factual information about lesbianism. However, late imperial literature describes some fictional lesbian encounters. These stories always take place in the inner quarters of a wealthy household. The presence of a wife, concubines, and female servants within a confined space facilitated sexual relationships. According to literary accounts, a senior woman with higher status or age would initiate the sexual encounter with someone of lower rank. People did not exhibit prejudice toward lesbianism. Because these relationships took place outside of the kinship bonds that organized society, men considered them unimportant. Instead of condemning lesbian encounters, they simply ignored them.

Motherhood was a key aspect of female social identity, so changes to the relationship between mothers and children had a major impact on women lives. Filial piety (*xiao*) regulated the maternal bond. In antiquity, this virtue developed out of the ancestral cult. Because people conducted elaborate rituals in remembrance of their forebears, they began to reason that living elders ought to be held in high regard as well.[49] This idea gradually became elaborated into a wide-ranging ideology. Although filial piety is most often associated with Confucianism, Buddhist and Daoist ethics assimilated this virtue and sacralized it.[50] Initially the concept of filial piety governed relations between fathers and sons, but it was extended to cover mothers as well. Children acted out filial devotion in many ways. Most often, they showed honor and obedience to their parents. They might go to some trouble to show their commitment, such as procuring a parent's favorite food. Occasionally offspring expressed filiality in extreme ways, such as cutting off a piece of flesh to concoct medicine that they could use to treat a sick parent.

In each era, people found new ways to express filial piety. At the beginning of the Qing, one painter created a series of album paintings depicting how a devoted son undertook a long and arduous journey through China's chaotic southwest in search of his missing parents.[51] Both the journey and the resulting artworks attested to his intense devotion to his mother and father. At this time, children praised their mothers as almost superhuman. Important men attributed their successes to being raised by a wise and loving mother. Many of them wrote essays commemorating maternal sacrifices and declaring their eternal gratitude.[52]

Yet in spite of all this high-flown rhetoric, not all women were good mothers. The failure of so many mothers made the successful ones seem even better by comparison. For various reasons, such as the high cost of dowering a daughter, women sometimes felt compelled to terminate a pregnancy or rid themselves of an unwanted baby. Chinese medicine had techniques to induce abortion, and the law did not prohibit the procedure.[53] However, abortion drugs were unreliable and extremely dangerous. Only an experienced practitioner could administer them safely, so dependable abortion was expensive. Due to these drawbacks, abortion could not serve as routine birth control. It seems that women resorted to abortion only as an emergency measure, when pregnancy seemed life threatening or else to cover up an extramarital relationship. Chaste widows and young unmarried women had the most to lose from becoming pregnant, so they were the most willing to risk having an abortion.

Given the danger and expense of abortion, people usually disposed of an unwanted child immediately after delivery.[54] It was customary to commit infanticide by drowning. Most commonly, people murdered a newborn baby daughter to avoid having to eventually pay out a costly dowry. Although generous dowries had some positive effects on female status, the practice also gave rise to widespread female infanticide. Qing records provide many examples of infanticide from across China and depict it as very common. The government regarded the murder of infants as a major problem. Although not specifically outlawed, as a form of homicide it was nevertheless strictly illegal. Even so, because so many newborns died of natural causes, the government could not possibly enforce this ban. Although officials could not prevent infanticide, they were horrified by the number of parents murdering innocent babies and spoke out about this dire social problem.

The government founded orphanages so that families could rid themselves of an unwanted child without resorting to murder.[55] During the Song dynasty, the state had founded a government agency dedicated to child welfare, and the Ming revived this bureau. During the Qing, some regions had similar agencies called "baby raising halls" (*yu ying tang*). However, instead of being overseen by the central government, local authorities managed them. These organizations cared for vulnerable children. Staff would take in unwanted babies and find nursemaids to provide them with breast milk and raise them to maturity.

Toward the end of the dynasty, reformers and missionaries targeted infanticide.[56] Progressives considered widespread infanticide not just immoral but also an embarrassing symptom of national backwardness. But while they may have discussed it using newly fashionable ideologies, they tried to solve it in much the same way as prior generations of literati. Reformers reached out to educate parents about the horrors of this practice and convince them not to kill daughters. They founded orphanages and family support societies that gave financial aid to poor families raising daughters. Yet despite their efforts, infanticide remained a major social problem up to the end of the dynasty.

Although a minority of women aborted, abandoned, or killed their babies, most looked forward to becoming a mother. Indeed, a wife's most important duty was to produce an heir to maintain her husband's line of descent. People often viewed motherhood in stereotypical terms. They praised the attentive mother and considered her almost heroic. Popular culture disseminated images of stern fathers and kind mothers, associating the maternal role with benevolence.[57]

Society also depicted motherhood as a challenging sacrifice. Late imperial writers emphasized the mother's suffering, enveloping her with an aura of martyrdom and sanctity.[58] A mother had to undergo the pain and danger of childbirth (figure 1.1). Then, in addition to a heavy load of housework, she spent years nursing infants, caring for sick children, and doing everything necessary to raise them to adulthood. Given the magnitude of these sacrifices, mothers expected their sons to express their gratitude. The best way for a man to do this was to become successful. The desire to repay maternal sacrifices with worldly success served as a key motivation for many ambitious men.

The state took steps to ensure that the intense tie binding mother and son did not undermine the justice system.[59] Under Tang dynasty law, a son could not accuse his mother of a crime. This provision was based on Confucian principles, which prioritized the dictates of filial piety over law. Yet allowing people to cover up malfeasance made it difficult to enforce justice. During the Song era, it become possible for a child to report a mother's crimes. By the Qing, mothers had lost their immunity in this regard, and a son could no longer legally conceal his mother's guilt from authorities.

The family was not the only kinship unit in Qing society. In many regions, lineages had a significant impact on the lives of their members.[60] A lineage is a corporate group that claims descent from a common ancestor (figure 1.2).[61] Through the course of China's history, lineages waxed and waned in importance. The medieval elite did not feel obligation toward extended kin. Aristocrats wanted to marry someone from a comparable background, so their brides often came from distant places, diffusing their kinship connections. In contrast, the Song dynasty elite preferred to take a spouse from the same area. This form of marriage kept extended kin close together and led people to identify more closely with their place of residence. From the Song onward, the gentry believed that they ought to serve as community leaders. They fostered the development of lineages and used their ties with extended kin as a strategy intended to help them dominate local society.[62] The Qing emphasis on ritual orthodoxy further stimulated the formation of lineages, as members conducted certain rites together. The popularity of these organizations varied by region. Lineages were most common in south China, where they often carried out important social, economic, and administrative responsibilities.

Figure 1.1. Mother and Baby
Metropolitan Museum of Art

Figure 1.2. Ancestor Portrait
Metropolitan Museum of Art

Lineages also affected the inheritance system. Because Chinese practiced partitive inheritance, with each son receiving a share of land, the average size of plots decreased every generation. From the Song dynasty onward, authorities enforced partitive inheritance to prevent the emergence of a hereditary aristocracy that might challenge the central government.[63] Yet under this inheritance system, a prosperous family could become impoverished in just a few generations. Putting some land under the control of a lineage helped members preserve wealth, as some income from the land would continue to benefit them even if the family declined. Anthropologists often refer to lineages that hold communal wealth as clans. These organizations managed their wealth professionally, somewhat like a business corporation. Lineage trusts provided a steady flow of income that provided credit for their members' business ventures and aided those in need.

Although historians emphasize the practical functions of lineages, participants focused on their collective ritual activities. According to custom, distant kinsmen had to come together to conduct certain ceremonies.[64] Late imperial scholars declared that only one person in the patriline had the authority to lead ancestral sacrifices—the eldest son in the main line of descent. His kinsmen performed supporting roles. Because extended kin had to come together regularly for these rites, some formed lineages for this purpose. The gentry enthusiastically promoted ancestral rituals, and over time these ceremonies gained respect. During the sixteenth century, the Ming state began to allow ordinary people to build ancestral halls, which soon became common.[65] Ordinary people established lineages, group cemeteries, and ancestral halls in imitation of the elite. Communal rituals promoted group solidarity. People became increasingly conscious of their membership of a lineage, and they considered it an important aspect of their social identity.

The rise of lineages in the late imperial era affected views toward women. Anthropologists assume that the emergence of large patrilineal descent groups often degrades overall female social position. Although women carried out important duties at home, they had marginal roles in their husband's lineage. As a patriline organized around male descent, a lineage tended to minimize the symbolic and ritual importance of female kin. Nevertheless, the actual impact of lineages on Chinese women seems to have been mixed.[66] In some parts of rural Guangdong, where lineages were particularly strong, women may have lost ground. Yet in other regions, women often maintained significant status and rights within the lineage kinship system.

Qing lineages tended to take a conservative line on ethical questions. Members had a collective identity, so the misbehavior of one woman shamed the entire group. Similarly, exceptional female virtue, such as a widow who refused to remarry, brought honor to all members. Consequently, lineage elders enforced stringent ethical standards for female kin.[67] Lineages sometimes even expelled a widow who remarried and purged her name from their genealogy, effectively severing their tie with her. However, lineages also supported vulnerable women. Some gave material aid to widows and their children and protected widows from greedy in-laws.

During the Qing dynasty, many people never married. Female infanticide had skewed the sex ratio, making it impossible for many men to find a wife. In addition, the custom of concubinage took large numbers of women off the marriage market. And poor men found it difficult to scrape together the requisite betrothal gift necessary for a wedding. Due to these problems, large numbers of men found it almost impossible to marry. Among the men recorded in one group of lineage genealogies, 22.1 percent never wed.[68] The men in this sample were attached to an active lineage, hence more likely to marry than men with tenuous kinship links. The most marginal men did not participate in these organizations, so the actual number of lifelong bachelors was even higher. The sex ratio became increasingly unbalanced over the course of the Qing, so the number of unmarried adult men rose steadily. From 1776 to 1850 the ratio of men to women in Jiangsu declined from 128.1:100 to 135.1:100. In Xuzhou county in Jiangsu, the ratio of men to women in 1874 was 129:100. In some places the ratio reached 194.7:100.[69] The skewed sex ratio meant that in many areas, more than 20 percent of men could not possibly marry.

Penurious and cut off from the family system, lifelong bachelors suffered immense hardship.[70] Many were poor farmers with too little land to thrive. Others worked for wages but lacked a fixed profession. They did hard labor and performed odd jobs. A poor man who never wed had no one to care for him in old age. Many faced the prospect of eventual destitution or even starvation when they could no longer work. They also endured the humiliation of lifelong celibacy in a society that celebrated marriage and fertility. People disparagingly referred to lifelong bachelors as "bare sticks" (*guanggun*).[71] This pejorative term referred to both poor bachelors and hoodlums, as the two groups tended to overlap. Government officials regarded these men with contempt. Men untethered from society's core institutions were more likely to cause problems, so the state and local community viewed them as failures and troublemakers.

Bare sticks tended to think and behave differently from those in the social mainstream. Normative gender roles emerged largely through the interaction of men and women within the home. The removal of so many men from family life disrupted this dynamic and caused bare sticks to develop marginal forms of masculinity independent of female influence. They often sought out sympathetic comrades who could provide support. Some joined criminal gangs and secret societies whose members shared resources, conducted group rituals, and worshipped a patron god. Many of these disaffected men participated in the large-scale rebellions of the nineteenth century, which weakened the Qing and left the dynasty unable to cope with pressing external threats.

Although most men dreaded a life outside of marriage, during the late Qing an increasing number of women sought to avoid conjugal life. Some did not want to deal with the restrictions and obligations of married life. Others probably wanted to avoid the dangers of childbirth or the necessity of sexual relations with a man. Qing literature and theater

Figure 1.3. Encounter
Metropolitan Museum of Art

depicted unmarried female characters, and this new social type intrigued audiences.[72] In romantic fiction and dramas, the young beauty hoped to wed a talented student (figure 1.3). The emergence of female characters uninterested in marriage departed from this stereotype, marking a major social shift. Traditionally, most women had wanted to marry, as the role of wife brought prestige and security. For increasing numbers to resist wedlock shows the emergence of a new and distinctive mindset.

Female characters in popular literature rejected marriage for various reasons. Some had been engaged to a man who died, and they vowed to remain faithful to their partner for life, even though the pair had not formally married. These women took the concept of conjugal loyalty to an extreme, extending it from husband to fiancé. Some famous courtesans also refused to marry, as they considered their lifestyle stimulating and financially rewarding. Female knights errant (*nü xia*) mirrored their male counterparts in declaring a lack of interest in sex and marriage. Sometimes an arrogant female character refused to marry because she considered all potential mates far beneath her. There were also female characters who rejected marriage due to psychological trauma. Youthful suffering made these women incapable of affection, and they wanted to keep other people at arm's length.

Traditionally, women who wanted to avoid marriage had become Buddhist or Daoist nuns. Monasticism legitimized a woman's unmarried state and provided her with an acceptable path in life. Otherwise, a woman could avoid having to deal with a husband by marrying a man who had recently died, allowing her to remain a virgin for the rest of her life.[73] This practice had the advantage of giving a woman a place within the patrilineal kinship system without entering an actual marriage. After she died, her spirit tablet would be placed beside that of her husband, ensuring that she would receive ritual attention from his family.

Occasionally a filial daughter would reject marriage so that she could remain at home and look after her parents in their old age.[74] There are records of this sort of filial sacrifice in Guizhou, a poor region. If a couple lacked a son, their daughter would have to take on his responsibilities. If a family was extremely poor and lacked a son, the parents might not be able to survive if their daughter left, in which case she might decline to wed out of filial devotion. Foregoing marriage also saved the family the cost of dowry. A lifelong virgin would usually devote herself to spinning and weaving to support her poor parents.

Early Catholic missionaries promoted an alternative type of virginity that combined native ethical concepts with imported religious beliefs.[75] In the early eighteenth-century, Spanish Dominicans established a secret Christian community in a remote mountainous region of Fujian. They reinterpreted virginity and chastity as expressions of Christian faith, harnessing conventional Chinese moral sentiments to attract converts. Chinese believers embraced Catholic teachings that associated virginity with moral purity. These beliefs had a major impact on community mores, convincing many pious women not to marry. Instead they continued to live with their natal families and dedicated themselves to filial piety and Christian worship. In 1746 Qing authorities discovered the covert Fujian congregation. They considered Catholicism strange and potentially subversive, so they executed five Spanish missionaries and exiled the most fervent Christians to other places.

In the late nineteenth century, after Catholicism became legal, missionary priests once again emphasized virginity.[76] When a Catholic girl reached the age of marriage, she could request to take a vow of virginity instead. To do so, she would kneel before a priest and ask for permission from the Church to become a lifelong virgin. If the priest and his superior both approved the request, she would be exempted from marriage and expected to devote her life to worship and mission work. Numerous Catholic women took a vow of virginity and spent their days doing charitable deeds, such as helping out in mission orphanages. Priests relied heavily on Catholic virgins for practical support. These women also helped assimilate foreign priests into the local community.

Native forms of virginity were particularly popular in certain areas, such as the prosperous region around Huizhou.[77] Families in this area had a strong commitment to female education. The Confucian curriculum taught conservative female ethics that justified extreme expressions of virtue. In some families, a young woman might decide not to marry so that she could remain at home and care for her parents. A few of these women were talented painters, and they sold their works to support their families. The thriving Huizhou art market presented female artists with opportunities to sell their paintings and give lessons to other women.[78] Justifying marriage avoidance as an expression of filial piety and associating it with high culture made it seem respectable.

Toward the end of the Qing dynasty, industrialization and the rise of factories presented women with new opportunities to earn money. Some female factory workers in the textile industry used their new financial power to permanently avoid marriage.[79] They invented rituals and organizations that institutionalized their lifestyle and provided tangible support. When a young woman renounced marriage, she underwent a ceremony during which she altered her hairstyle. This unique coiffeur signified a new social role as a lifelong virgin. She continued to work in a factory and saved money to buy a room in a communal residence for unmarried women. This was not just a place to live. The residents acted as a surrogate family who helped members in times of need. They nursed the sick, cared for the dying, and venerated the ancestral tablets of the deceased. Lifelong spinsterhood allowed women to avoid the duties and constrictions of married life. Parents often supported this choice because they received a share of their unmarried daughter's wages, which she gave them out of filial piety, and also avoided paying out a dowry. This arrangement illustrates the fact that many Qing women and men often maintained unconventional ties to their families. Although the ideology of kinship consisted of prescriptive principles, in real life many people constructed expedient forms of kinship that responded creatively to their particular circumstances.

2

Marriage

Because women married young, they typically spent most of their lives as a wife. With few exceptions, a wife lived in her husband's house and depended on him financially. Given the importance of this bond, the spousal relationship determined a woman's basic circumstances. However, this institution was not static. People conceptualized marital relations in various ways and arrangements changed over time, affecting how women lived.

The government embraced assertions by the Song dynasty Neo-Confucian thinker Zhu Xi as the official ideology of marriage. Most importantly, Zhu believed that the ancient rites should serve as the basic template of marital relations.[1] The Neo-Confucian movement sought to reinterpret family rituals to suit current conditions. This was not a simple task. Zhu Xi and like-minded thinkers lamented the many contradictions between deeply rooted contemporary practices and the classic rites.[2] In trying to implement a stringent Neo-Confucian vision of marriage, Qing dynasty officials encountered similar challenges.

Ritualists viewed marriage as a hierarchy. A wife resided in her husband's home, where she lacked natural allies, making it easier for her husband to dominate her. Wives were customarily younger than their husbands by several years, and age inequality gave men even more power.[3] The husband also served as family elder and controlled common resources. Society expected a wife to fulfill demanding obligations.[4] Most importantly, she was to bear children and carry out her allotted domestic duties. She also had to serve her in-laws without complaint. After a husband's death, she was not to remarry while still in mourning. Ideally, a widow was not supposed to enter into a second marriage at all. However, most women lacked sufficient economic resources to stay chaste. Widows in families of ordinary means usually remarried out of necessity.

Although society had clear expectations for wifely behavior, in fact marriages took many forms, so women behaved differently depending on their circumstances. For example, the lives of merchant wives often contravened conventional expectations.[5] Merchants spent much of their time away from home, and their wives had to manage the household in their absence. Out of necessity, merchant wives handled many matters usually considered the purview of men. Some also helped their husbands with their work. If a merchant married a woman who turned out to have a head for business, his peers considered him fortunate. More often, however, merchant wives took care of the home while their husbands handled trade. Yet despite the autonomy that these women enjoyed, people pitied them. They did not consider it easy for a woman to take on male responsibilities and manage the household by herself. Merchants were frequently on the road, and wives complained about unwelcome separation. Also, a wife feared that her husband might be keeping a concubine or second wife in a distant place, compounding loneliness with jealousy.

During the cultural ferment of the late Ming dynasty, thinkers and fiction writers explored the emotive side of human nature. Song Neo-Confucians had a generally negative view of *qing* (emotion or sentiment). They believed that even though our emotions might motivate us to do good, they might just as easily inspire evil behavior. However, many late Ming literati went against previous thinking on the matter and began to see emotion in a positive light, identifying it with authenticity and naturalness.[6] They even promoted *qing* as an antidote to sterile Confucian platitudes and ritualized formality.

An increasingly positive view of emotion affected popular views of marriage. During the late Ming era, many people considered the ideal marriage a relatively egalitarian relationship grounded in shared feelings. In a successful marriage, husband and wife were not merely united by shared obligations but engaged with one another on a deep emotional level (figure 2.1). Literature celebrated the companionate marriage, and many husbands treated their wives with respect and empathy.[7]

This new view of marriage can be seen in the epitaphs that men wrote for deceased wives.[8] Epitaphs became increasingly common over time. By the seventeenth century, a husband in mourning would often commission an epitaph for his deceased wife or write one himself. In earlier eras, women's epitaphs employed formulaic language and they portrayed the departed as a paragon of virtue. In contrast, Qing epitaphs praised women for a wider range of qualities, such as intelligence and educational

Figure 2.1. Wife and Husband
Metropolitan Museum of Art

attainments. Qing epitaphs of wives often included mundane details that demonstrated a couple's intimacy. These texts also became increasingly emotional. Men no longer felt embarrassed to express love for a departed spouse. Some even admitted that they had survivor's guilt and found life unendurable without the company of their beloved wife.

These sentiments were not limited to epitaphs. Hao Yixing (1757–1829), also known as Langao, wrote enthusiastically about his happy marriage with fellow poet Wang Zhaoyuan (1763–1851).[9]

> On the wedding day, I dressed in finery and jewelry, fetching her in person. And finally we became husband and wife, treating each other like guests and friends. That two people should share the same taste is not likely innate. However, spiritual connections have started before the actual meeting. What we two have experienced is really extraordinary. Langao says, "It is a romantic story and has to be made known to the world."

The couple even compiled a collection of poetry to celebrate their happy marriage. In previous eras, such a project would have been almost unthinkable. Spouses would have been embarrassed to discuss their romantic feelings in public. Yet Wang and Hao were proud of their passionate relationship. The writings of these contented spouses show that contemporary readers approved of companionate marriage and even looked to it as an ideal.

Many women had forthright relationships with their husbands and wanted their marriages to be grounded in shared feelings. Qing gentry women enthused about the joys of married life. Many female writers emphasized shared feelings as the basis of a successful conjugal relationship. Women from educated families also felt more confident in showing off their learning and talent. They sought to share their husbands' intellectual and literary interests so that they could become cultured companions.[10] Ming literati had cultivated refined relationships with elite courtesans, but by the Qing, courtesan culture had come to seem tawdry, and men preferred to seek elegant female camaraderie from their wives.

Some women used their literary skills to express extravagant devotion to a beloved husband. Pang Buyan's writings exemplified intense wifely sentiments.[11] Pang lived during the late nineteenth century and belonged to an ethnic minority on Hainan Island. She married at age eighteen and just one year later her husband drowned, leaving her grief stricken. Pang composed a long song of mourning consisting of 360 lines in Be (Lingao), her native language, which became popular locally. Even though Pang was not Han and did not write in Chinese, the Qing government nevertheless recognized her as unusually talented, filial, and chaste. They awarded her a commendation, and a memorial arch was constructed to honor her chaste widowhood.

People viewed marriage in highly positive terms, even if they emphasized different aspects of the relationship. The government encouraged people to consider it a solemn expression of the ancient rites, even as many couples hoped for a marriage based on deep shared feelings. Nevertheless, not all marriages succeeded. Records frequently describe the failures of married life. Most often they viewed these problems from a female perspective and stressed the unhappiness of the wife trapped in a miserable marriage.

Stories about romance and happy marriages raised women's expectations, making them more easily disappointed. Many stage dramas depicted the search for a loving marriage. Scripts portrayed the ideal relationship as beginning with romantic attraction and turning into a joyful partnership based on shared interests and emotions.[12] Yet reality was often quite different. Many women found themselves disillusioned by the mundane reality of conjugal life. Some felt trapped in an intolerable situation with no realistic hope of escape. A poem by He Shuangqing (b. 1715) expressed the misery of a woman bound to a man she detests. She had expected love but discovered that married life consisted of little more than tedious household chores.[13]

> I deem my whole life wretched—but I'll bear it to the bitter end
> Even if I turn into powder and ash.
> I foresaw this when I married:
> Beautiful thoughts and romantic feelings,
> All would be suffocated in cooking smoke.

Literary critics condemned the works of women who dared to complain about marriage. They expected female writers to confine themselves to polite themes couched in delicate language. Nevertheless, some women dared to complain about their situations. Gu Zhenli (1623–1699) wrote scathing poems about her dismal marriage.[14] Her parents had married her to a mismatched husband who failed in his career. Gu had to pawn her dowry and take in needlework to support the family. She wrote 160 poems that still survive, but only three mention her husband. Gu seems to have thought it best to simply ignore him. Instead she focused on her own hardships. Whereas boudoir poetry traditionally described a woman's bedroom as a gorgeous and romantic space, Gu depicted it as a prison enclosing a bitter inmate.

Many men acknowledged the unhappiness of the women close to them. The epitaph was the best medium for expressing these sentiments. A husband writing an epitaph for his wife would not admit that she had resented their relationship. However, men writing epitaphs for deceased sisters often empathized with their hardships.[15] Some epitaphs rued a sister's failed marriage and blamed her husband and parents-in-law for condemning her to an unhappy life.

In extreme cases, wives had to endure a violent husband with little hope for escape. Married women had few protections against domestic abuse, which could sometimes even be fatal. Judicial records describe numerous cases of husbands murdering their spouses.[16] Men gave various excuses for killing their wives. Sometimes a jealous murderer suspected his wife of having an extramarital affair. Other men accused spouses of theft or mistreating their parents. In many cases, a murder resulted from incompatibility. Sometimes a petty argument escalated and the husband became violent. Even if a woman returned to her family in search of safety, an angry husband might track her down and kill her. In some cases, authorities determined that a murderous husband was simply insane.

Wives reacted to domestic violence in various ways, depending on their circumstances. It seems that most put up with physical abuse. With no easy escape from marriage, they usually had no choice but to endure mistreatment. However, some women resisted and fought off their violent husbands. A few wives resorted to violence themselves and murdered their spouses. Mariticide had a range of causes. Not all murderous wives were lashing out against battery. Some killed a husband for infidelity or unfilial behavior. In some cases, a woman murdered her husband during a heated argument. Others reacted to abuse with self-destruction. If a woman felt that her circumstances had become unendurable, she might commit suicide. Some suicides allegedly committed for virtuous reasons were probably in fact an escape from long-term abuse.

Unhappy couples could divorce.[17] Chinese divorce law changed over the centuries. In antiquity, the government had nothing to do with divorce. A husband could simply expel his wife from the house, or his wife might abscond, with no legal process or ceremony to mark the separation. Over time, the legal system developed systematic rules, and by the Qing these procedures had become extremely sophisticated. Divorce could be initiated by the husband or by common consent. A wife could only initiate divorce if her husband had disappeared for at least three years, he had forced her to commit adultery, sold her to someone else, or beaten her so severely that she had suffered visible bodily harm.[18] A wife could also obtain a divorce if a parent-in-law had beaten her without "reasonable cause" and the beating was so serious that she had been disabled. The law also facilitated the dissolution of improper unions, such as bigamy or forced marriage.

Qing law followed earlier precedents by requiring a husband to justify divorce by specifying which of seven serious faults his wife had committed. Divorce could be granted if she had been unfilial to her parents-in-law, infertile, licentious, jealous, seriously ill, loquacious, or thieving.

Even if a wife had committed one of these transgressions, her husband could still not divorce her under three circumstances: she had nowhere to go, she had mourned his parents for three years, or he had been poor when they married and subsequently became rich. These provisions originated in the ancient rites as ways to protect wives from expulsion without due cause and had been incorporated into medieval law. However, the vague wording of these justifications made it easy for a man to find an excuse to rid himself of an unwanted wife.

Because marriages involved an exchange of wealth between families, a couple would often draw up a divorce contract that specified the financial settlement. Unlike the Song dynasty, when women's dowries had firm legal protections, during the Qing a wife lost her dowry if she left her husband's home. For this reason, most wives likely put up with a failed marriage, or even physical abuse, as the alternative was usually destitution.

If a wife left her husband's home without having been granted a divorce, according to the law she had absconded. A woman usually abandoned a husband due to unendurable poverty.[19] Others were escaping domestic violence or fled to avoid infection with a dreaded disease. Usually only women from the lowest ranks of society absconded, as this act was illegal. If authorities apprehended a runaway, they forcibly returned her to her spouse. In the meantime, a wife who had absconded could not legally marry a new husband, as this would constitute bigamy. Most runaway wives fled to their natal families. Although it was illegal for a woman to abscond, the law permitted her to return to her own family. This loophole allowed an unhappy wife to leave her husband without receiving a divorce. In these circumstances, it was almost impossible for a husband to force his wife to return. Although a woman could not legally remarry after absconding, this recourse allowed her to escape from domestic violence or some other intolerable situation.

Not all women had only one husband. Although technically illegal, people at the bottom reaches of society often practiced de facto polyandry, with a wife having two or more husbands. In this respect, Qing society departed from the global norm. One anthropologist has calculated that polygyny is 141 times more frequent than polyandry in cultures around the world.[20] Polyandry does not arise from a single cause.[21] In each society, it emerges to address local challenges. It seems that people never consider polyandry an optimal form of kinship organization, as it can easily give rise to jealousy and quarrels. However, it can sometimes be an expedient way to cope with pressing problems.

The unusual demographic structure of Qing society, together with widespread poverty, led to the emergence of polyandry.[22] Female infanticide and concubinage had skewed the sex ratio to such an extent that many men could not possibly enter a monogamous marriage.[23] The number of unmarried men seems to have increased during the eighteenth century, perhaps tripling in number. A lifelong bachelor who lacked offspring faced terrifying insecurity, as he would not have anyone to care for him in his old age. When he became too feeble to work, he might starve to death. Polyandry arose as a way for unmarriageable men to raise children. The women involved were usually extremely poor, so they consented to the arrangement to improve their own circumstances. People commonly referred to this practice as "getting a husband to support a husband" (*zhao fu yang fu*). This term highlights the poverty of the people involved. A wife took a second husband to support her first husband and his family. For both sides, polyandry helped them avoid destitution or starvation.

Records from previous eras occasionally mention polyandry. In the year 972 the Song dynasty government even prohibited it, implying that it was not rare.[24] However, it seems that this unorthodox practice became much more frequent during the Qing era due to the rising number of lifelong bachelors. There was already a large market for female bodies, as the wealthy purchased concubines to provide sex and bear children. The widespread commoditization of women for wealthy buyers made it easier for people to accept a corresponding practice among the poor.

In polyandrous relationships, an unmarried man would have sex with a married woman, usually with her husband's approval, in exchange for a fee. Sometimes a husband would rent his wife to another man, a practice little different from prostitution. More often the connection was more substantial. A woman might move away from her husband and live with another man until she bore a child. Then she would return to her first husband and leave the child behind. Or she might split her time between the two men in a long-term arrangement lasting up to a decade. Sometimes the second man would move in with the couple and become part of their household. Even if the two men resided in different places, they might take meals together with their common wife and pool their resources. To make this embarrassing relationship less awkward, the parties involved might refer to one another by fictive kinship terms. Sometimes the men became sworn brothers. People believed that sworn brothers should share everything, so it seemed reasonable for them to share a wife.

The law mandated monogamy, so these relationships were illegal. Even so, those involved often specified the terms of their bargain in a contract. If one of them was literate, they might write down the details. Otherwise the agreement was verbal. Most importantly, the parties involved specified which man would receive custody of the children born from the polyandrous arrangement. The main point of these relationships was reproduction, so the male outsider would receive custody of at least one of the sons that the woman bore.

A legal case from 1743 highlights the financial motivations of polyandry. Wang Yuliang, a forty-nine-year-old peasant living in the countryside near Beijing, worked hard but had little to show for his toil.[25] He owned a small plot of marginal land that yielded little, so he also worked for others as a hired laborer. Wang suffered from bad health and no doubt worried about his future, so he approached an even poorer man named He Shixin, age thirty-seven, and proposed a polyandrous arrangement. The younger man and his wife, named Li Shi, moved in with Wang, who began to sleep with Li. He Shixin was supposed to farm Wang's land and support the family. However, he was also sickly and did not turn out to be a good provider. Wang became extremely jealous and began to abuse Li. In response, she conspired with her first husband and the two of them killed Wang. Authorities uncovered the plot and they were sentenced to death.

Polyandry was neither legal nor respectable. The state prohibited it and the community condemned it. Yet even though neighbors and relatives might mock those involved, they would not intervene. Polyandry may have been embarrassing, but society tolerated it nonetheless. Neighbors realized that those involved did not want these associations but entered them unwillingly out of crushing poverty. Nor did the women at the center of these triangular relationships consider themselves victims. Unlike women kidnapped and forcefully sold into prostitution, concubinage, or marriage, authorities presumed that women in polyandrous relationships consented to them. In fact it seems that in about a third of the cases, a wife took the initiative. She established the polyandrous relationship on her own and only informed her first husband after initiating it. Poor women knew that their sexual and reproductive capacities were valuable resources, so they used what they had at their disposal to solve their financial problems. Despite the shame involved, people resorted to polyandry due to its utility, as both sides could benefit substantially. The bare stick gained a child who could support him in the future, and the wife and her legal husband raised their standard of living. Polyandry offered people in seemingly hopeless circumstances a way to survive.

Although the polyandrous relationships of the poor were both illegal and shameful, the rich could purchase concubines to achieve a similar result. Concubinage had a long history in China.[26] Not only was it acceptable, but buying a woman advertised a man's wealth and status. A man could purchase a concubine from either a woman's parents or a professional agent. The government licensed brokers and regulated transactions to prevent human trafficking. There had to be a written contract, and local authorities kept track of each purchase. A concubine's price depended on her qualities. A beautiful virgin with dainty feet cost much more than a plain older woman. If a concubine could sing or compose poetry, she could command a higher price. Men also prized women born into wealthy families that had suffered ruin, as they had refined manners and an elegant bearing. The wording of concubine contracts implies that both buyer and seller regarded these women as chattel.[27] Because concubines were purchased outright, they had low status and few rights.

The governments of previous dynasties carefully distinguished wife from concubine, seeing the latter as far inferior. During the Tang era, people looked on concubinage as a form of servitude. However, concubines gained more respect during the Song dynasty. At that time, social shifts led people to take a broader view of kinship, so they began to regard concubines as a kind of family member. Neo-Confucians emphasized the importance of kinship bonds as the fundamental principle for organizing society and encouraged the integration of marginal relations as full family members. Ming dynasty law treated wife and concubine similarly in many respects, as both had comparable relationships with the husband and family elders. This change made concubines much closer to wives in status. However, Ming authorities saw concubinage as a threat to the institution of marriage, so they tried to limit it to members of the officialdom.[28] Men who were not officeholders were not supposed to take a concubine until age forty. Even then, they were only supposed to purchase one if they did not yet have a male heir. However, this law was rarely enforced and concubinage remained common among the elite. It remained on the books during the early Qing but was eliminated in 1740. Overall, the relative positions of wife and concubine were closer during the Qing than before.[29]

Men of varying ages bought concubines.[30] Most were middle-aged, and few were elderly. In contrast, concubines tended to be young. Most were about the same age as a bride, and three-fourths were age nineteen or younger at the time of purchase. Although grooms were usually a few years older than brides, there was usually a much larger age gap between concubines and their masters. More than half of these women were fifteen or more years younger than the men who purchased them.[31]

The mechanics of Qing concubinage differed according to ethnicity.[32] Han men generally took Han women as concubines, and they were not supposed to have a Manchu concubine. The concubines of Manchu men were also usually ethnic Han, but the children of these pairings were considered ethnic Manchu. It seems that concubinage was much more popular among Manchus than Han. There were far fewer Manchus than Han, so it was hard for a Manchu man to find a suitable wife of the same ethnicity. Also, like their Han counterparts, Manchu families frequently practiced female infanticide, reducing the number of marriageable Manchu women. Because Manchu men were forbidden from marrying a Han wife, they often had no choice but to take a Han concubine to bear them children.

The prevalence of concubinage should not be exaggerated. Bringing a new woman into the home could easily lead to friction with other family members, and most men wanted to avoid complicating their domestic life unnecessarily. In most places, even the wealthy rarely took concubines.[33] Among a sample of 884 men who had obtained a prestigious *jinshi* in the civil service examination during the second half of the nineteenth century, only 8.6 percent had a concubine. Another study of 3,455 men with a *jinshi* had similar results, as only 7.24 percent had a concubine.

Concubinage was more popular among the elite in certain regions, depending on local conditions and customs. Taiwan had a relatively high rate of concubinage.[34] Because the Qing government prohibited women from legally migrating to Taiwan, the cost of marriage was unusually high. The proportion of women in Taiwan's population steadily increased over the course of the dynasty, but in 1896 there were still 119 men for every 100 women. Previously the ratio had been even more skewed. Due to the unequal sex ratio, men had to pay out an extremely large betrothal gift to obtain a wife. Given the expense of marriage, concubinage was sometimes a cheaper option. The economy of Taiwan centered on the export of cash crops, and some merchants used their profits to purchase a concubine smuggled in from the mainland. Taking a concubine instead of a wife could have financial advantages. Although a concubine's main function was usually to bear a son, they were considered akin to servants. Their masters often worked them hard, so a concubine could be much more productive than a wife. Also, sometimes a man migrated to Taiwan after he had married and left his wife behind in Fujian. If he prospered, he might buy a concubine because he was already married.

Fujian was overpopulated, so many poor families were willing to sell their daughters into concubinage. Some ended up in Taiwan. It seems that wealthy Taiwanese men bought concubines more frequently than elsewhere. For three generations, men of the Lian family of Mabinying had one concubine each. Fifty-one men of the wealthy Lin family of Wufeng took concubines. Most had a single concubine, but some purchased as many as four.

During the Qing, it became much more common for masters to compose a commemorative epitaph for a deceased concubine.[35] This trend was largely due to the increasing popularity of epitaphs. Even ordinary people were honored with written commemorations. If a concubine bore her master a son, she would be much more likely to have a funerary epitaph composed in her honor. A man writing an epitaph for a deceased concubine faced a quandary. While clear standards existed for lauding deceased mothers, wives, and sisters, masters and concubines shared an ambiguous tie, so this tribute lacked clear guidelines. As with the commemorations of other women, a master often praised a concubine for possessing conventional female virtues and qualities appropriate to her social role, such as humility and submissiveness. If a wifeless man had took a concubine to manage his household, he might laud her domestic skills.

The situations that concubines faced varied considerably. Many ended up exploited, maltreated, and degraded. When a concubine entered a man's home, her presence implicitly raised the wife's status in comparison.[36] Even so, wives often resented concubines and treated them badly. Despite these problems, becoming a concubine could have advantages. A woman who helped her poor parents by selling herself into concubinage would win praise as an exceptionally filial daughter.[37] And for someone born into poverty with no good prospects, entering the household of a wealthy man might seem like a big step up the social ladder. If she bore her master a son, her treatment would likely improve. After her son grew to maturity, she would be respected and attain a decent standard of living.

No one saw the concubine's life as the best possible option, but it was sometimes better than the other possibilities available to the poor. If a poor woman was not desirable enough to become a concubine, she might end up as a servant.[38] In the late Qing, it was more economical for the rich to purchase a maid than to hire one, so there was a large market for female bondservants.[39] Servants had an even lower place in the home and almost no hope for upward mobility. Worst of all, a poor family might sell their daughter into prostitution.

Despite the degradation that concubines had to endure, this custom might have had some positive effects on society. By allowing poor families to sell their daughters and avoid dowries, concubinage lowered the rate of female infanticide. It also allowed the poor to obtain a share of resources from the rich. Selling a daughter could provide desperately needed financial relief for indigent families. Authorities saw concubinage as a pragmatic way to reduce hardship among the poorest sector of the population and quell potential unrest. The officialdom even justified concubinage as an expression of Confucian benevolence. From today's standpoint, buying another human being seems barbaric, but at the time people considered it normal and even virtuous.

3

Government

The rich corpus of Chinese literature includes many stories about strong and capable women. For centuries, many authors wrote about "knights errant" (*xia*) who resorted to violence in the pursuit of justice. Although these figures were mostly men, women behaved in a similar fashion—at least on the pages of fiction.[1] Sometimes a female knight errant had no relation to the person she helped but attacked a villain simply because he had treated others unjustly. Other times she punished someone who had impugned her reputation. Most frequently, a female character avenged a major wrong that she herself had endured. Audiences also enjoyed stories of women who took to the field of battle to defend their country. Hua Mulan is by far the most famous, but there were others as well.[2]

These narratives provided female readers with food for thought. While ordinary women gained approbation for meekness and reclusion, female heroes were lauded for behaving in the opposite manner. Naturally, some women found these martial role models compelling. Chai Jingyi (fl. mid-seventeenth century) wrote a poem celebrating Liang Hongyu (1102–1135), a Southern Song dynasty female general who led troops against Jurchen invaders.[3]

> Jade-white face and cloud coiffure brushed with the dust of war,
> The little "Lotus Battalion" clustered at the river's edge.
> Carrying—not well-bucket and rice mortar—but the drums of battle,
> Who would believe the hero was a fair maid?[4]

Although a few female warriors were real people, most were fictional. Law and custom kept women tied to the home, and a fighter with bound feet would not be very effective in battle. Nevertheless, audiences enjoyed fantasizing about female warriors. Over the centuries, the prominence of female characters in fictional tales of war increased. Many were historical dramas. Qing audiences enjoyed stories and plays about the generals of the Yang family (*Yangjia jiang*), which developed out of folktales about a Song dynasty family that fought to defend China from foreign invasion.[5] The threats that China faced from foreign powers in the late Qing made this a timely theme, so playwrights transposed this classic story into new genres and styles. Historians note that the warriors involved in these battles were all male. Even so, legends described the family's women also heroically fighting against enemy troops, so nineteenth-century Chinese opera scripts included female warriors.

Besides warfare, government also provided possibilities for women to exercise power. Yet few women had a chance to participate in affairs of state. Blocked from both warfare and public life, usually only proximity to the throne gave a woman the chance to influence important matters.[6] However, China's institutions deliberately made it difficult for women to accrue authority within the state apparatus. For this reason, historians often prefer to discuss female agency instead of power.[7]

Prior to the invasion of China, Jurchen women seemed well positioned to influence politics. They rode horses, practiced archery, hunted, and even fought when necessary. These physically active women did not bind their feet. This vigorous demeanor affected attitudes toward women, and Jurchen men assumed that their mothers and wives might participate in important affairs. Among steppe peoples, a khan's wife or mother often assumed the role of regent when he died and ruled until tribal leaders met and selected his successor.[8] The potential for regency elevated the political status of elite Jurchen women.

Early Manchu rulers were polygynous, and some of their consorts attained a degree of influence at court. Although a consort lacked authority herself, she might affect policy by counseling her powerful spouse. Many consorts came from important families, and this prestigious background lent their opinions greater weight. The early Manchu leader Nurhachi (1559–1626) used political marriage to forge useful alliances. Fourteen of Nurhachi's sixteen wives came from the families of Jurchen chieftains and the other two were related to important Mongols.[9] After 1653 the ruling family began to marry the daughters of banner officials.

Hong Taiji, founder of the Qing dynasty, had a Mongol wife named Bumbutai (1613–1688), eventually known as Empress Dowager Xiaozhuangwen (figure 3.1).[10] The nascent Qing system as yet lacked systematic rules and procedures, allowing her to garner a degree

Figure 3.1. Empress Dowager Xiaozhuangwen (Bumbutai)
Wikimedia Commons

of influence. Bumbutai was a significant presence at court for more than forty years over the course of three reigns. As empress dowager, she helped manage matters during the reign of her son, the Shunzhi emperor. When her grandson Kangxi ascended the throne as a child, her faction continued to dominate administration through the early years of his reign. Bumbutai used her authority well. She helped construct a consistent administrative system, selected able officials, and stabilized the new state. Her prudent guidance saw the dynasty through its uncertain early decades.

At the beginning of the Qing, emperors and high officials handled many important issues in an ad hoc manner. The mechanics of Qing government coalesced during the long reign of Kangxi. To establish robust institutions, Kangxi and his advisors took heed of the lessons of history. Previously, empresses dowager had periodically seized control of the state. To maximize their influence, they subverted the regular procedures and institutions of government, sometimes fomenting chaos as a consequence. Reactions to the controversial reign of Wu Zetian (624–705) crystallized negative views toward female power. Wu not only ruled as an emperor (*huangdi*), the only woman ever to assume that male title, but she also overthrew the Tang and declared the start of a new dynasty. Memories of that traumatic episode poisoned male attitudes toward powerful women.[11] Eleven of the subsequent Tang emperors did not even dare to name an empress for fear that their consort might use the title to seize power. Rulers of the Five Dynasties and Song once again ventured to call their consorts empresses, but they put stringent safeguards in place to prevent them from accruing authority.

Over the centuries, the posthumous reputation of Empress Wu plummeted.[12] Even though she had been a competent ruler overall, she was increasingly condemned. Scholars criticized her reign as unorthodox and inept, while the authors of novels depicted her as a depraved villain with an insatiable libido.[13] By the Ming and Qing, the demonization of Wu Zetian had led people to regard her reign as an utter catastrophe. Officials wanted to ensure that no woman would ever overthrow the patrilineal political order again. Many rules regulating the behavior of empresses emerged in reaction to Empress Wu's extraordinary reign.[14]

The founder of the Ming, Zhu Yuanzhang (1328–1398), ordered that the dynasty's rulers should all take their wives from the lower elite. He wanted empresses to enter the palace with minimal prestige. The Ming imperial clan also observed primogeniture to ensure a smooth transition of power and prevent an empress dowager from enthroning a puppet.[15] These provisions had the desired effect. Eleven out of fifteen Ming emperors were the eldest sons of prior rulers and no woman ever became an official regent.

The Qing employed different measures to prevent empresses from gaining power. Although the Jurchens traditionally practiced polygyny, the Qing followed Chinese custom in designating only a single empress as the true wife. Although lesser consorts were theoretically akin to concubines, emperors muddied the distinction between the two roles to degrade the position of empress.[16]

Unlike the Ming emperors, most Qing monarchs were healthy and capable, reducing the possibility of female influence. They rejected Ming primogeniture, as this practice had often put a feeble ruler on the throne. Instead rulers tried to select a capable successor from among their offspring. Under the Qing, the son of an empress did not outrank his brothers and he would probably not succeed his father, reducing his mother's status. Moreover, empress and emperor were usually not very close, and their relationship was not expected to have a sexual dimension. Imperial concubines bore most of sons of Qing emperors. Although the mechanics of succession varied over time, an emperor would usually secretly select the most talented of his sons to be his heir. In some instances, after a ruler's death the court assembled to hear the reading of his will, at which time the name of his successor was dramatically revealed. The flexibility of Qing succession helps account for the high quality of the dynasty's rulers. In addition, the air of uncertainty surrounding succession weakened empresses dowager. Because no one knew which of the emperor's sons would succeed him, a woman could not begin to consolidate power prior to her son's accession. Also, many of the emperor's sons were born to low-ranking palace concubines or even servants, further decreasing the possibility that they might intervene in matters of policy.[17]

Like their Han subjects, the Manchu emperors wed a woman of a different surname. Qing empresses were usually descended from Manchu generals who participated in the conquest of China or imperial bondservants with an intimate tie to the imperial clan.[18] The in-laws of the emperors rarely had any influence. A strong bureaucratic apparatus gave them few opportunities to intervene in affairs of state.[19] Moreover, the palace machinery carefully limited interactions between empresses and their natal families. A Qing wedding custom symbolically demonstrated the alienation of empresses from their blood kin. When an emperor married, the wife's dowry was supplied by the palace, not her family. The court intended this unusual custom to emphasize that henceforth she belonged to the imperial clan, not the family of her birth.

Empresses and other consorts spent most of their time confined in the massive palace complex in the center of Beijing. Palace ladies enjoyed certain freedoms denied most Chinese women. They could ride horses, wear men's clothes, and frequently attended operas and other performances.

However, as even Manchu women from elite families were usually illiterate, the Qing empresses were poorly educated and unsophisticated.

When a woman's son became emperor, she could be elevated to the role of empress dowager. However, a woman from a low background lacked the prestige that traditionally accompanied this position. Emperors treated their mothers with respect, but with the exception of Empress Dowager Cixi, who ruled at an unusual time, Qing emperors usually managed to prevent their mothers from influencing policy. The Qing maintained the Chinese institution of empress but reduced these women to symbols of propriety and motherhood.

Palace organization changed somewhat over time.[20] At the beginning of the dynasty, Manchu rulers initially managed their households according to steppe custom. Palace life was fairly informal and the harem lacked a clear hierarchy. Nurhachi had sixteen consorts, all of whom had a status akin to wives. An incident involving one of Nurhachi's wives, named Gundai, illustrates the atmosphere of the early Qing palace.[21] Nurhachi suspected Gundai of stealing valuables from him, but he did not execute her, as was his prerogative. However, Gundai's children felt tainted by her disgraceful behavior, and one of her sons killed his mother to remove the stain on his honor. Chinese considered matricide perhaps the most terrible crime of all, but according to the traditions of northern nomads, this sort of honor killing was acceptable and even laudable.

The palace walls in Beijing enclosed an immense warren of buildings that housed thousands of residents and laborers, in addition to subsidiary palaces and lodges. A comprehensive palace bureaucracy with standard rules and procedures managed these vast establishments. Palace management had been refined over the centuries, so in most respects the Qing followed the precedents set by previous dynasties.

As palace organization developed, harem women began to have varied ranks. The empress dowager stood above all other palace women in status. Below her, the emperor chose one consort as his senior spouse and granted her the title of empress, in line with Chinese custom. Originally, all of the other consorts were just called madam (*furen*, or *beile* in Manchu). Beginning in the late eighteenth century, the sixty highest-ranking women of the harem were classified into eight distinct ranks. Women residing in the two imperial palaces had different titles, with the empress at the top of both hierarchies. Below the titled consorts, numerous concubines of lower status lacked a clear rank.

The Kangxi emperor instituted a simplified system with sixteen titled consorts classified into three upper ranks, as well as an empress. Below these women were an unspecified number of lesser consorts occupying three lower ranks. Then came myriad minor concubines (*yingqie*). Although a son of any of these women might possibly become emperor, a boy born to a concubine did not automatically receive an aristocratic title, unlike the sons of major consorts.

Consorts of the highest ranks had an elite background, while lower-ranking women came from ordinary families. Under previous dynasties, a harem woman could change her status. The mother of a prince or one of the monarch's favorites might rise in the palace hierarchy. However, Qing palace ranks were relatively static, and a consort's status usually did not change much over the course of her life.[22]

Most palace women were Manchus or from allied nomadic peoples. There were women of other ethnicities as well. Qing officials forced attractive Han women from good families to become imperial concubines, as they considered them a kind of tribute from the conquered.[23] Chinese detested this custom and considered it akin to kidnapping. Some parents even married off their daughters prematurely to keep them from ending up as minor concubines in the imperial harem. The Qing empire included many minority groups, and the palace took in women from the various peoples inhabiting the borderlands. The residents of Beijing considered women from remote regions extremely exotic and their presence in the harem evoked comment. They even circulated paintings of palace women who came from the Yi people in the far south.[24] These women may have been exoticized, but people still treated them with due respect. Artists portrayed them in dignified poses appropriate to their station.

Empress Dowager Chongqing (1693–1777), wife of the Yongzheng emperor and mother of Qianlong, represents the model Qing consort.[25] She kept a low profile during her husband's lifetime and lived uneventfully within the confines of the inner palace. After Yongzheng died, her son gave her the title of empress dowager and she took on a more public role. Qianlong clearly loved his mother. He visited her frequently, took her along with him when he traveled, and held a lavish banquet to celebrate her sixtieth birthday. Nevertheless, Chongqing lacked tangible authority, and Qianlong confined her to ceremonial duties. Mostly he used his mother as a prop to demonstrate his own virtue. He insulated her from administration but made a show of treating her with deference and respect, thereby publicly demonstrating his commitment to filial piety. She played the part of the virtuous mother and he took on the role of the dedicated son. In this way, they used each other to elevate their reputations and garner praise.

Although the Qing emperors did not choose their empresses for political reasons, they often used their daughters' marriages to bind useful allies to the throne.[26] The dynasty's twelve emperors bore eighty-two daughters. Many died young, as the rate of infant mortality in the crowded palace precincts was surprisingly high. Of the survivors, forty-five married on schedule and twelve remained in the palace, perhaps held in reserve in case they were needed to quickly make a useful match. Princesses wed from age eleven to thirty, with fifteen being the average. Only four married before age fifteen.[27]

Jurchen leaders had traditionally married off their daughters for political gain. Immediately prior to the invasion of China, Manchu rulers wed daughters to useful allies to build up a large coalition for the coming conflict. After the conquest, the emperors did not marry princesses to Han gentry or officials, even though Han dominated the bureaucracy. Instead they married their daughters to the leaders of various ethnic groups living in strategically important border areas. Throughout the Qing, emperors continued to marry off their daughters to forge and reinforce ties with foreign leaders.

Unlike most dynasties, the Qing did not limit the title of princess (*gongzhu*) to daughters of the monarch. Because these marriages were so useful, the rulers wanted even more princesses, so they also granted the title to the unmarried daughters of important nobles. The emperors then married off these so-called princesses to cement political alliances. The office managing the imperial clan (*zongren fu*) oversaw the affairs of princesses and helped arrange their marriages. Emperors granted the husband of a princess the title *efu*, which elevated him to a privileged position within the Qing hierarchy. Because so many women bore the title of princess, their marriages became an important aspect of Qing foreign policy. The Manchus were deeply involved in north Asian affairs and used political marriage to continuously renew their bonds with the region's leaders. Besides marrying princesses to allied khans, the emperors also wed them to members of the Mongol nobility and important figures in the Mongol and Chinese banners. The Manchu emperors put great stress on maintaining close ties with their Mongol allies, as they considered Mongol support vital for keeping the northern frontier stable.[28] Even so, they did not marry their daughters to minor khans living in distant wastelands. They tended to favor leaders in regions closer to the Chinese border. After the Qianlong era, most princesses married men living in the capital region.

When a princess married, she received a generous dowry that included gold, silver, and other precious items. Brides also received fields and buildings that could be rented out to generate a regular stream of income. A princess leaving the palace took along luxuriously crafted items for daily use, including furniture, toiletries, sedan chairs, clothing, and jewelry. Up to the late eighteenth century, most princesses married steppe allies, so the trousseau had items that allowed them to live comfortably in a tent. A princess' dowry also included a mansion in Beijing for her to use when she and her husband visited the capital. A princess did not own

Figure 3.2. Empress Cixi
Wikimedia Commons

the real estate in her dowry, but only had usage rights. When she died, the sitting emperor could decide what to do with this property.

Kangxi and his successors followed procedures intended to block women from affecting policy, so most palace women had no influence over affairs of state. However, when the Qing dynasty slumped into terminal decline, Empress Dowager Cixi (1835–1908) seized control of the government and handled key matters for more than four decades (figure 3.2). Cixi stands out as one of the most important figures not just in women's history but in the general history of China. She was the most powerful force in the government when China faced threats from the industrialized outside world, dooming the imperial system. When Chinese today look back on empresses of the imperial era, they visualize Cixi as emblematic of the powerful consort.

Three empresses stand out as particularly important in Chinese history. Empress Lü (241–180 BCE) was the wife of the Han dynasty founder Gaozu who established the standard characteristics of the imperial system. After Gaozu died, Lü took control of the government. Her bold actions set an important precedent. Thereafter many empresses dowager imitated Lü and involved themselves in governance. She was the crucial figure who first inserted palace women into the heart of administration.

Seven centuries later, Wu Zetian (624–705) transformed the nature of female power during the Tang dynasty. After she became empress dowager, she seized control of the government from her son, usurped the dynasty, declared herself emperor, and ruled in her own name. Wu left behind a mixed legacy. Judged from the standpoint of her age, she seems to have been a successful ruler. Empress Wu was intelligent and competent, and she usually used her authority to pursue good ends. Nevertheless, the sight of a woman lording over the realm devastated male pride. Thereafter rulers took elaborate steps to make sure that a woman could never again wield so much authority. These measures were generally very successful. After Empress Wu, few consorts had much authority. They mostly confined their attentions to benign activities such as religion, patronage, and court ceremony.

Cixi was the final member of this trio of major empresses. Despite the battery of elaborate rules and institutions designed to prevent female ascendency, Cixi nevertheless managed to seize control of the machinery of state. She ruled China at a crucial time in the nation's history. Not only was the Qing dynasty disintegrating but a series of traumatic failures called into question the entire edifice of Chinese civilization. Faced with unprecedented threats from imperialist powers, Chinese had to suddenly confront such confusing alien ideas as modernism, industrialization, capitalism, and imperialism. Cixi led the government's response to these existential challenges. Her actions shaped the nation and helped make China what it is today.

Contemporary Chinese views toward female power emerged largely in response to Cixi. She did not write memoirs or leave behind her version of events. This silence allowed rivals and critics to portray Cixi as a profligate, greedy, and foolish woman who deserves a major share of the blame for the dynasty's collapse.[29] Denunciations of Cixi appeal to popular sentiments. Chinese want a villain to take the blame for the nation's repeated humiliations, and an extravagantly dressed Manchu woman with extremely long fingernails made an ideal scapegoat. The popular image of a haughty and imprudent woman at the helm of a failed government poisoned contemporary Chinese views toward female power. It is no coincidence that almost all of the high officials in the current government of China are male.

Although most Chinese still see Cixi as one of history's great villains, and her ultimate failure is indisputable, revisionists have recently begun to reassess her actions and legacy. This debate continues to rage, making Cixi one of the most controversial figures in Chinese history. Yet whatever judgment one renders, it must be admitted that she faced almost insurmountable challenges. Cixi tried to push through essential changes in response to a long series of crises, in the face of steadfast opposition from reactionaries and rivals. Her failure resulted in the fall of the Qing dynasty and an end to the imperial system.

Cixi was born into one of the most important Manchu families, surnamed Naha.[30] No one bothered to record her given name, as they did not consider it important. Following Manchu custom, she did not receive much schooling. Although no one considered Cixi a beauty, she was poised and charismatic, so palace administrators selected her as a minor consort for the Xianfeng emperor (r. 1850–1861). The emperor already had an empress named Zhen (1837–1881), whom he chose for her easygoing personality. However, Cixi bore Xianfeng his first son, so she was promoted to the second most important consort after the empress. Initially Cixi did not express any political opinions. She quietly observed what was happening around her and learned about the immense challenges facing the empire.

When the sickly Xianfeng fell terminally ill, his son by Cixi was only five years old. Xianfeng appointed a committee of eight experienced officials to act as regents during his son's minority. However, Xianfeng was a poor judge of character and selected xenophobic reactionaries who opposed vital reforms. Their bad advice had previously resulted in foreign forces occupying Beijing and burning down the Old Summer Palace.

Xianfeng died in 1861 and Cixi's son was enthroned as the Tongzhi emperor (r. 1861–1875). At first, Cixi had no power. Officially, Tongzhi was the son of Empress Zhen, who assumed the title of empress dowager. Cixi received the same title as a courtesy. In the past, when two women held the title empress dowager, they often fought for supremacy. Unusually, this pair of dowagers got along well. They became firm allies and plotted to bring down the inept regents. Just two months into the new reign, the empresses dowager accused the regents of disrespecting the monarch and ousted them from the court. With this palace coup, Empresses Dowager Cixi and Zhen became the de facto rulers of the Qing Empire. Cixi was only twenty-five years old.

The two dowagers selected moderate officials to serve on a Grand Council that managed routine administration. The Manchu nobleman Yi Xin, known in English as Prince Gong, was chosen to head this body because he was pragmatic, open-minded, and got along well with foreign diplomats. Thereafter Cixi made key decisions and Yi Xin implemented them. However, Cixi found herself handicapped by insufficient education. She had trouble understanding the arcane language of bureaucratic documents and could not compose the formal prose used at court. Although she studied with eunuch teachers in the evenings, she never became a proficient writer.

Rules that prohibited mixing of the sexes also posed a problem. Cixi could not appear in public or meet with officials, making it difficult for her to deal with important matters. However, she could interact freely with castrated men, so she used palace eunuchs as her intermediaries. By operating outside the conventional power structure, Cixi practiced a style of governance known as intimate politics.[31] She promoted eunuchs to posts formerly held by imperial bondservants, putting them in positions capable of carrying out her orders. Although Cixi found eunuchs useful, they had a reputation for corruption and dissipation, so the prominence of so many eunuchs evoked criticism.

Although Chinese people today regard Cixi as a reactionary, in fact she backed many reforms. She realized that the dynasty had to change to survive. However, she also understood that Chinese society had become extremely fragile from invasions, rebellions, and severe economic pressures, so she introduced changes gradually. Even so, her early reforms met with shrill hostility from conservative officials and literati. The officialdom opposed the construction of railways because they feared that noisy trains would disturb ancestral tombs. And they selfishly resisted the teaching of science, mathematics, and engineering because they did not want to render their own hard-won classical learning obsolete. Reactionaries wanted to close China off from the West and seek vengeance for past defeats. Given the unrealistic attitude of much of the Chinese establishment, it is impressive that Cixi was able to achieve as much as she did.

The Tongzhi emperor suddenly died of smallpox at age nineteen. Because he had not yet produced an heir, Empresses Dowager Cixi and Zhen had a three-year-old child posthumously adopted as Xianfeng's son. This arrangement allowed the boy to assume the throne as the Guangxu emperor (r. 1875–1908). Cixi continued to dominate the government during the young ruler's long minority. At this time Li Hongzhang, an enthusiastic and outward-looking reformer, became extremely influential at court. The government embarked on a military modernization program and began to improve infrastructure and basic industry. China established a telegraph network, railways, and steamship lines. Students began to learn about science and mathematics. Cixi also launched a military campaign that recaptured Xinjiang.

The dowagers had to retire when Guangxu reached the age of majority in 1889. Unfortunately, the young emperor had been handicapped by a narrow classical education. Guangxu's tutor was an ardent reactionary and xenophobe, and he taught his impressionable student an archaic Confucian worldview. Outdated schooling rendered the monarch unable to deal with the unprecedented challenges facing China. Guangxu was also extremely shy and tongue tied, so he had trouble communicating with officials. When he started to handle matters on his own, Guangxu turned away from reformism and instead instituted a passive bureaucratic routine.

In 1895 Japan unexpectedly defeated China, sending shockwaves through the realm. The victors demanded that China hand over the island of Taiwan and pay an enormous indemnity. This setback delivered an immense psychological blow. Not only was the Qing Empire many times bigger than Japan, but Chinese had always dismissed the Japanese as exotic barbarians living on the fringes of the civilized world. This unforeseen humiliation shattered Chinese self-assurance. It also highlighted the failure of Guangxu's passive style of rule.

Overwhelmed by this catastrophe, Guangxu called Cixi out of retirement to help him cope with the crisis. The indemnity demanded by Japan wrecked the government's finances. China had to borrow huge sums from foreign governments just to maintain basic services, and there was nothing left to pay for modernization projects. Guangxu began to spend a considerable amount of time with Cixi, and she taught him the principles of statecraft. She counseled a new round of restructuring, and the emperor heeded her advice.

Consultations between Cixi and Guangxu resulted in the reform movement of 1898. Although Cixi's enemies claimed that she opposed this round of reforms, in fact she fought hard for them in the face of conservative opposition. These measures went beyond previous restructuring. The military received modern training. Students were sent abroad to learn about science and technology. The government encouraged agricultural improvements and Western-style commerce. Numerous machines were imported and factories established.

The charismatic public intellectual Kang Youwei (1858–1927) posed the most determined challenge to Cixi.[32] Even though both Cixi and Kang both supported reform to some degree, they detested one another. Kang's circle eventually plotted a coup. They planned to assassinate the head of the military and capture Cixi. Perhaps they even intended to kill her. However, the plot was exposed and forestalled. Although Kang failed to take over the government, he nevertheless exerted considerable influence over the pliable emperor and convinced Guangxu to favor Japan. Although most Chinese considered Japan their most dangerous enemy, Kang saw it as the best role model for China, as Japanese had quickly industrialized and built a formidable army. He hoped to establish a union between Japan and China, as he assumed that this would be the fastest way to modernize China. Kang managed to win Guangxu's support for this naive vision.

Cixi had other ideas. She feared Japan, detested Kang, and despised Guangxu. To keep China from sliding into Japan's orbit, Cixi seized power outright and imprisoned Guangxu in the palace. But whereas she had previously handled matters capably, this time she made a disastrous error. In 1899 xenophobic militias formed to counter foreign bullying and avenge repeated humiliations. They called themselves the Militia United in Righteousness (*Yihetuan*), but because many of their members practiced martial arts, foreigners referred to them as Boxers. These violent nativists wanted to massacre foreigners and restore the nation's vigor. Although the Boxers opposed Cixi's moderate reformism, she feared that if she actively opposed them, they would turn their wrath against the Manchus and bring down the dynasty. Although Cixi officially banned the Boxer movement, she did not try to restrain them.

Eventually Boxer forces entered Beijing to target the foreign legations there. The city's residents were surprised to see virgins and widows among the Boxer ranks. Female fighters called themselves Red Lanterns, as they carried both a spear and a red lantern. Each of them also had a red handkerchief believed to have magical properties. This female brigade shocked onlookers by defying the norms of female modesty and marching through the streets.

Foreign governments wanted to protect their diplomats and quell the antiforeign movement, so they dispatched an international army to capture the capital. In response, Qing soldiers shot a foreign ambassador and China declared war on eight foreign countries. Cixi aligned herself with the militias, and the Boxers fought alongside government forces to defend Beijing. However, the militias were undisciplined, and many fighters were no more than bandits. The allied army easily overcame this feeble opposition and occupied Beijing. Cixi and Guangxu fled westward to safety, accompanied by a ragtag entourage. If they had wanted to, the invaders could probably have captured the emperor and empress dowager. However, foreign generals realized that if they destroyed the monarchy, China would probably collapse into civil war, so they were allowed to escape. Although foreign governments resented Qing support for the Boxers, they continued to support the dynasty as the only viable guarantor of order.

Eventually the occupiers allowed the monarch and dowager to return to Beijing. The rigors of the flight into exile had caused the fragile emperor to have a physical and mental breakdown. Henceforth Guangxu was sickly and withdrawn. He rarely spoke during audiences and officials had trouble hearing what little he said. With the emperor incapacitated, it fell to Cixi to take charge of the government.

The empress dowager repudiated her previous support for xenophobes and pursued a new round of reformist policies that went much further than before. In addition to building up the economy, Cixi tried to modernize society. She urged Chinese to abandon footbinding, a custom that she had always detested. She tried to break down barriers between the sexes and founded a school for the daughters of the aristocracy. Cixi also rescinded the ban on marriages between Manchus and Han. Cixi had begun to fear that Manchus would be massacred when the dynasty inevitably fell, so she promoted the assimilation of her people into the Chinese mainstream. Under these far-reaching reforms, China's cities changed rapidly. Local authorities installed streetlights, running water, and telephone lines. They built museums, sports facilities, public parks, and zoos. Newspapers and magazines espoused a wide range of opinions, allowing the public to participate in the ongoing social and cultural ferment.

Cixi also reformed the government. She abolished the traditional examination system, which required students to memorize ancient texts and classical commentaries. Thousands of new schools opened and an educational system based on a modern curriculum took shape. Cixi also reformed China's legal system to bring judicial procedures and punishments into line with those of industrialized countries. The government set up a commerce ministry and state bank and issued a modern national currency. Ultimately, Cixi hoped to salvage the dynasty by establishing a constitutional monarchy with an elected parliament. In 1905 she sent a commission to travel abroad and study the political systems of foreign countries in preparation for instituting a new form of government.

Despite these far-reaching reforms, many influential people continued to steadfastly oppose the Qing. They believed that the decayed dynasty was holding China back. Instead of curtailing the powers of the emperor, they advocated replacing the imperial system with a republic. Growing ethnic hostility made the Qing increasingly unpopular. Not only was the ruler a Manchu, but the Qing had traditionally reserved top posts for Manchu officials and advisers. Ethnic bias had limited opportunities for talented Han Chinese. If the Qing had been a native Han Chinese dynasty, perhaps it could have evolved into a constitutional monarchy and China would be a very different place today. However, as traditional institutions fell by the wayside, many people embraced republicanism to rid China of detested Manchu domination. Widespread ethnic resentment ultimately doomed the dynasty.

As the elderly empress dowager's health deteriorated, she made provisions for how matters would be handled after her death. Cixi had no faith in Guangxu and feared that he would hand the country over to Japan. She ordered him poisoned, and the emperor and empress dowager died just one day apart. Cixi arranged for the child emperor Puyi to ascend the throne after Guangxu's demise. At the end of her life, Cixi had no hope for the survival of the Qing. She just wanted a smooth transition to a republican government to prevent the Manchus from being wiped out in a genocidal massacre. Puyi was a child, so real authority went to the Empress Dowager Longyu (1868–1913). Cixi trusted Longyu to yield to the republicans at the right time, preventing the massacre of Manchus. The final plan of Cixi worked as intended. When rebellions broke out, Longyu approved an edict of abdication in 1912 and declared an end to the Qing dynasty.

Like many powerful women, Cixi came to prominence during a time of crisis. The government's inability to cope with a series of catastrophes threw institutions into disarray. People yearned for strong and competent leadership, wherever it might be found. This atmosphere of desperation allowed Cixi to overcome longstanding prejudice against female power and take control of the government. However, the history of the period was largely written by her rivals. For centuries, historians had portrayed powerful women as licentious and depraved. Likewise, Cixi's rivals cast her as a villain responsible for the fall of the Qing dynasty. Such a negative portrayal is unfair. In her long stretch of involvement in government, she made one major mistake—her support for the Boxer Rebellion. It seems that she saw no alternative, as she feared that the Boxers would turn their wrath on the government and bring down the dynasty. This destructive episode stands out as an anomaly. Overall, Cixi accepted the necessity of cautious reform. She sought to modernize and strengthen her country at a measured pace intended to avoid instability.

The failure of Cixi's reformist endeavor had terrible consequences. The collapse of the Qing dynasty was followed by decades of civil war. Japan took advantage of China's weakness to invade and occupy the eastern portion of the country. If Cixi had succeeded in establishing a constitutional monarchy, a stable government might have maintained unity and overseen rapid modernization. In that case, China could potentially have followed in the footsteps of Japan's Meiji Restoration. However, she failed, so that alternative path was never taken. In sum, although Cixi was ultimately unsuccessful, at least she was on the right side of history.

4

Wealth

The financial condition of a woman's family determined her basic circumstances. Successive economic shifts over the course of the Qing altered family finance, presenting women with new challenges and opportunities. Because of rampant overpopulation, increasing numbers of peasants lacked sufficient land, and many women were born into families on the edge of destitution. Demography condemned them to a life of hard labor that yielded little reward and no hope of escape. Yet at the same time, commerce, manufacturing, and technology were all becoming increasingly sophisticated, giving wealthy women access to an unprecedented array of consumer goods. Items that had previously been considered luxuries were now readily available to the elite. This plethora of merchandise sparked a consumer revolution.[1] The wives of the gentry and prosperous merchants were the prime customers for many products, and their lives became increasingly comfortable and opulent. Consumerism also made women more important economically, with female demand driving a large proportion of economic activity. As the power of women's consumption increased, it became an increasingly important aspect of elite female identity. A privileged woman could express her social station and individual character through her choice of consumer goods.

The most fortunate women owned significant amounts of wealth. The nature of historic Chinese property ownership is extremely complicated. Scholars have articulated two very different views of the matter.[2] One side holds that families owned property in common, making women co-owners of collective wealth. An opposing school of thought distinguishes between budgeting and ownership and argues that while women belonged to a common budget group and benefited from family wealth, they did not own it. Instead men owned family property and passed it down the male line of descent, while women received a dowry separate from communal family wealth. Historians continue to weigh in on both sides of this debate, and a consensus has yet to emerge. At the very least, it seems that most women had some money of their own from dowry wealth, pin money, and perhaps gambling.[3] A large dowry could yield regular income from investments such as rents or profits from a pawnshop.

For a woman to protect her property rights, she would have to be able to access the justice system. In earlier eras, women had been able to bring lawsuits before magistrates on their own, but Qing authorities curtailed this right.[4] A woman could still file a lawsuit, but a male intermediary usually handled the matter on her behalf. This measure seems to have been intended to prevent tawdry legal proceedings from impugning women's reputations. The government also assumed that women could be easily coerced. Having a man handle a case on a woman's behalf helped ensure that she would not be pressured into acting against her best interests. Qing law enforced the ancient ritual ideal that an unmarried women ought to obey her father and a wife should yield to her husband. Forcing women to use male intercessors made them dependent on men for legal redress. If a woman wanted to bring a lawsuit and male family members refused to support her, she would find it difficult to seek justice on her own. In effect, she was a ward of her kinsmen.

In spite of these constraints, some women still handled lawsuits in person, and courts accepted these cases. It seems that young women who had not yet married did not dare to file a suit on their own behalf. They used male intermediaries so that they could maintain a reputation for cloistered virginity. An unmarried woman who exposed herself to public view in embarrassing circumstances might find it hard to marry well. Although most wives used male liaisons, some dealt with magistrates on their own behalf. Sometimes a woman handled her own lawsuit because her husband was away from home, sick, or under arrest. Most women who filed lawsuits were widows.

A woman could own land and other property in her own name. Like men, women used commercial contracts to transfer ownership of land. Surviving land and contracts list women as property owners, buyers, and sellers.[5] Women could also write wills, confirming their ownership of land. Records from Qing dynasty Taiwan show that magistrates took women's wills seriously and tried to enforce their wishes, sometimes overriding the standard principle of equal inheritance among sons to do so.[6] Women engaging in land transactions were most likely to be selling their dowry land. Sometimes a widow sold off some land from her husband's estate to pay for pressing expenses.

Women received most of their wealth from their families through dowry and inheritance. The standards and laws governing women's inheritance altered considerably over time.[7] Women's inheritance rights reached a zenith during the Southern Song dynasty. At that time, a daughter inherited a share of her parents' estate equal to half that received by each brother. If a family lacked male heirs, a magistrate declared it extinguished (*hujue*) and daughters would inherit the property. These generous inheritance provisions removed considerable amounts of wealth from the male line of descent.

As conservative officials schooled in Neo-Confucianism gained influence, the government reduced female inheritance rights to keep property within the patriline. Yuan authorities made considerable changes to the inheritance system. They deprived daughters of the right to inherit property from their parents, even from an extinguished household. Instead the government confiscated an extinguished household's estate. Although the Mongol regime did not last long, these alterations had major long-term consequences. The Ming and Qing codes maintained key provisions from Yuan law. Like the Yuan, they embraced the principle that property should remain within the patriline, severely attenuating female inheritance rights. A woman normally had no claim on the property of a deceased parent or husband.

During the Yuan and Ming eras, the property rights of Chinese widows declined as part of the overall reduction in female financial autonomy.[8] A childless widow did not inherit her husband's property outright. Instead she acted as custodian for the property for the remainder of her life. The state mandated that her deceased husband's property remain within the circle of her husband's kin, so she had a legal obligation to appoint an heir from among his kinsmen. The designated heir was supposed to be a nephew, although widows had some leeway in making this appointment, so they would try to appoint someone unlikely to cause trouble.

Qing inheritance rules for women varied by ethnicity. In theory, Manchu women had somewhat more substantial rights than their Han counterparts, as they could inherit a share of the wealth generated by certain ancestral lands held in common by their lineage or banner.[9] Like Han counterparts, Manchu women bought, sold, and rented out land to tenants, showing that they were full owners of their personal properties. A widow could retain the right to use her deceased husband's land. If she lacked heirs, the government would confiscate her estate and that of her husband upon her death. Ethnicity also influenced lifestyle and consumption patterns, so the items purchased by Manchu women often differed from the Han.[10]

The rising cult of chastity affected the legal position of widows.[11] Increasing respect for chaste widows made the government want to treat them well. Officials no longer expected that a widow would choose a husband's nephew as heir to her husband's estate. They allowed her to select any man from her husband's lineage. Allowing a widow to freely choose from such a large pool of candidates gave her considerable leeway in selecting an amenable person for this role. She might take several factors into account, including her deceased husband's wishes, lineage rules, the opinions of his family's elders and lineage leaders, and ritual norms. Occasionally a widow prioritized her own interests and appointed an heir of a different surname from her husband. Some even remarried and brought in a new spouse to take over the first husband's estate.[12] This way she could continue to control her deceased husband's property, maintain the integrity of his household, keep her dowry, and have a man to work the land. Although this sort of expedient arrangement was technically illegal, it happened nonetheless.

Some widows received financial support from the lineages of their husbands. In the nineteenth century, many lineages established charitable estates to provide widows with a regular income so that they would not have to remarry.[13] Charitable estates prioritized the access of widows to common resources. Widows came to consider this income a right and they might initiate litigation if they did not receive sufficient support. Wealthy widows also founded charitable estates to aid less fortunate peers. The rise of charitable estates affected how family elders selected spouses for their children. A man from a lineage with a charitable estate was deemed a good match, as his widow received a regular income. This fact helps explain the increasing popularity of this practice. In part, lineages established charitable estates so that members could attract desirable brides and realize collective upward mobility.

Although women saw their inheritance rights curtailed significantly after the Song dynasty, they still received dowries from their families. Classical ritual did not even mention dowry. Instead the rites emphasized the betrothal gift given by the family of the groom to that of the bride as essential for a legitimate marriage. Without this gift, a woman was considered to have eloped, or else she entered a man's home as a concubine. During the Qing, the value of betrothal gifts varied considerably, ranging from a token amount to an impressive sum.[14] However, ever since the Song dynasty, dowry had exceeded bridewealth in value, so Qing families considered dowry by far the most important financial factor in marriage negotiations.

Dowry affected women's status in various ways.[15] Most fundamentally, it distinguished wife from concubine. While men spent money to obtain a concubine, wives brought wealth into their husbands' homes. Dowry raised a wife's domestic status and gave her a degree of autonomy. A lavish dowry also publicly displayed her family's wealth and generosity, elevating their social standing. Most importantly, dowering a daughter gave her a sense of security. Because grooms were older than brides, wives often outlived their spouses. It was assumed that a woman would likely spend her final years in widowhood. A dowry would help support a woman in old age after her husband's death, regardless of his family's circumstances.

A dowry consisted of two components. The trousseau was made up of personal items such as clothes and jewelry. A dowry could also include tangible wealth such as real estate and other valuables. Prior to finalizing an engagement, the families of bride and groom negotiated the dowry's contents in detail and set them down in the marriage contract.[16] Dowries varied considerably depending on social status, wealth, region, and ethnicity.[17] Manchu women received especially large dowries. In addition to a luxurious trousseau, they might gain ownership of property that generated a stream of income, such as fertile fields, buildings, and pawnshops. Because of dowry wealth, a Manchu wife had a relatively high standing within her husband's family.

The dowries of Han women from wealthy families could also be considerable, particularly in vibrant commercial centers such as Huizhou.[18] Prosperous families included numerous luxury items in their daughters' dowries to flaunt their wealth. These might include finely crafted everyday items, furniture, jewelry, embroidered fabrics, and expensive foodstuffs. A dowry sometimes included high-quality wood for constructing the bride's coffin. This would ensure that she would eventually have a good funeral, hopefully in the distant future.

Most importantly, many dowries included land.[19] Brides preferred to receive wealth in the form of fertile land because it could generate a reliable stream of income. It was also difficult for rapacious in-laws to appropriate a woman's land, so real estate gave a wife more security than moveable wealth. However, dowering a bride with land had drawbacks. For a woman living in seclusion, managing dowry land could be problematic, as she would find it awkward to communicate with male tenants. Also, women from wealthy families often married men who lived in another place. Because their dowry land was located near their hometown, they would have trouble managing it from a distance. Moreover, dowry land often gave rise to disputes. Under the complex Qing property system, land ownership rights, usage rights, and rental contracts were often ambiguous and confusing. If the various parties involved refused to cooperate, disputes and lawsuits would result.

Even ordinary families felt obligated to send a daughter off with a proper dowry, and they often went into debt to obtain the requisite sum.[20] Qing society was intensely competitive. Presenting a daughter with a large dowry publicly demonstrated a family's respectability and helped preserve their social position, even if they were experiencing downward mobility. However, generous dowries became a source of intense financial pressure. People commonly attributed the high rate of female infanticide to the expense of dowry.[21] Parents preferred sons to daughters not just due to misogyny but for a practical reason. When a son married, he brought in a betrothal gift, but the wedding of a daughter saw a large exodus of wealth from the family coffers.

Due to this financial calculus, people realized that drowning a newborn daughter would preserve their family's assets. Both rich and poor murdered their daughters. The high rate of female infanticide elicited considerable hand wringing and discussion. In nineteenth-century Fujian and Taiwan, the custom of sending a young daughter away to be raised by her future in-laws emerged as an alternative to infanticide. Because she left home at such an early age, she did not require a dowry, so poor families in that region did not feel as much pressure to murder their daughters. This expedient arrangement saved the lives of an untold number of women.

Over time, women's hold over their dowries loosened. Song dynasty authorities had actively protected dowries. At that time, a woman had clear ownership and control of this wealth, and she could take it with her if she returned home or remarried. Dowry law changed under the Yuan.[22] If a husband expelled his wife from the home without due cause, she could still take her dowry with her. However, from 1303 onward a widow who remarried could not bring her dowry into her new household. Instead her deceased husband's family kept her dowry. Mongol women did not traditionally receive a dowry. Also, Mongols traditionally practiced levirate, so to them, the idea of a widow leaving her deceased husband's family seemed extremely alien. Due to these Mongol customs, Yuan authorities had little interest in protecting these assets. The idea of a woman not only leaving her deceased husband's family but taking wealth along with her struck them as simply wrong. The Ming and Qing codes maintained Yuan legislation restricting female property rights, including the provision that a widow had to forfeit her dowry to in-laws if she left to remarry. In other words, when a woman remarried, she lost her dowry. The threat of destitution no doubt helps account for the clear rise in widow chastity from the Yuan dynasty onward.

Although wives continued to own their dowries, they felt increasing pressure to employ these funds to benefit their husbands and in-laws. Neo-Confucians lauded this sort of sacrifice. Although the influential Song dynasty thinker Zhu Xi did not believe that a woman was obligated to use her dowry to help her husband or his kinsmen, he deemed this behavior exemplary and encouraged it.[23] By the Qing era, this sentiment had become widespread, and records show that wives frequently spent their dowry wealth to advance the interests of others.[24] They paid for the funerals of parents-in-law, the education of husbands and sons, and the marriages of children. Sometimes they even helped a husband's distant kinsman. Because the community considered this sort of behavior exceptionally virtuous, a lavish dowry allowed a woman to publicly demonstrate Confucian virtues such as benevolence, filial piety, wifely fidelity, and maternal love and to prove herself a moral exemplar.

Economic changes affected female work roles.[25] In spite of overpopulation and widespread impoverishment, improving technology and commercial methods made the economy increasingly productive and diverse overall, giving some women unprecedented opportunities. For example, people living in the lower reaches of the Qingshui River in the far south began selling large amounts of wood to other parts of China, making the region far more prosperous than before.[26] As the general economic level rose, women from the Miao and Dong (Kam) ethnic minorities began to participate in the commercial economy. They even started to buy and sell using written contracts.

Despite this progress, as before women had far fewer opportunities than men to work outside the home. Major work roles had been associated with one sex or the other since the Neolithic era, effectively locking women out of most professions. The increasing emphasis on the propriety of female reclusion made many women unwilling to work outside the home even if the opportunity arose, restricting their productive capacity. And women with mutilated feet were physically incapable of doing many jobs.

Gendered labor roles restricted women from participating in some of the most important and profitable types of labor, affecting the structure of the overall economy.[27] Generally speaking, women and children worked at home while men did heavier work and wage labor outside. Wage rates in the labor market applied mainly to men. The labor of women had little opportunity cost, so it did not matter if they devoted their time to activities with little economic return. Removing women from the paid labor market reduced the number of workers, keeping wages artificially high for men. Because women and children worked at home for little or nothing, family labor remained cheaper than wage labor, holding back the development of China's economy.

In previous eras, large numbers of women had done heavy agricultural work. The state allotted land to women during the medieval era, requiring them to do all types of agricultural labor. Starting from the Song period, when the rate of economic development markedly quickened, women increasingly left the fields.[28] But even though men carried out the most important agricultural work, women still helped out when necessary. Female labor participation in agriculture depended on the type of crop and the agricultural cycle.[29] Men did most of the work in the grain fields, but women and children might assist them during the busy harvest season. Women also did the lighter work of processing grain, such as threshing, winnowing, and milling. Cotton was a highly profitable cash crop but required intensive labor, and picking cotton was often a female task.[30] Some regions and social groups clung to more traditional ways of life, with women doing substantial agricultural labor. Hakka women did not bind their feet and were not embarrassed to be seen working in the open, allowing them to perform heavy agricultural tasks.[31] Natural feet became a cultural marker. Hakka women in prosperous families did not bind their feet, even though they did not labor outside the home.

Women tended to have far less capital than men, and their training was limited to traditionally female tasks, so working women usually did domestic labor such as weaving on small looms. Women working at home often had no control over the fruits of their labor.[32] Parents, husbands, and in-laws frequently sold their output and received the benefits. Even if a woman sold her handicrafts on the open market, she probably earned far less than the hourly market wage for male laborers.

People traditionally considered sericulture, spinning, weaving, tailoring, and embroidery the most important types of women's work.[33] Up through the medieval era, rural women weaving at home produced almost all textiles. During the Song, sericulture spread to a much larger area than before, allowing more women to manufacture a relatively expensive product. The shift from agriculture to textiles raised female productivity. From the sixteenth to eighteenth centuries, household incomes in the Jiangnan region increased about 15 percent, largely due to a rise in female cloth production.[34]

As the textile industry became more lucrative, professional male artisans entered the field. Urban factory owners did not hire female workers, as they considered the mingling of the sexes inappropriate. Instead men staffed factories with better equipment. Capital investment and technological innovation allowed male workers to produce large amounts of a high-quality product at lower cost. These developments gained momentum during the Qing, so during the eighteenth century the value and amount of women's textile production decreased.[35] Also, at that time cotton became the most common fabric. Cotton threads were especially suited for mechanical looms, making manufactured cloth even cheaper than before. Increasing numbers of female weavers abandoned manufacturing for the market and returned to producing small amounts of cloth for their families, consigning them to the subsistence economy. From 1750 to 1840, women's income from spinning and weaving declined by about a third. Those who produced cloth for the marketplace turned away from

Figure 4.1. Women Raising Silkworms
Metropolitan Museum of Art

cotton to concentrate on sericulture, as handmade silk cloth remained competitive (figure 4.1).[36]

Even though the economic significance of female textile production declined, it maintained strong associations with normative femininity. Many women continued to spin and weave, even though they did not need to do so for financial reasons. Since antiquity, people had considered cloth making a sign of female virtue.[37] Although wealthy families purchased high-quality fabrics in shops, their wives and daughters might nevertheless produce a token amount of cloth as an expression of diligence and thriftiness.[38] A woman who failed to undertake this symbolic labor would be considered lazy or even dissolute.

Even as the value of homespun textiles diminished, women could still earn money from embroidery.[39] People appreciated elaborately embroidered clothing, beddings, and shoes, and they were willing to pay high prices for top quality needlework. As women abandoned spinning and weaving, they increasingly turned to embroidery to make money. Women from ordinary families could sell embroidered cloth for ready cash or accumulate a store of embroidery to be sold if they suddenly needed money. A pile of embroidery in the cabinet served as a trove of accumulated wealth.

Women confined at home also used embroidery as an outlet for their creativity. Needlework techniques became increasingly elaborate and refined, and museum visitors today are still awed by the virtuosity of

Qing embroiderers. Even as cloth making lost economic importance, poets emphasized a dedication to embroidery as a sign of female virtue. While conservatives might have felt uneasy about women who dedicated their time to scholarship and writing, they saw embroidery as a safe outlet for female energy. Even women in wealthy families did embroidery work, both as an enjoyable leisure activity and also to demonstrate their virtue.

As female reclusion intensified, women retreated from jobs that put them on display.[40] There seems to have been fewer female vendors and restaurant workers than before. Even so, women still undertook jobs outside the home. Certain professions, such as the matchmakers essential for a legitimate marriage, were traditionally female. And because women were willing to work for lower wages than men, some found work doing unskilled jobs in workshops. For example, female workers performed some of the tasks in printing workshops.[41] Highly trained male artisans carved the wooden printing blocks and printed premium editions. But for inexpensive books, publishers often lowered costs by employing women and children to do the unskilled work of applying ink to the blocks and pressing them onto paper.

Some women worked as healers. As before, female shamans performed ceremonies to cure the sick, particularly in less developed regions.[42] Because shamanistic treatments cost far less than conventional herbal medicine, it was often the only recourse for poor patients. Uneducated people had little interest in religious orthodoxy, so they readily embraced beliefs that literati derided as base superstition. Overall, the reputation of spirit mediums had fallen considerably since the medieval era. The elite upheld Confucian orthodoxy and regarded shamans with scorn. However, Jurchen shamanism influenced China during the Qing period, giving it a boost of popularity. The Manchus respected these ancient religious practices, and there were even shamanistic ceremonies held in the palace. Some were aimed at curing disease.

Women served as the primary healers for family members, so they were often familiar with medical treatments.[43] Chinese medicine usually consisted of boiled plants and other ingredients, and female cooks learned recipes for healthy decoctions. It was common for patients to diagnose their own illnesses and prescribe medicines and treatments based on oral lore or the many popular medical manuals in circulation. These writings included specific descriptions of female ailments. Men wrote almost all medical texts, as people considered it unseemly for women to publicly discuss such intimate and disturbing matters. Barred from publishing their medical lore, women passed it down orally from one generation to the next. There seems to have been a considerable body of oral medical wisdom, but because it was not recorded, most has been lost. Some women often did medical work professionally, using their experience and healing lore to treat people from other families. Because women disliked being physically examined by an unrelated male, they preferred to consult a healer of the same sex.

Women also worked as servants. Jurchens traditionally practiced slavery, so during the Qing dynasty high-ranking Manchus could own slaves. Far more commonly, parents sold an unwanted daughter as a bondservant, obliging her to perform a specified period of servitude. After the term expired, she reclaimed her free status. Some wealthy women wrote poems about their bondservant girls, providing glimpses of their lives.[44] Although many bondservants worked hard and suffered abuse, others were treated as marginal family members. Some mistresses even expressed affection for their serving girls and depicted them as vivacious, innocent, and loveable. The most fortunate bondservants could receive an education, have a suitable marriage arranged for them, and be mourned by their masters if they had an untimely passing.

Women with no better options sank into prostitution. China never had many independent streetwalkers. Not only was this illegal, but a woman who openly solicited clients in public exposed herself to considerable risk. Prostitutes preferred to work in brothels, which protected them from troublesome officials and abusive clients. In prior eras, prostitution had been legal but highly regulated. The Ming government had an elaborate bureaucracy that managed prostitution. In the eighteenth century, the Yongzheng emperor wanted to raise the moral tenor of society, so he outlawed all prostitution and even discouraged masters from using servile women for their sexual pleasure. The Manchus wanted Chinese to regard them as the guardian of Confucian ethics. They repudiated the louche excesses of late Ming culture and took stern positions on ethical issues such as prostitution to win over their skeptical Chinese subjects. The Qing prohibition of prostitution also reflected changes to the social structure. As status became increasingly unmoored from heredity, the state put greater emphasis on personal conduct in determining a person's position in society.[45]

Qing laws on sexual matters served as propagandistic expressions of political values rather than realistic legislation, so they were never strictly enforced. Even so, laws against prostitution stigmatized sex workers even further. Society held these women in contempt, and they suffered institutionalized discrimination.[46] Prostitutes could not own land or enter respectable occupations. Even their family members suffered by association and were barred from taking the civil service examinations.

During the Qing, private bordellos emerged to replace the government-managed prostitution system of the previous dynasty. Brothels had different grades.[47] Courtesans worked in expensive establishments with a luxurious ambiance called guesthouses (*keguan*) or teahouses (*chafang*)

Figure 4.2. Courtesan
Cleveland Museum of Art

(figure 4.2). These women were usually performers and companions, not true prostitutes. Customers went to these venues to enjoy performances and conversation. Many actresses also served as prostitutes, and they used their performances to advertise themselves to potential customers.

For this reason, the government took a dim view of actresses, so the number of women on stage declined and men began to play most female roles.[48] Ordinary bars, restaurants, and opium dens often had prostitutes on their staff. Some could sing or play an instrument, but they were also readily available for sex. The most inexpensive brothels catered to poor men who could not afford to get married, as well as itinerant laborers such as sailors and porters. The women in these grim places endured constant sexual abuse and crushing poverty.

As society and government changed in the late nineteenth century, the conduct of prostitution altered as well.[49] The administrators of China's most developed cities began to emulate European civic administration. Because many European municipal governments regulated prostitution, Chinese civic authorities followed suit. They licensed prostitutes and brothels and required them to pay nominal taxes. Authorities regulated prostitution and the police enforced these rules. These establishments had limited hours of operation and could not accept certain kinds of clients, such as underaged boys or government officials. In some places, prostitutes could not dress like respectable women but had to wear special clothing and hairstyles to mark their profession. They had to undergo regular health checks, and city officials helped women who wanted to leave prostitution find a new job. City authorities also tried to prevent brothel owners from abusing sex workers.

Courtesans occasionally had sex with their clients, but they were usually just performers. The status of courtesans fell precipitously during the transition from Ming to Qing.[50] The late Ming had been the apex of courtesan culture. At that time, talented female performers attracted the attentions of leading literati, allowing them to influence literary trends and elite taste. However, the Manchus took a dim view of courtesans, whom they associated with Ming decadence. The government forbade courtesans from performing at official functions. Moreover, the new stress on classicism and orthodoxy led the elite to scorn courtesans. Those loyal to the previous dynasty continued to respect these women as a holdover from a vanished world. Over time, however, the reputations of these performers declined, and most people dismissed them as tawdry and pathetic.

The declining status of courtesans had a major impact on Qing culture. During the late Ming, young women had to undergo rigorous training before becoming courtesans.[51] Their skill in singing, performing music, and dance was legendary. But as the demand for courtesan performances decreased, standards plummeted. Some performance arts went into decline as a result.

Changing perceptions of courtesans affected popular views toward female talent in general.[52] Ming literati had honored courtesans as talented women (*cainü*) and lauded them as exemplars of female artistic ability. During the Qing era, they lost this distinction. Instead talent became associated with respectability, so it only applied to gentry women. The model talented woman of the Qing was the educated gentry wife who wrote poetry and played the lute. The artistic accomplishments of courtesans seemed shallow and disreputable in contrast.

Even though the courtesan world went into abeyance for most of the Qing, at the end of the dynasty it experienced an unexpected resurgence. In late nineteenth-century Shanghai, courtesans once again became glamorous public figures on the cutting edge of fashion.[53] They positioned themselves on the forefront of the city's emerging new fusion culture that mixed East and West, old and new. Some deliberately behaved in an outré manner to attract attention. Shanghainese saw courtesans not as Ming dynasty relics but as modern women suited to the vibrant new mercantile culture. Women from wealthy families looked to courtesans as trendsetters in fashion and emulated their wardrobe and appearance.

The Shanghainese courtesan became an icon of the city. Illustrations of Shanghai courtesan houses depict them as luxurious and merry places. Other regions of China were still much more traditional, so Shanghai's courtesan realm distinguished the city from stodgy inland areas. Shanghainese redefined courtesans to fit into the city's forward-looking culture. Ming dynasty illustrations had depicted courtesans in traditional interior settings and the homes of wealthy patrons. In contrast, Shanghainese artists portrayed them as an integral part of the modern urban cityscape. They were often shown standing amid a Westernized street scene.

Shanghai's courtesans may have embodied sophistication, but most were extremely young. The ideal age was fifteen, and they found it difficult to continue working after age twenty. Most of these girls came to the big city from towns in Jiangsu. Their families sold them to courtesan houses, so they were akin to bondservants. A courtesan could not leave her bordello unaccompanied and all of her earnings went to the brothel proprietor who had purchased her. Although Shanghainese considered these women analogous to the fabled Ming courtesans, in fact they were very different. Because they began working at such a young age, there was no time to train them, so few could sing or play an instrument. Instead of emphasizing talent, brothel owners dressed the girls in flamboyant fashions and used them as visual props.

Relations between Shanghai courtesans and their clients had many rules, making their interactions akin to a ritual. Meeting a top-grade courtesan was not a simple matter. A prospective customer had to be introduced by one of the brothel's trusted clients. If he lacked this sort of contact, the only way to meet a courtesan was to hire her to entertain a group of his friends at a restaurant. Although Shanghai courtesans usually lacked artistic accomplishments, people nevertheless considered them entertainers, and they rarely had sex with clients.

The unexpected resurrection of courtesan culture at the end of the Qing hinted at far more radical changes yet to come. The social ferment that accompanied the dynasty's decline blurred gender roles and threw time-honored ideals into doubt. People struggled to construct new types of womanhood that suited a society increasingly dominated by capitalism, alien values, and unfamiliar new lifestyles. The increasing rate of change and dynamism at the end of the Qing led people to reassess women's economic roles along with every other gendered activity.

5

Education

Education means different things to different people. For most Qing women, it consisted of learning manual tasks such as cooking, cleaning, and weaving. They also had to understand how to behave so that they could fit into their family and community. In addition to this basic knowledge, they might also learn about the world beyond their immediate horizons. Most were illiterate, so they usually absorbed knowledge in informal and indirect ways, such as listening to stories and so-called gossip and watching performances. Religion was also an important educational resource. Buddhism and Daoism allowed women to transcend their immediate surroundings and engage with profound ideas about abstract matters. Religion taught them about the cosmos and netherworld, and they learned rituals alleged to influence the supernatural.

Although most women could not read, the rate of female literacy had been on the rise for centuries, and the number of educated women continued to increase during the Qing era. As literate women became more common, intellectual leaders discussed the impact of learning and talent on female character and what position educated women ought to hold in society.[1] Scholars had long shown respect for talented women (*cainü*). However, the meaning of this term shifted over time, and it had various implications. During the seventeenth and eighteenth centuries, the nature of female talent became an important topic of discussion.[2] Gazetteers included sections devoted entirely to biographies of talented women, lauding them as exemplary role models. In the late imperial era, the talented woman was usually a poet. Some were painters or calligraphers. The talented woman thus represented a female foil to the refined male literatus. A family with competent female poets impressed bystanders as highly cultured, so they could be a source of honor. To publicly emphasize a daughter's refinement and education, gentry families often included cultured items such as books, paintings, and art supplies in the bride's dowry.[3]

Educated men often expressed admiration for talented women. At times, it seems that they even envied their female counterparts. The world of male scholarship was highly competitive. Men came under intense pressure to conform to rigid standards of literary and scholarly orthodoxy, so they often did not dare express their true opinions. Not surprisingly, much of their writing now seems sterile. In contrast, women faced no pressure to excel, so they were allowed to express certain kinds of feelings in a more authentic manner. In fact readers expected female authors to employ an intimate and emotional style. Some men even considered female learning as superior to that of men due to its purity.[4] Men studied hard to pass examinations and attain office. The pursuit of worldly success sullied the male curriculum, which could seem like a cynical path to fame and fortune. In contrast, women's education had no connection to salary and rank, so it seemed noble in comparison.

Despite the benefits of female education, as learned women became more common, some people fretted that literary pursuits might distract them from more important matters and lead them astray. Above all, people expected a woman to be virtuous. Conventional female ethics stressed traits such as humility, submission, and dedication to domestic tasks. Conservatives feared that education would make women arrogant and inattentive, and they saw virtue and talent as incompatible.[5] Even some women held this view. As female education became increasingly common, some illiterate women proudly defended their ignorance by stressing the primacy of virtue over education.[6]

Ethical training remained the focus of female education, and a virtuous reputation became a prerequisite for a woman to be considered talented.[7] Literati no longer took notice of the poetry of courtesans and held up gentry women from respectable backgrounds as ideal female litterateurs. In praising female talent, literati put moral probity at the forefront. Epitaphs of female authors deliberately put far more emphasis on virtue than skill to render their achievements unthreatening.

Talented women did not necessarily lead happy lives.[8] The most accomplished female authors tended to die young. In one sample of 272 talented Qing women, half died by age thirty. Many women of talent suffered from ill health. Confined to the home, the bones in their feet crushed, denied exercise and fresh air, and spending hours at the loom to prove their diligence, they were trapped in an environment conducive to neither creativity, health, nor happiness. Moreover, biographies of female poets portrayed their appearance in unflattering terms, describing them as ugly and asexual.[9] In response, talented women endeavored to present their abilities and achievements in ways that allowed them to overcome negative stereotypes.

During the early Qing, gentry women replaced courtesans as the preeminent icons of female talent. Some families became well known for the learning and accomplishments of their wives and daughters.[10] By passing down education and artistic training, some cultured families maintained a high level of female refinement for generations. However, even though critics lauded the authenticity of female poets, gentry women had to be careful about what they wrote lest they disgrace their family. Most importantly, gentry women usually did not dare write love poetry. If they took up the topic of romance, they approached it very tastefully.[11] Overall, they wrote and acted in ways calculated to avoid censure.

So-called worthy women (*xianfu*) gained prominence at this time.[12] This term dates back to the Han dynasty and originally referred to any virtuous women. During the Qing, however, the worthy woman referred to a very specific social type. She was learned, came from a respectable family, and successfully educated her children. Eventually the son of a worthy woman distinguished himself in the civil service examinations and obtained the coveted *jinshi* degree, attesting to the success of her maternal instruction. National and local records document large numbers of worthy women. This social type was largely a regional phenomenon, as 90 percent lived in south China. The general education level of southern women exceeded that of their northern counterparts, so southerners employed this archetype to make the learned woman seem moral as well as capable.

Qing writers praised respectable female poets and artists as famous beauties (*mingyuan*).[13] Despite this choice of words, these women did not gain recognition for their appearance. Since antiquity, many writers had taken a comprehensive view of beauty, including intelligence and talent as well as looks. Famous beauties came from respectable backgrounds, usually wealthy merchant families, had received a good education, and gained attention for their skill at poetry, painting, or calligraphy. Their families were sophisticated, worldly, and well traveled, so these women often displayed a more cosmopolitan outlook than gentry ladies. Because the gentry looked down on commerce, the merchant elite educated their daughters and encouraged them to excel in the arts to help their families appear cultured and reputable. In Huizhou, a vibrant mercantile center, 145 women received recognition as famous beauties over the course of the dynasty. However, that region was particularly prosperous. Most places in the south had far fewer famous beauties.

Figure 5.1. Mother and Child
Wikimedia Commons

Many Qing women embraced education and made it a cornerstone of their personal identity. When a learned woman fell on hard times, her educational attainments continued to make her seem respectable. Such was the case with the talented Wu Qi, who wrote during the turbulent mid-seventeenth-century Ming Qing transition. She had a cultured upbringing but fell into poverty after her husband died, so she began selling her paintings to earn a living. Wu wrote about the consolation she received from her refined sensibilities, even as she suffered privation.[14]

> Paintings and history texts are our friends in the women's quarters.
> Our modest skill at poetry composition takes us beyond worldly affairs.
> . . .
> Our beautiful eyebrows outshine the color of the mirror,
> Our sleek hair puts other scholars to shame.

Not only did Wu consider talented women as good as men, but she even staked a claim to female superiority. She argued that women can enjoy educated pursuits as much as men, and they have beauty as well. According to her, this combination of refinement and good looks put them above male literati.

While people today associate education with literacy, the average young woman of the Qing mostly just learned how to perform stereotypical female work roles.[15] Most tasks were gendered, so it was clear which forms of work she should master. Older women would teach girls domestic tasks such as cooking, cleaning, and how to care for infants and elders. Even women born into wealthy households had to become competent at spinning and weaving. Since antiquity, various thinkers had valorized cloth making as a tangible expression of a woman's goodness, so almost all women did at least some token weaving. Women of all backgrounds also learned about society and their place within it.[16] By observing the people around them, they understood how they ought to behave in various situations. Attaining social competence allowed a woman to form and maintain relationships. If she mastered the canon of unwritten social rules and observed them, the community would regard her as a worthy person.

The female members of gentry households received a literate education as a matter of course. Nevertheless, relatively few Qing women were literate. Historians estimate the rate of female literacy in nineteenth-century China as somewhere between 1 and 10 percent.[17] This figure varied considerably by region and family background, with more prosperous areas having higher educational standards.[18] Southerners were much more likely to educate their daughters, as were city dwellers. Among the peasantry, however, female education was exceptional. A comprehensive study of rural women in 1930 found a literacy rate of only about 1 percent, and circumstances in the Qing era were probably similar.

Peasant women would have had little use for Confucian ethics and poetry. Out of necessity, they devoted themselves to everyday tasks. It might seem that women in privileged families did not have much need for education either, as they had little contact with the wider world. Even so, among the elite, female education could bring practical benefits to both individual women and their families. Gentry families sought to distinguish themselves from the hoi polloi, so they actively tried to present themselves to local society as different from the peasants around them. Female education constituted an important aspect of their symbolic capital, as it helped them stand out as socially superior.

Educated gentry women were also likely to attract a better spouse. Many people considered an educated wife an ideal companion for a cultured husband. Shared knowledge and interests would strengthen their bond and increase the chance of conjugal success. His family would also welcome the addition of an educated woman, as her presence confirmed their dedication to high culture. She could even put her learning to practical use. The ability to read and write would also make a wife a more effective household manager.[19]

Most importantly, a learned woman could educate her sons. Ever since the civil service examinations became the prime path to office during the Song dynasty, ambitious families had embraced maternal instruction. They expected the competent mother to begin teaching her sons at an early age, giving them a useful head start. Society celebrated educated wives (*xianfu*) whose sons became successful, and they attributed these men's accomplishments in part to a patient mother's early lessons. Epitaphs and biographies praised these maternal paragons. Given the utility of women's learning for elite families, important men actively promoted female education.[20]

The textual education of daughters varied according to family status.[21] In most families, girls who learned how to read usually only acquired basic literacy. They typically studied a simple didactic textbook for female students that inculcated ethical values appropriate to her sex. Although Confucianism demanded that men and women both lead moral lives, the virtues expected of each differed. Many key male virtues involved public life, so they had little relevance to women confined to the domestic sphere. To the average woman, virtue consisted primarily of keeping an orderly household, maintaining the distinctions between the sexes, and observing the family rites.

Only the most cultured families would give their daughters a classical education. In such cases, girls studied some of the same texts as their brothers, albeit with far lower expectations. A smattering of classical learning would put a woman at ease in the household of a cultured husband. This knowledge could also allow her to help her sons prepare for the civil service examinations. Instruction in the classics emphasized ethical training, and female students learned to appreciate the moral implications of these works. In addition, women often received considerable instruction in poetry appreciation and composition, as this was the most conventional medium of female self-expression. They might also study painting, calligraphy, and music. Even a concubine in the home of a wealthy family might study poetry and other arts, as this made her a more interesting companion for the master of the house. Some of these women became accomplished poets.[22]

Unlike boys, who could study in schools, girls almost always took their lessons within the inner quarters of the home.[23] Most often their parents taught them. A girl's primary tutor was usually her mother. This custom imbued the relationship between mothers and daughters in elite families with an intellectual dimension. Mother and daughter were not just bound by family ties. They were also teacher and student who had read the same books and shared common ideas.

A major problem with female education was its ambiguity. A female student did not have a clear plan of study. Men followed a standard curriculum geared toward the official examinations. In contrast, women's learning had little practical use, so it was far more varied.[24] A mother's interests and expertise, the family's resources and cultural level, and a girl's own inclinations all influenced what she learned. While her brothers were busy memorizing the ancient classics, a girl might be reading Buddhist sutras or learning how to compose poetry. As an adult, she could participate in sutra reading societies or poetry clubs to continue learning.[25]

During the eighteenth century, women's education became increasingly widespread. To cater to the demand for learning materials, publishers put out inexpensive textbooks aimed at female students. Most commonly, girls studied the *Four Books for Women* (*Nü sishu*).[26] A publisher in the late Ming era released a quartet of ethical works as a set, marketing it as a systematic curriculum for female education. The *Four Books* continued to sell very well during the Qing. Moreover, due to rising educational standards and a vibrant publishing industry, other books written earlier belatedly found a large audience, giving them a far greater impact than before. *Analects for Women* (*Nü lunyu*) had been written during the Tang dynasty, in an age before commercial mass printing, so it initially had a limited readership. During the late imperial era it became a popular textbook.[27] Women also studied some classical texts, particularly the *Classic of Filial Piety* (*Xiaojing*), which was short, easy to understand, and revered as a cornerstone of Confucian ethics.[28]

The level of women's education may have risen, but it remained far below that of men from the same background. Women's educations tended to be patchy. Even gentry families had illiterate female members. Because parents had low expectations for their daughters, girls usually only studied basic texts. The authors of textbooks for female students used easy language and kept the contents simple. Many of these books had woodblock illustrations to make them more appealing and help semiliterate readers understand the content. Images also increased a book's emotional impact. A woman who felt sufficiently moved might want to transform herself to accord with the ethical injunctions that the artist depicted, so illustrated textbooks could serve as effective tools for ethical training.[29]

Because men and women received different educations, they tended to have distinctive perspectives on the world. Education can expand a student's horizons, or it can teach a student to accept a lower position in the world. Sometimes education made a woman more critical. After studying *Changes* of Zhou (*Yijing*), a key classical text, Qian Fenglun (fl. 1690) wrote a poem expressing how it affected her.[30]

> With inkstand and red paste
> I study the *Changes* of Zhou,
> More aware than ever
> how remote from the world
> is my little window.

This text represented the apex of the classical curriculum, so Qian obviously had considerable learning. However, she realized that however much she learned, she would have little opportunity to use her knowledge. It was unseemly for a woman to discuss the classics, so she could not participate in academic debates or talk to others about profound philosophical ideas. Studying exciting ideas and then being denied the opportunity to talk about them only intensified her intellectual isolation.

Women and men had different positions in society, affecting what they knew. The wide gap in educational background exacerbated these differences, causing female and male tastes and values to diverge.[31] Elite men received an extensive classical and literary education, and they used this learning to interpret the world around them. In comparison, women usually had a more limited education, so popular culture exerted a far greater influence on their worldview, values, and inclinations.

Because women acted as major consumers of popular culture, they affected its development. A great deal of popular literature catered to female taste. Fiction included female protagonists and situations of interest to female readers. For example, mass market fiction described women confronting quandaries that arose from competing priorities in female ethics. Most famously, the novel *Dream of the Red Chamber* (*Honglou meng*) features numerous female characters and much of the action centers on women's activities. The novel attracted female fans, and women referred to it in their poetry.[32] Women also helped transmit and perpetuate oral literature such as religious stories, legends, and ballads. Men found the close engagement of women with popular culture suspect, as a great deal of popular culture had vulgar or even pornographic content. Male critics cautioned that women should be kept away from dissolute works lest they be tempted to imitate what they have read.[33]

A vibrant publishing industry allowed many women to see their writings in print.[34] An enthusiastic audience of female readers consumed these works, providing a commercial foundation for literature by women. The confluence of these two factors in the late Ming and early Qing gave rise to a new kind of literary culture centered on female writers and readers, a trend that lasted up to the mid-nineteenth century. There are at least 3,671 known female writers from the Qing.[35] This figure represents more than half of the known total of women authors from the entire imperial era.[36] There are about five times as many published female authors from the Qing as the Ming, attesting to the explosion of literary activity among women from the seventeenth through nineteenth centuries.

The rise in women's literature began amid the effervescent cultural atmosphere of the late Ming.[37] At that time, many intellectual figures rejected the stringent Neo-Confucianism of Zhu Xi and his peers and turned to more subjective and inclusive forms of thought. They criticized rigid formalism and instead promoted psychological authenticity and the exploration of authentic emotions. These intellectual and cultural changes facilitated the growth of female literary culture. Unlike previous surges in women's literary activity, at this time almost all female writers belonged to elite families. Qing gentry women held the writings of courtesans in contempt, as they saw these women as lowly and likely debauched. The quality of works by courtesans and nuns fell, and readers showed little interest in their writings.

The literary world of Qing women differed significantly by region. Jiangnan had the most writers. Changzhou, Hangzhou, and other cultural hotspots had well-known female authors and groups of women readers who critiqued and discussed the latest writings. In contrast, even though wealthy families in the Lingnan region and Ningbo educated their women, they emphasized feminine modesty and so discouraged their women from circulating their writings. This was a widespread sentiment. A sequel to *Dream of the Red Chamber* describes two female characters who wrote a commentary to the work. However, they refused to show it to anyone, even the author of the novel himself, out of a sense of decorum.[38] Families usually destroyed a woman's writings after her death lest these potentially embarrassing works fall into the wrong hands.

Although far more women were writing and publishing during the Qing, they remained at a disadvantage compared to men. Reclusion limited women's life experiences, so they found it harder to come up with fresh material. Luo Qilan, active in the late eighteenth century, wrote about this problem in her preface to an anthology of works by female authors.[39]

> Confined to their boudoir, Chinese women are extremely limited in experience. They have no friends for discussion whereby to open up their sensibilities, no mountains and rivers to visit and behold whereby to fructify their literary propensity. Unless they have a father or an elder brother to teach them about the origin of different schools of literature or to point out for them what is real and what is specious, they cannot really complete their education. Then, after they are married, when they must take over household chores, serve their husband's siblings, and tend to such trivialities as the supply of salt and rice, they often find no time for poetry.

Although domestic isolation posed challenges for female writers, it also made them value literature as a medium that they could use to explore the wider world. Some women appropriated the literary concept of recumbent travel (*woyou*).[40] In earlier centuries, men of letters had seen literature and painting as imaginative vehicles that allowed them to take vicarious journeys. They realized that books allowed them to imagine beautiful scenes and interesting people without having to undergo the inconveniences of travel. Literati often resorted to recumbent travel in old age, when ill health limited their mobility. However, this sort of cultured fantasy suited women of all ages. By exploring the world through books and images, a woman could safeguard her good name while entertaining herself, expanding the boundaries of her life, and obtaining a degree of psychological liberation.

The increasing availability of women's literature presented readers with a problem. Female authors often chose different topics than men and used distinctly feminine styles of writing. Yet conventional literary criticism had evolved to evaluate men's writings. When male critics applied these criteria to female literature, they complained that women's poems were inferior in quality, trivial in theme, and often lacking moral content. Mainstream critics felt obliged to hold women's writings to lower standards than men's works.

As conventional literary criticism could not evaluate women's literature on its own terms, incisive male and female readers constructed a suitable critical apparatus. Scholars collected women's writings from previous eras and pieced together a lengthy tradition of women's literature that could inform the judgments of contemporary authors and critics.[41] They also tried out new modes of critique that elevated the place of women's writings in the literary canon.[42] Most critical theory focused on poetry, by far the most common type of women's literature.[43] The poet

Wang Duanshu (1621–ca. 1685) discussed how women's works ought to be evaluated. She believed that readers should assess poems and writers individually, based on their characteristics, rather than using uniform standards of critique. She also held that works must be positioned within the context of an appropriate poetic tradition to be properly evaluated.

Although men usually took a patronizing attitude toward women's writings, some appreciated these works as a fresh alternative to mainstream male literature. The erudite literatus Zhang Xuecheng (1738–1801) considered the output of female writers a respectable counterpoint to the works of male authors.[44] Zhang argued that while both men and women can express the Dao hidden beneath perceived reality, each sex does so differently. In this way he justified the deviation of women's literature from male standards as an acceptable variation. Zhang even believed that female writers have certain advantages over their male counterparts. A man often wrote poetry to curry favor with the powerful or attract an influential patron who could help him obtain a promotion in the civil service. The exclusion of women from office, salary, and fame allowed them to express the Dao in a purer form. Zhang concluded that women's literature was often more sincere and authentic in consequence.

Views toward women's poetry evolved over the course of the Qing.[45] In the early part of the dynasty, critics concentrated on rediscovering talented female writers from the past and assembling a comprehensive canon of women's literature. To this end, editors put together many collections of women's poems from previous eras. As critics became more familiar with the female literary tradition, they could appreciate the differences between female and male literature and make informed judgments. Many literati began to praise the distinctiveness of women's poetry, portraying it as significant and skillfully executed. During the mid-Qing, critics singled out refinement as an important characteristic of good women's poetry. They emphasized that women ought to write poetry that exhibits purity (*qing*) and elegance (*ya*), as they considered these attributes appropriate to their sex. During the nineteenth century, critics looked back to the late Ming era for inspiration and once again lauded the emotional authenticity of the best female works. They appreciated women who wrote in an individualistic or even idiosyncratic manner and expressed genuine emotions.

Whereas previous female authors had mostly written poetry, during the Qing era they began to explore a wider range of genres. Previously people of both sexes had written letters to family members, friends, and cultured contacts.[46] As female literacy became increasingly widespread, more women wrote letters. At the time, publishers put out many books of model letters that included templates specifically for use by women. Aside from writing to family members about practical matters, educated women often wrote one another to exchange ideas and works of poetry. Letter writing allowed them to maintain cultured friendships without leaving home. Sometimes two women maintained an active correspondence over a long period of time even though they never had an opportunity to meet in person. Most women did not publish their works, so they valued feedback from epistolary contacts. Talented women exchanged letters to encourage one another to persevere with painting and poetry. They treasured this encouragement because they knew that few people would probably ever see their writings.

Female authors wrote for a public audience in a wide range of genres, including scripts for the performance arts. Women of all backgrounds were enthusiastic fans of stage plays. Actors performed not just in cities but in villages as well, exposing small town women to the wider world. Beginning in the Ming dynasty, some women wrote opera scripts. The number of female script writers increased over time, and thirteen are known to have been active during the Qing.[47] A script writer could not have her work staged unless she had connections with an opera troupe, so female script writers usually belonged to families of performers. By writing engaging scripts, these women were helping out with the family business. Writing an opera script gave a woman an unusual opportunity to imitate the male voice and insert dialogue into the mouths of male characters. While men had long written about female characters and had them express stereotypical sentiments that men expected from women, for a female author to do the same for male characters allowed her to put forward new visions of masculinity.

Women also appreciated a type of ballad called *tanci*. Performers chanted or sang a ballad consisting of alternating prose and verse, often accompanied by a stringed instrument.[48] The authors of *tanci* scripts wrote lyrics in simple language and set them to easy melodies. Performers did not need much skill and audiences found the works readily accessible. *Tanci* ballads resembled popular fiction in many respects. Originally authors intended them to be sung before an audience, but as scripts became more sophisticated, they began to write more complicated ballads intended to be read.

During the eighteenth century, educated women showed great enthusiasm for *tanci*. Few men were involved with the genre, so most male critics had a negative opinion of these works. They belittled the literary value of ballads and fretted that the lyrics often had ambiguous or immoral content. A minority of male critics rejected this condescending stance. They even supported *tanci* as effective vehicles for female education. Open-minded male critics assumed that the creations of women would have a greater impact on female audience members, increasing their self-awareness and spurring moral self-cultivation.

Because both *tanci* authors and audience were largely female, the contents differed from male-dominated literature.[49] *Tanci* authors often wrote about matters of concern to women. Many ballads were based on the writer's personal experience or events in the lives of women she knew. *Tanci* writers criticized patriarchal domination and expressed a desire for greater gender equality. They hoped that the institution of marriage could become more equitable and condemned concubinage. Ballads also expressed women's desire for greater economic autonomy. Authors emphasized the importance of women controlling their dowries and the need to safeguard female inheritance rights. A few writers even cast doubt on fundamental gender arrangements such as the cult of widow chastity and female exclusion from government.

Talented women did not limit themselves to writing. Some gained attention for their mastery of painting or calligraphy.[50] A few noted painters were concubines or courtesans from humble backgrounds. They cultivated artistic talent to gain respect from influential men and raise their social standing. However, most female artists came from refined gentry families and learned how to paint as part of their educational training. Although female artists usually confined themselves to polite themes, some showed an adventurous spirit. A few imitated idiosyncratic paintings by a controversial group of eighteenth-century avant-garde artists known as the Eight Eccentrics of Yangzhou (Yangzhou baguai). Some cultured men working in a similarly adventurous style appreciated works by the most daring female painters.

Since antiquity, female education had often included training in poetry appreciation and composition. People expected an educated woman to be able to write competent verse, as it was the most common outlet for female creativity.[51] When a woman wanted to convey her ideas and feelings, she would most likely do so in poetic form. By communicating in such an elegant but oblique format, she could use indirect language and thereby avoid awkwardness and embarrassment. Writing poetry also brought her prestige, as it marked her as a woman of talent and refinement.[52] Given these advantages, even when a woman wrote to an absent husband about practical matters, she often used poetry rather than prose. Yet despite the prestige of poetic composition, many women considered it an activity for the young. Wives often abandoned literary pursuits to concentrate their full attention on home and family.[53]

Poetry allowed women to interact with a wider circle of contacts, providing them with the means to break out of their isolation in the home. Most importantly, poetry exchanges allowed a married woman to stay in contact with blood relatives.[54] After sisters married, they usually rarely met. Sending one another poems allowed them to keep in touch, share news, express their feelings, and inform siblings about their lives. Sisters had received comparable literary training, so they wrote in a similar style, making it easy for them to appreciate one another's writings. Gentry women also exchanged poems with in-laws and other distant relations to strengthen family bonds.[55]

Women could also build friendships with counterparts in other households by exchanging poems.[56] By repeatedly sending each other poetry, often written in response to one another's writings, women could engage in satisfying literary friendships even while physically separated. Women cherished these exchanges and often thought of like-minded literary companions as surrogate sisters. They even wrote poems in response to poetry published by women they had never contacted. Wang Duan (1793–1838) wrote several poems in reaction to works by contemporary female poets.[57] This sort of formal interaction, with writers responding to one another's works, established a public literary circle of talented women, even when they were not in direct contact.

During the Qing dynasty, it became common for a group of women to write linked poems (*lianyin changhe*).[58] Women in different households would compose a poem together by sending it back and forth, with each participant adding a new line in turn. In this way, two or more women could have fun creating a poem together. Participants in this literary game were called poetic companions (*shilü*). Unmarried girls, wives, and widows all found linked poetry a useful way to break out of their seclusion. Sometimes family members would compose a poem together. Some linked poems were even published. Although these works were rarely very good, cloistered women nevertheless appreciated this activity as a useful social tool that allowed them to expand their horizons.

Groups of women met in person to discuss literary matters and write poems together.[59] The refined tenor of these gatherings gave them an excuse to socialize by sharing an enjoyable activity. Sometimes women established a formal poetry club that met regularly. Some groups consisted solely of female residents in a large household. Home-based clubs were extremely common, as they gave the members a reason to gather periodically for a special event while staying hidden from public view. Sometimes women from an area's literati families would attend a poetry club in the inner quarters of a member's home. During the nineteenth century, the scope of women's poetry clubs expanded. Some included women from different places. Others became more diverse and allowed respectable women from diverse backgrounds to participate.

Sometimes a teacher's female students would gather to write poetry together. Usually, these groups were all female. However, male poets occasionally took on the role of patron to a group of literary women, teaching, critiquing, and encouraging them.[60] Such intimate interaction between men and women, even in the most high-minded setting, could lead to trouble. The talented writer Yuan Mei (1716–1797) surrounded himself with numerous female protégées, and meeting so many attractive young women in his home raised a scandal.[61] In addition, some literati condemned Yuan Mei's efforts to bring women into the realm of male culture. They believed that associating female authors with the grubby male world of practical concerns degraded their art.

The novel *Dream of the Red Chamber* describes a home-based poetry group called the Crab-Flower Poetry Club (Haitang shishe). Most of the members of this fictional club were women in the same family who held festive meetings in their beautiful garden. They met in private and did not circulate their poems. In contrast, the Plantain Garden Poetry Club (Jiaoyuan shishe), active in late seventeenth-century Hangzhou, was a public female literary society.[62] The members consisted of highly educated women from literati families. By limiting membership to women from impeccable backgrounds, these women escaped censure, even though they left their homes to meet together.

Although most female poets never dared to release their works to the general public, the number of women's poetry anthologies nevertheless increased. Over the course of the Qing it became increasingly common for a woman to share her poetry with people outside the home. Women edited some anthologies, but production was usually handled by literati.[63] Male editors were usually former students who had failed the civil service examinations. Editing the works of talented poets, whether male or female, provided an unsuccessful student with a chance to affirm his identity as a man of culture. The publication of numerous anthologies spurred female creativity. The possibility of publishing a poem in one of these collections gave female poets a tangible goal, and they strove to take their art to a higher level.

Most female poets resided in just two provinces: Jiangsu and Zhejiang.[64] Almost 70 percent of the 1,930 Qing dynasty female poets with works in one major anthology lived in those two places. Overall, more than 90 percent of female poets resided in the seven southern provinces. Not coincidentally, about 70 percent of men with a *jinshi* degree came from Jiangsu and Zhejiang as well. Clearly, most notable female poets belonged to highly educated official families. Women in other regions either wrote little poetry or else did not feel free to release their poems to the public.

Although female poetic talent was concentrated in the most cultured realms, other places produced some accomplished female poets as well. Wei Yizhen (b. 1832) belonged to the Zhuang minority in Guangxi.[65] She distinguished herself as an extremely prolific poet, and her poems were well regarded. Some Manchu women also became notable poets.[66] Although Jurchens traditionally did not educate their women, some elite Manchu families in Beijing embraced the Chinese cult of education and encouraged their women to study. A few Manchu women in the capital became respected poets. Gu Taiqing (also known as Gu Chun, 1799–1877) gained attention for her mastery of *ci* poetry.[67] Gu's wrote in a conventional style akin to that of contemporary Han women. She used a feminine poetic voice and expressed gentle emotions. Skill rather than originality made her work stand out. Gu Taiqing's poetry reveals that the taste and mentality of some high-ranking Manchu women in Beijing closely resembled that of their Han counterparts, attesting to the cultural assimilation of portions of the Manchu elite.

Thousands of female poets published their works, and their poetry covered a range of themes and styles.[68] As with men's poetry, most of it was extremely conventional. Women rarely used literature as a social critique or to demand more autonomy.[69] They mostly accepted their restrained circumstances as inevitable. Nevertheless, poetry gave them a public voice, and they used it to express heartfelt feelings, allowing readers to appreciate their humanity.

Many poems by Qing women had a heavily moralistic tone, reflecting the values that they had absorbed from a female curriculum that emphasized ethics. Like male poets, women often used their writings to project a reputable public façade. Readers had great respect for poetry that expressed virtue, so a great deal of women's poetry centered on moral themes such as filial piety, chastity, maternal love, and wifely fidelity.[70] In fact, readers expected to see these moralistic sentiments in women's poetry. If a female author departed too far from stock sentiments, her readers would feel confused or look down on her.

Women also wrote poetry in some of the same genres used by men, albeit using a female perspective. Many famous Tang dynasty poems dealt with historical topics, and Qing men often imitated this sort of classic poetry, describing famous incidents and personages from the past. Highly educated women also read historical works, so they could compose knowledgeable poetry on historical themes.[71] Like men, they portrayed historical events in ways intended to express their own ideas and beliefs. The standard female perspective on history differed from that of men. Educated men read historical works to prepare them for politics, administration, and war. In contrast, women had no practical use for history, and they were under no compunction to study it. They considered historical works leisure reading, so they had a more detached view of the past.

Women also used their poetry to convey stories about themselves and their families. A woman who felt that she had little time left to live would often write a farewell poem to sum up her life.[72] In previous eras, a few women had written deathbed poems, but this genre became common during the Qing. Women who died in poverty or other unhappy circumstances wrote deathbed poems to lament their fate. Others knew they would likely be killed in an impending battle, or else they were about to commit suicide to avoid rape. Whatever the context, deathbed poems often expressed a woman's life intentions. Poems in this genre also usually took a strong moralistic tone.

Like men, some women wrote poems on the walls of public places such as inns and temples while traveling.[73] Wall poetry became common during the Tang dynasty and increased in popularity over time. Many educated women accompanied their husbands and fathers on their travels, usually because a male family member had to take up an official posting in a distant locale. When women traveled, they would sometimes write poems on walls along the way to record their impressions and publicly express deeply held feelings. Passersby occasionally recorded and published an exceptional wall poem, bringing it to a wide readership. Both male and female readers enjoyed women's wall poems. Some men even took on a female persona and wrote wall poems in a feminine style. In fact this ventriloquistic practice was extremely common. Because most wall poetry was anonymous or obscure, in many cases it is not certain whether a poem was written by a woman or by a man writing in a female voice.

Most women's poetry was set in the inner quarters of the home, most often in the bedroom (*gui*).[74] Women focused on that place for the simple reason that they spent a great deal of time there. Setting poems in the boudoir also suggested a commitment to integrity by implying that the poet kept her distance from men. Yet despite these positive connotations, traditionally a great deal of boudoir poetry dealt with ambiguous themes. Male writers had long written about a lonely woman waiting in her bedroom for an absent lover who never arrives. Qing women disliked these erotic insinuations, and they also usually found this premise inapplicable to their own lives, so they wrote about the boudoir differently. During the late imperial era, women reinvented the tired boudoir genre by describing the wide range of activities that took place in the inner quarters. Instead of portraying a solitary beauty miserably pining for her loved one, they wrote about quotidian matters that took occurred in the bedroom, such as doing needlework, reading, playing games, listening to music, teaching children, painting, chanting sutras, chatting, and sleeping. Respectable female poets purged boudoir poetry of erotic associations and instead depicted the bedroom as the locus for a rich and cultured life.

A great deal of men's poetry had political undertones. Because women could not hold office, their poems rarely had political content.[75] Even so, as China reeled from increasingly dire problems toward the end of the dynasty, some women expressed their concern about the fate of the nation. Sometimes they even mentioned military matters in their works. When writing political poems, women cast aside customary delicacy and instead called for heroism and martyrdom. These political writings sometimes dealt with gender relations. Authors not only expressed concern about difficulties plaguing society but railed against the weak state of women in general. As China suffered a string of humiliations, women increasingly identified with the nation. They saw the problems facing their sex as analogous to those confronting Chinese as a whole. In this way, they transformed nationalistic literature into a new and highly effective mode of gender discourse. Male critics struggled to cope with poetry that departed so far from gender stereotypes. While they agreed with these women's sentiments, it disturbed them to see women expressing forthright opinions about war and government policy, not to mention interrogating patriarchy.

Many women wrote about war and upheaval from a personal perspective. Works that include details of the poet's personal suffering come across as authentic and deeply moving. Cai Runshi (1612–1698) was the wife of a Ming loyalist who had been executed for refusing to surrender. She was a talented poet and painter accustomed to a life of ease but suddenly lost everything when her husband died. Cai wrote frankly about her miserable life as a refugee.[76]

> How happy our life was, and how miserable it is now!
> After the calamity, we've suffered more misfortunes as refugees;
> I lost two sons on Heyang's post station road
> And collapsed in sow in the valley of Mount Huaimeng.
> Running into an old servant, I was able to survive;
> Three months in an old shabby temple, I grieved at my homelessness.
> In the howling wind, I often heard noises of killing and plunder;
> Smelling the stench of blood, I felt more worried and afraid.
> Thousands of words cannot describe what I've suffered;
> Facing each other, we cried with tears like rain and dew.

Although women usually composed uncontroversial verses, some such as Cai Runshi put forward disturbing emotions and documented traumatic experiences. In this case, the writer had fallen so low that she had nothing to lose by speaking her mind. The depth of feeling that Cai reveals in this poem shows that even though most women kept up appearances by adhering to polite cultural conventions, these could mask a tumultuous inner life. In reading Qing dynasty poems, the modern reader confronts women who, in spite of the restrictions they faced, maintained an interior sense of psychological authenticity.

In imperial China, people saw religion as far more than just an expression of faith. To women in particular, religious teachings and activities gave them precious opportunities to learn about both this world and the supernatural. Even so, the impact of religion on popular culture had declined markedly over the centuries. Up through the Tang dynasty, the teachings of Buddhism exerted immense impact on mainstream values and ideas. The intellectual level of religion had been in decline ever since, and secular learning eclipsed religious training. By the Qing era, religious institutions had decayed considerably. Because religion had previously been such an important intellectual and cultural resource for women, this decay affected them more than it did men.

Late imperial literary depictions of clerics attest to a decline in the reputation of religion in society at large. Literature often depicted monks and nuns as cynical and licentious. Many anomaly tales (*chuanqi*) described Buddhist and Daoist nuns in romantic terms.[77] Authors sexualized female monastics and made them into romantic protagonists to create an entertaining variation on stereotypical "scholar and beauty" romances. Even though the nun characters in these stories are usually good people, presenting them in erotic terms nevertheless shows a marked decline in their reputation. Readers now wanted to read about the beauty and romantic liaisons of nuns, not their holy acts.

As Buddhist clerics developed a shady reputation, officials repeatedly issued declarations forbidding laywomen from visiting temples, going on pilgrimages, and performing certain religious practices.[78] It seems that the pious ignored these prohibitions. Even so, the fact that government functionaries wanted to keep women away from temples shows deep prejudice toward religion among the elite. Officials were trying to protect naïve female worshippers from being seduced by rogue monks or led astray by lascivious nuns. They also wanted to keep women inside their homes for the sake of propriety. Visiting a sacred venue for the purpose of worship potentially exposed a woman to humiliation or seduction.

Even as authorities tried to keep women secluded, female worshippers still found ways to visit temples. Pious women even went on religious pilgrimages to distant holy sites.[79] Poor women were most likely to expose themselves to the public gaze in this way. But in the prosperous Jiangnan region, women from wealthy families went on pilgrimages as well. However, instead of traveling on foot, these women were carried in closed sedan chairs, and they tried to hide their faces from strangers as much as possible. Women also looked forward to raucous and colorful temple festivals.[80] Every city and village in China held periodic religious festivals, and it was considered permissible for women to attend.

Women did not visit holy sites simply for the sake of piety. Worship gave them a convenient excuse to leave the house and break out of reclusion.

As a woman made her way to the temple, she would be exposed to the sights, sounds, and smells of the outside world, allowing her to enjoy the panorama of life beyond the walls of her home.

Religious excursions gave women precious firsthand opportunities to learn about what lay beyond their immediate horizons. When confined to the home, they had to rely on books and hearsay to learn about the outside world. Religious outings confronted them with a plethora of new experiences, enriching their lives and providing them with precious knowledge.

For centuries local gentry leaders and government officials had been working to simplify and standardize popular religion.[81] Chinese had long worshipped a confusing pantheon of local deities, some of which struck educated observers as strange and morally dubious. During the late imperial era, the elite encouraged people to forsake minor local gods and concentrate their devotions on a small number of approved deities. This religious simplification movement had great success. Before the advent of the Qing, the number of deities being worshipped had already begun to decline. Over the course of the dynasty, people abandoned most unique local gods and turned their attentions to major gods approved by the state.

Religion also became increasingly secularized.[82] Believers turned away from abstract religious doctrines and instead embraced teachings and rituals that addressed real-life concerns. The Buddhist bodhisattva Guanyin originally attracted devotion as a symbol of compassion. During the late imperial era, her identity merged with that of popular maternal deities, and many women worshipped her as a fertility goddess. Various streams of religion also integrated considerable secular content. Confucian ideas became absorbed into Buddhism and Daoism, then presented to believers as religious imperatives. Secularization brought religious beliefs closer to mainstream knowledge, so when a female believer learned about religion, she assimilated many secular concepts as well.

Dozens of the deities venerated in popular religion were female, inviting the empathy and devotion of pious women.[83] Most had a maternal image. Some goddesses were credited with creating the world, such as the ancient figure Nü Wa and the newly popular Eternal Mother (Wushengmu). Various late imperial religious movements also included female deities in their pantheons. Goddesses embodied stereotypical female virtues such as compassion and maternal love. New Year folk paintings pasted on the walls of their homes frequently featured fertility symbols, celebrating an important female characteristic.[84] By giving female values a tangible identity and making them objects of worship, popular religion provided an important avenue for women to learn about normative femininity.

Religion had an especially important role in the lives of poor women and those living in marginal communities. Because they were usually illiterate, they learned largely through firsthand experience and hearsay. Religion provided them with a valuable opportunity to engage with abstract ideas and ethical teachings. Women at the bottom of society tended to prefer popular religion over Buddhism and Daoism, as they felt alienated by hierarchies and complicated teachings. Hakka women appealed to homey popular gods for blessings, fertility, and curing disease.[85] Women with the fewest resources were most likely to turn to religion in times of need, as this was often their only alternative. The utility of popular religion made it an important component in the worldview of the poor.

In addition to long-established religions, numerous mystical popular faiths also emerged during the Qing. The most successful of these new religions promoted ideas that appealed to the disadvantaged. Women tended to be especially enthusiastic about new and unorthodox religions, as they often offered appealing alternatives to conventional gender expectations.[86] Many popular religions taught social equality or the equality of all living things. Some scriptures advocated overcoming gender distinctions so that believers could treat everyone with uniform benevolence. They also assimilated practices from female shamanism. Not surprisingly, these doctrines attracted women worshippers. Some women took on important roles in new religions. Certain families in each area constituted a religious elite, and the leaders of popular religious organizations often inherited their positions. Hereditary religious leadership sometimes gave a woman the opportunity to become a religious leader when her family lacked an adult man capable of assuming the position.

The White Lotus (Bailian) sect exemplifies Qing dynasty popular religious movements.[87] This sect became extremely popular in the sixteenth century and persisted for the remainder of the dynasty, even after the state branded it as heterodox. Believers venerated the Eternal Venerable Mother (Wusheng Laomu), said to have created humanity. They believed that they could attain salvation by following the teachings revealed by her emissaries. White Lotus gained popularity by mixing appealing beliefs with tangible benefits. The religion's leaders built up a supportive community that provided believers with practical aid, drawing in poor women. Widows and virgins could live in a female residence hall, allowing them to maintain their chastity. The practicality of this religion explains why so many women found it appealing, despite its motley content.

Some religions had extensive written scriptures that assimilated popular beliefs and presented them as holy writ. So-called precious scrolls (*baojuan*) circulated among various sectarian groups from the Ming dynasty onward. These scriptures described useful religious practices such as healing, divination, and exorcism.[88] Some texts included ideas that appealed to women, advocating equality of the sexes and emphasizing the powers of divine female figures such as Princess Miaoshan and Guanyin. Some encouraged women to be brave and take control of their own destiny. Many of those who publicly recited these texts were women, and they often attracted a female audience, so the content became increasingly suited to female believers. In the nineteenth century, religious writers produced precious scrolls specifically for a female readership.

Even established religions adopted increasing amounts of secular and popular content, and believers presented mainstream values in a religious guise. In particular, chastity became an increasingly important measure of female integrity during the Qing. Buddhists found comparable ideas in the Indian epic *Ramayana* and offered the Indic version of this virtue.[89] Many Indian stories included supernatural elements, and these affected the Chinese Buddhist interpretation of chastity. By embracing chastity and reinterpreting it according to their own teachings, Buddhists adapted to the changing value system of contemporary society and kept their religion relevant. Buddhist teachings thus ended up reinforcing conventional gender values in the minds of the female faithful.

Buddhism differed from popular religion both for the profundity of its intellectual content and also for its assimilation of high culture. Educated women often used Buddhist imagery in their writings to appear spiritual and refined. Yuanduan was an early Qing Chan (Zen) nun renowned for her poetry. She used her writings to present herself not as a typical nun but as the female equivalent of the cultured male recluse.[90]

> Leisurely we rest on the couch by the window,
> And hand in hand reminisce over past excursions.
> We brew some tea and all is elegant and refined,
> Perusing books is enough for this pure seclusion.
> In the night rain, the flowers begin to glisten,
> In the gentle breeze, the birds start to chatter.
> As if to detain the shadows of the fading light,
> I silently strum the white silk strings in the dark.

Yuanduan describes obligatory female reclusion as a religious practice that allows her to commune with nature and enjoy a cultivated lifestyle.[91] In this case, the writer was a nun, so the link between reclusion and spirituality seems obvious. However, cloistered laywomen also declared themselves as engaging in so-called boudoir reclusion (*guiyin*). Their lives may have outwardly resembled those of other women, but they saw themselves as hermits in a psychological sense. By deliberately rejecting some of the core values of secular society, they imbued their isolation in the home with a spiritual dimension. During the early Qing, some female hermits drew inspiration from Ming loyalism, as men loyal to the previous dynasty had gone into reclusion for the sake of principle. They portrayed their withdrawal as a deliberate political position and implicitly compared themselves with Ming loyalist recluses.

Qing religion gave women a wide range of ways to learn about the world beyond the home. The beliefs and practices that a believer assumed depended on her background and what she wanted to achieve. An educated woman might use Buddhism to portray herself as an elegant recluse while the poor sought practical benefits. By selecting features that suited individual situations from this rich body of thought and practice, women from a wide range of backgrounds could improve their lives and imbue their existence with a sense of meaning.

6

Virtue

As ideas about female virtue hardened during the Qing dynasty, a woman had to undertake difficult sacrifices to be considered a moral exemplar. The amplification of female ethical duties had various causes. The gentry emphasized the virtue of their mothers, wives, and daughters to gain esteem and distinguish themselves from wealthy merchants, who often followed looser codes of conduct. Simultaneously, they tried to elevate the moral tone of society by encouraging people of all backgrounds to embrace ritual propriety and Confucian virtue.[1] This ethical shift also had political motivations. The Manchus were a small minority trying to keep control of a vast empire. Their Chinese subjects resented their initial cruelty and despised the nomadic lifestyle of their ancestors, so to gain respect, the Manchu establishment promoted stringent Neo-Confucianism as state orthodoxy.

Since antiquity, moralists had demanded that the sexes be distinguished in appearance and behavior and kept physically separate as much as possible.[2] In earlier periods, most people observed these injunctions loosely. But over time, increasing numbers of women secluded themselves in the inner quarters of the home. Boys and girls played together when very young but separated at about age seven or eight.[3] Thereafter they largely stayed apart and had divergent ways of life. Domestic architecture fostered gender separation, removing women from view and keeping male and female family members apart within the home. Even the poor would try to maintain a degree of separation between the sexes, perhaps hanging a curtain in front of the kitchen to provide a hidden refuge for women when male visitors arrived.[4]

Women's isolation shaped their worldview.[5] The sexes had different degrees of mobility that conditioned their experiences, taste, and values. For creative women in particular, reclusion could be a major handicap. Some men considered women's poetry uninteresting because women's constricted lives gave them little to discuss. Female writers worried about the psychological effects of extended seclusion.

Women in wealthy families faced the harshest restrictions. Whereas a poor woman might visit a crowded temple, those in prominent families felt uncomfortable exposing themselves in a public setting, as society held them to the highest standards. Even so, they were not completely isolated. Women read travel literature written by men to engage with the wider world. Those from privileged backgrounds could visit the homes and gardens of other wealthy families. And women could appear in public or travel long distances to fulfill family obligations. Most importantly, if a man died far from home, a dutiful wife would want to escort his body home for burial.

Keeping the sexes apart posed practical problems. Isolated within the home, women were effectively barred from most professions, reducing China's overall economic output. Women found it inconvenient to perform important tasks themselves, as they found it awkward to deal with men. And when women of good family appeared before magistrates to handle legal matters, their emergence from reclusion embarrassed everyone concerned.

Women even had trouble seeking medical treatment because they did not want a male physician to touch their body or even look at them.[6] Many women ended up forgoing proper medical care for the sake of propriety. Doctors tried to come up with ways to ascertain the health of a cloistered woman. Chinese medicine emphasized the diagnostic importance of the pulse, but women did not want to be touched by a man, so sometimes a woman would tie a silk thread tightly around her wrist and the physician would try to feel her pulse by holding the other end of the thread.

Gynecological conditions, especially sexually transmitted "secret diseases" (*yinji*), confronted male physicians with the greatest difficulties.[7] It was considered indecent for a physician to examine the affected area, so he had to rely on the patient's description of the problem. However, women found it mortifying to describe their genitalia to a man, so they often misrepresented the symptoms or refused to discuss the subject altogether. Male physicians had to be very sensitive to the feelings of their female patients. They might couch their questions in indirect language and euphemisms. Or they might reason with an embarrassed woman and urge her to describe her condition clearly so that she could receive proper treatment. Occasionally a male physician and female patient would even hold a ceremony to become fictive kin so that the sick woman would submit to an examination. Doctors and patients responded to these awkward encounters in various ways, but both parties usually felt abashed and confused.

Even under normal circumstances, it was not easy for a woman to remain isolated, and many resented having to stay hidden. Keeping women concealed in the home denied them opportunities to use their abilities and gain recognition for their achievements. The poet Wang Yun (1749–1815) complained, "Buried deep in the boudoir for more than a decade, I can earn neither honor nor immortality."[8] Even so, flouting these restrictions could expose a woman to terrible shame. A poor woman named Chen Susu wrote a poem expressing her regret at having foolishly besmirched her reputation.[9]

> I'm from a poor family.
> I grew up in Yangzhou.
> At the age of thirteen I learned embroidery.
> At the age of fifteen I learned to play the zither.
> During difficult times I found I was unable to protect myself:
> Without intending to I lost my chastity.
> Though I have only one blemish in a lifetime,
> Who will again believe in my sincerity?
> This is very hurtful, how can I talk of it?
> My life is cast away like the feathers of a swan.

A woman who defied ethical norms could even face prosecution. The state put enormous stress on the integrity of patrilineal descent, so magistrates punished adulterous wives severely. An adulteress would be degraded to chattel and her husband could sell her to another man against her will.[10] A husband could even kill an adulterous wife and her lover if he caught them *in flagrante*.[11]

Qing rape law treated victims differently depending on their perceived character. If a magistrate considered a victim licentious, both she and her rapist would receive the same penalty. But if the victim of a rape had been a chaste and loyal wife, the rapist was to be executed.[12] Women had to maintain a reputation for probity, regardless of the sacrifices required, simply to stay safe. Someone who gained a louche reputation put herself in danger.

Qing authorities changed laws covering sex crimes, including rape law, to safeguard chastity.[13] The Qing code punished the rape of a respectable married women heavily, as the state valued wifely chastity. A convicted rapist could be executed. Yet because the penalty was so severe, the government introduced stringent standards of proof, making it difficult for a woman to conclusively prove that she had been raped. When a victim reported a rape, she had to prove that the sexual act had been involuntary.

To do so, she had to convince the magistrate that she had struggled with the rapist throughout the entire ordeal. She was required to produce three kinds of evidence: the testimony of witnesses, bruises or wounds on her body, and torn clothing. If the magistrate deemed the evidence insufficient, he would assume that she had willingly submitted to the sexual act. She could then be convicted of "illicit intercourse by mutual consent" and punished. These demanding requirements made it almost impossible for a victim to report a rape without being condemned as a criminal herself. Given the legal system's hostility to rape victims, it made sense for women to seclude themselves in the home for their own protection.

Women faced tangible threats from numerous sexual predators. The skewed sex ratio meant that large numbers of men would never take a wife, and some of these "bare sticks" became extremely aggressive toward vulnerable women and threatened them with sexual violence.[14] In some places, gentry and officials went to great lengths to protect widows from harm. In addition, human traffickers abducted numerous women and sold them off as prostitutes, concubines, and wives.[15] Most often they abducted the poor, victims of domestic violence, those unhappy with their family situation, and women working outside the home. Some women eloped with a supposed lover only to end up being sold. Among a sample of sixty-nine abducted women, 39 percent were forced into prostitution and 28 percent were purchased as wives. The rest ended up as concubines or servants. The oldest abductee in the group was thirty-seven years old and the youngest only four. A third of them were ages sixteen to nineteen, the most desirable age for both prostitutes and brides. Although the government battled human trafficking, these incidents remained common. A woman who left the safety of the home exposed herself to unknown dangers.

Nevertheless, some women still moved about in public. The poor had no choice but to labor outside the home. Even secluded women went out on special occasions to participate in religious festivals and attend open-air opera performances.[16] Manchu women faced far fewer restrictions than Han. Jurchen men and women had traditionally worked side by side, and Manchu women maintained much of their traditional freedom of movement. The Spanish Dominican friar Domingo Navarrete, who visited Beijing in 1665, remarked on their boldness: "The Tartar women wear boots and ride astride like men, and make a notable figure either afoot or a-horseback."[17]

Not all women observed the imperatives of Confucian ethics. Popular stories described so-called wanton women (*yinfu*) whose transgressive behavior titillated and disgusted readers.[18] They pursued men in search of romance and even physical intimacy. Although authors portrayed wanton women in a negative light, in fact these characters were just behaving like men. Society considered it acceptable for a man to seek satisfaction for his emotional and physical needs. This sort of character was the female counterpart of the male philanderer. But in a woman, this sort of behavior seemed shocking and immoral.

The shrew presented an even more transgressive female image. This character had long been a staple of popular fiction and remained a common presence in Qing novels, short stories, and opera scripts.[19] Shrews terrorized, humiliated, and even assaulted their husbands, overturning expectations about the marital relationship. Shrews existed in real life as well. Qing magistrates handled cases of termagants mistreating their husbands.[20] Magistrates often blamed the henpecked man for his predicament, criticizing him for having failed to exercise the prerogatives of manhood.

Men discussed possible cures for female ferocity and jealousy.[21] Some advocated using violence to tame a shrew. However, Confucians counseled a gentler approach. They believed that a misbehaving woman should be educated to teach her to observe conventional female ethics. Alternatively, Buddhists reminded the shrew of the terrifying results of bad karma. They urged her to respect conjugal propriety so that she could have a good rebirth. Some physicians considered shrewish behavior the result of a physical ailment and tried to treat it with a proper diet or medication. As a last resort, government functionaries could invoke the law to punish viragos, forcing them to fulfill their wifely duties.

Widows faced particularly complex ethical quandaries.[22] Wives were almost always younger than their husbands, so they frequently ended up as widows. Although female life expectancy varied depending on region and social background, it was not unusual for a woman to outlive her husband by decades.[23] A widow could either remarry or declare herself chaste and remain faithful to her deceased spouse for the rest of her life. Widows faced very different expectations than widowers. People regarded men's remarriage as completely uncontroversial and commonplace.[24] In fact a widower without a son had a moral obligation to remarry or take a concubine to bear an heir and maintain the family line. In contrast, a woman's remarriage usually carried some stigma.

Manchu women could remarry without opprobrium.[25] Even though the Manchus encouraged widow chastity among their Han subjects to prove their commitment to Confucian virtue, they encouraged their own women to remarry. Until the mid-eighteenth century, the government even used financial pressure to coerce young Manchu widows to marry a new husband. This policy grew out of native Manchu culture. Widow chastity was not a native Jurchen custom. To the contrary, the Jurchens practiced levirate before entering China and required a widow to marry one of her husband's kinsmen to keep her attached to his family.

Encouraging the remarriage of Manchu widows also had practical goals. The law required Manchu men to take a Manchu wife, but female infanticide had resulted in a severe shortage of marriageable Manchu women. The government wanted Manchu widows to remarry so that more Manchu men would have a chance to wed, thereby maintaining ethnic exogamy and keeping their numbers from decreasing. The Manchus expected their men and women to follow different cultural norms. Men maintained much of their traditional appearance and lifestyle to preserve Manchu identity, yet they allowed their women to adopt Han ethics to demonstrate their collective virtue and refinement. From the mid-eighteenth century onward, some Manchu women began to observe Han ethics and practice widow chastity.

Han women had a very different view of remarriage. During the Ming and early Qing eras, the prestige of widow chastity rose dramatically.[26] By the start of the Qing dynasty, widow chastity already had a special place in the pantheon of female virtues, and it continued to increase in importance over time. The law forbade anyone from forcing a widow to remarry.[27] Nevertheless, authorities regarded widow chastity as laudable but not mandatory.

A widow had to consider many factors when deciding whether to enter a second marriage. Remarried women had to contend with increasing social disapproval. No man saw a widow as an ideal spouse, so she would probably marry a man of lower status and less wealth than her first husband. Also, when she entered her new husband's home, she would have to leave her dowry behind with her first husband's kin, rendering her impoverished. Many widows probably stayed chaste not out of a dedication to virtue but just to keep their dowries. Also, as children belonged to the husband's family, a remarrying widow would usually have to leave her sons behind with their paternal kinsmen. A loving mother would be loath to remarry if she would have to abandon her offspring. Popular superstition also reinforced chastity ethics. Many people believed that a deceased husband might turn into a ghost if his wife remarried, making widows hesitant to take a new husband for fear of retribution.[28]

If a widow wanted to remain with her in-laws, they might not welcome her decision. Her deceased husband's kin might resent the financial burden of having to support her. Or they might try to bully her into remarrying so that they could reclaim their kinsman's property. If they convinced the widow to remarry and leave, they would gain ownership of her dowry as well. They might even receive the betrothal gift for arranging her new marriage. It was never clear who was to receive the betrothal gift when a widow remarried, as this had to be decided during the marriage negotiations, and sometimes it went to the family of a widow's first husband.[29]

Given the practical advantages of chastity and drawbacks to remarriage, many widows decided to remain chaste. A poor woman had no choice but to remarry, as she would find it difficult to survive on her own. But if she had sufficient resources, a widow could declare herself chaste and live out the remainder of her life in her deceased husband's home, managing his estate until her death. In doing so, a widow took on certain responsibilities. She was expected to continue caring for her parents-in-law, and she had to remain faithful to her former husband. If she had sexual relations, it was considered adultery and she would be sent back to her family in disgrace.[30]

During the Qing dynasty, widow chastity became increasingly common. The massive compendium *Complete Collection of Illustrations and Writings from the Earliest to Current Times* (*Gujin tushu jicheng*), completed in 1725, contains the biographies of thousands of female paragons from the span of Chinese history, including more than nine thousand women from the early Qing. A quarter of chaste widows described in the collection date from the Qing era, even though the dynasty was only a few decades old when compilation began.[31]

The number of chaste widows escalated through the course of the dynasty. This trend began soon after the establishment of the Qing. Suzhou had more than three times as many chaste widows in the first century of the Qing than during the entire Ming era.[32] Similarly, a gazetteer from Xiangshan county in Guangdong province lists the names of thousands of exemplary women, mostly chaste widows, with the number increasing notably over the course of the Qing.[33]

In 1879 22,987 women in Guangdong gained recognition for their exceptional morality. Half came from just two counties, Xiangshan and Sanshui. These numbers show that the popularity of chastity differed markedly by region. Even within the same province, people in different counties had very different views of the practice.

Table 6.1. Number of Chaste Widows by Era

Reign Era	Date of Reign	Length of Reign (Years)	Number of Chaste Widows in Xiangshan County, Guangdong
Kangxi	1661–1722	61	37
Qianlong	1735–1796	60	209
Daoguang	1820–1850	30	1,876
Tongzhi	1861–1875	13	5,445

The Han dynasty scholar Liu Xiang had described many types of praiseworthy women. Over time, however, female virtue became increasingly identified with chastity. By the Qing, chastity was by far the most highly regarded female virtue. Biographies of chaste women became extremely popular, and records of faithful widows and women who died to preserve their chastity from bandits or rapacious soldiers make up a large proportion of the total biographies in local gazetteers.[34] Of 518 female paragons from a nineteenth-century gazetteer about Jimo county in Shandong, 98 percent were either chaste widows or martyrs.[35] Even many female relatives of the emperors decided to remain chaste after the death of their husbands. In 1846 the imperial clan included 1,263 widows, who received a stipend from the government to allow them to stay chaste.[36]

Chastity rhetoric not only became more common, but it also extended over a greater geographic area than before. The Qing Empire included large regions inhabited by peoples other than ethnic Han. Due to overpopulation in the Chinese heartland, many Han migrated into marginal regions and married local women of various ethnicities. Encounters between Han and other peoples had mixed results. Many Chinese migrants adopted local customs and melded into local communities.[37] But over time, ethnic groups along the empire's margins absorbed many Han Chinese values. The situation in Yunnan illustrates this trend.[38] Tang dynasty records do not indicate that the native peoples of Yunnan had any concept of Chinese-style chastity. Subsequently, many Han soldiers, farmers, merchants, and exiles moved into the region, exposing the local people to Confucian ethics. Chinese education introduced new ideas about proper female behavior, which clearly influenced people's thinking and behavior. Qing gazetteers from Yunnan record 9,645 virtuous women, many of them chaste widows. A similar process of acculturation occurred along much of the empire's margins.

A widow could only be recognized for model behavior after remaining unmarried for a long time. Young widows rarely received recognition from the government or in local publications. A woman had to stay a widow for decades for her fidelity to be considered worthy of recognition, so it was almost impossible for a widow to be publicly honored if her husband died after she was thirty years old. Among the chaste widows in the gazetteer of Jimo county, 95 percent were widowed in their teens and twenties and 98 percent had been a widow for at least three decades. A quarter had maintained chaste widowhood for fifty years or more.[39] Four of the Qing-era exemplars noted in the Xiangshan gazetteer had been widows for more than seventy years.[40]

Scholars of women's history have long referred to Chinese widow chastity as a cult, as the underlying principles seemed like religious faith and the practices of widowhood seemed like sacred ritual.[41] Most people accepted chastity as a major virtue and believed that loyal widowhood elevated a woman almost to the point of saintliness. Moreover, only widows with sufficient wealth could forego remarriage, so chastity also became identified with prosperity. This exclusivity elevated the reputation of chastity even further by making it a marker of elite status.

The surge in chaste widowhood during the Qing resulted from a concatenation of factors. The government and gentry both supported chastity as a source of prestige.[42] The Qing court employed Confucian ethics as a tool for stabilizing and governing local society, which could often be fractious. Manchus hesitated to promote male loyalty, as they feared an outburst of loyalism toward the previous dynasty. However, women's loyalty, in the form of widow chastity, did not threaten the state. Traditionally the faithful wife had been seen as a counterpoint to the loyal official, as both were loyal to a male superior.[43] By promoting widow chastity, the Qing also implicitly emphasized the importance of loyalty in general, helping to garner support for their regime.

This project allowed the state apparatus to cooperate closely with local notables, constructing a model of social order centered on the value system of the minor gentry.[44] The state expected the gentry to exercise leadership over their communities. To legitimize their guidance, the gentry emphasized their commitment to orthodox Confucian values, including chastity. The Qing government then recognized the moral stature of the gentry, winning their invaluable support. As the civil service examination system became increasingly competitive, the proportion of men from gentry backgrounds who obtained a degree decreased, rendering them unqualified for government service.[45] Taking a hard line of female ethics allowed gentry to claim moral superiority in spite of a failed career.

The inclusion of so many thousands of women in local gazetteers shows that widow chastity symbolized the community's collective honor. It was in everyone's interest to encourage widows to decline remarriage because it made their community appear virtuous. Women came into the home as outsiders, so they had long been seen as agents of tension who might potentially disrupt the patrilineal order.[46] Using women to represent the ethics of a much larger group demonstrated that even society's least trusted members were behaving righteously, affirming the moral tenor of the group. When compiling local gazetteers, literati included the names of numerous chaste widows from the area to garner the respect of outsiders.

The most common curriculum for female students centered on conservative Confucian ethics. They were taught to regard widow chastity as a lofty virtue. This rhetoric infiltrated popular culture as well. Stage plays, ballads, and lowbrow literature often featured chaste women in their plots, familiarizing women from the lower rungs of society with this moral ideal.⁴⁷ Inventive authors presented this theme to audiences in unexpected ways. Some stories featured a loyal courtesan who devotes herself wholeheartedly to one man.⁴⁸ Even though the couple cannot possibly marry due to their difference in status, the courtesan nevertheless remains faithful. Their fidelity is based entirely on love, making it seem heartfelt. The reputation of courtesans plummeted during the early Qing, so by portraying a courtesan as loving and devoted, authors demonstrated how this virtue could even evoke praiseworthy sentiments in base people.

Cloistered wives and faithful widows might seem like victims from today's standpoint, but these lifestyles could only endure with the complicity of the women involved.⁴⁹ Throughout imperial history, women rarely opposed the prevailing gender system, however unfair it may have been. To the contrary, many women enthusiastically supported and promoted the ethical ideals that restrained them, as embracing conventional morals won them respect. Because women participated in the creation of gender values, these principles included ambiguities and openings that women could exploit.

A commitment to chastity could even give a widow a sense of psychological well-being. Regardless of what hardships she may have had to endure, she could always take pride in having lived a life of integrity. The poet Wu Xun (1693–1735) summed up this sense of satisfaction.⁵⁰

> When I mend clothes, the dawn light is warm,
> As I weave silk, the night lamp is chill.
> The lot of the chaste is disregard and difficulty
> But together with my children in poverty
>   I am at peace.

Beginning in the Han dynasty, governments periodically issued official commendations (*jingbiao*) to female moral exemplars to encourage behavior believed to benefit state and society. Soon after establishing themselves in China, the Manchus revived this practice and started issuing commendations for virtue in 1651. Commendations served as part of the moral education (*fengjiao*) movement that began in the early Qing and became very active in the early eighteenth century. Under the Qing system, a woman could earn recognition for various types of outstanding behavior. At the beginning of the dynasty, authorities wanted to increase the population, so they presented mothers who gave birth to male triplets with a commendation.⁵¹ Overall, however, the Qing state took a narrow view of female virtue. Officials downplayed female bravery, talent, and intelligence and focused on the faithful widow as the premier icon of womanly morals.

Table 6.2 Number of Commendations of Women

Era	Number of Commendations	Average Number of Annual Commendations
1652–1661	403	40
1661–1722	4,822	79
1722–1735	9,995	769
1735–1796	32,521	2,323
1821–1850	93,668	3,122
1862–1873	190,040	15,537

In earlier eras, men had received most of the commendations for outstanding moral behavior. But during the Qing, most recipients were female. The state handed out many tens of thousands of awards to women, but far fewer to "righteous men" (*yifu*).[52] Moreover, the number of women receiving commendations increased considerably over the course of the dynasty.[53]

Commendations followed bureaucratic procedures based largely on Ming dynasty precedents.[54] A woman first applied to a local county magistrate for recognition to initiate the process. The application then passed up the bureaucratic hierarchy and was successively reviewed and approved at each level of administration. Final approval came from the court, so in theory the emperor bestowed each honor. Because the national commendation system was so complex, time consuming, and rigorous, women sometimes applied for a lesser award handed out by local authorities. Although local commendations were less prestigious, they were much easier to obtain.

As the commendation system expanded, officials relaxed some requirements. During the Ming dynasty, a widow could only receive a commendation if she was over age fifty. Qing rules reduced the requisite age to forty.[55] The government also made it less expensive to construct a commemorative monument celebrating chaste widowhood. Under Ming procedures, the families of chaste widows had to pay for commemorative archways themselves (figure 6.1). The government merely gave them permission to construct the monument. In contrast, the Qing state paid for memorial arches. As a result of this change, these monuments became extremely common, altering China's landscape.[56] Yet even as the Qing made it easier and less expensive to obtain official commendation, the government also demanded that a widow remain chaste after she received this award. During the Ming, if a widow received a chastity commendation and subsequently remarried, the award would simply be rescinded. But under Qing law, it was illegal for a widow who had received a commendation to remarry, and magistrates could punish violators.[57]

Figure 6.1. Memorial Arch
Wikimedia Commons | Panoramio

Whereas the rulers of previous dynasties had often singled out women from elite families for recognition, the Qing targeted commoners. The government considered chaste widows from poor families most deserving of commendation, as these women had to endure the most hardships to stay faithful to a deceased spouse. The state also saw this system as a means to promote Confucian ethics among the lower ranks of society. Official support for chaste widows increased rapidly in the nineteenth century, as the government encouraged virtuous behavior to stabilize an increasingly fractious society. During the dynasty's decline, authorities responded to successive rebellions, incursions, and humiliations with the administrative tools at their disposal, which included commendations of female virtue. Because commendations focused on women from ordinary backgrounds, few women from official families applied for this honor. Instead a man with an official post could request that his wife or mother receive an honorific title.

Attitudes toward widow chastity varied considerably by region.[58] Locales with high rates of widow chastity tended to be densely populated and have relatively large numbers of degree holders. A high rate of education also affected women's mores. Most of the widows who declined remarriage lived in provinces along China's southeast coast. Certain areas were hotspots of chastity, and widows there who remarried might suffer ostracism. Communities where women's physical safety was highly threatened also tended to emphasize chastity. Amid the chaos of the late Ming and Manchu conquest, many women in Huizhou were raped or else committed suicide when threatened with sexual violence. An extremely high proportion of widows in that region subsequently declared themselves chaste.

Fujian and neighboring Taiwan exhibited starkly different views toward chastity, despite their proximity and cultural similarities.[59] Among 33,562 chaste widows from the administrative region that encompassed both Fujian and Taiwan during the late Ming and Qing dynasties, only 239 lived in Taiwan. In Fujian, chastity was mostly practiced by the landed elite. In contrast, chaste widows in Taiwan often came from a poor background. These women could only decline remarriage if they received financial aid from charitable gentry and officials, so Taiwanese did not associate widow chastity with social status.

The paucity of chaste widows in Taiwan has several explanations. Fujian was densely populated, whereas Taiwan was a frontier society with relatively few Han residents. Taiwan also had perhaps the most highly skewed sex ratio in China. Because the Qing prohibited women from legally migrating to Taiwan, the Han population was mostly male. With women so rare, widows were expected to remarry. Taiwanese also exhibited a different mindset from their counterparts on the mainland. Taiwan's economy, based on trade, fostered an atmosphere of pragmatism. Women felt much less pressure to observe restrictive ethical injunctions or remain secluded. In addition, Taiwan had far fewer lineages and clans than Fujian. Newcomers to this immigrant society found it difficult to gather enough close relatives to establish a lineage, so unlike Fujian, Taiwanese widows lacked the financial support of charitable estates.

The unusual situation in Taiwan highlights the connection between widow chastity and the strength of lineages during the late imperial era. Members considered chaste widows to have brought honor to the entire lineage and elders recorded commendations in the official genealogy.[60] Many lineages in Fujian and other places used income from their common estate to support chaste widows by giving them enough for food and housing.[61] Widows in some lineages considered this support a right of membership and sued the lineage if they were not receiving this aid. Lineages also helped protect the property of widows against the incursions of greedy kinsmen.

The gentry, particularly those in the Jiangnan region, also embraced widow chastity. Local gentry leaders funded benevolent societies that built institutions to house poor widows in their communities. Funding these ventures allowed them to prove themselves moral leaders. Gentry support for chaste widows differed from religious charity. Whereas Buddhists allocated aid according to need, Confucians judged the moral tenor of potential recipients and helped those they deemed virtuous, particularly chaste widows.[62] This sort of charity emerged in the late eighteenth century and reached a height of popularity a century later. Gentry began by providing housing for the widows of poor literati and gradually broadened their support to help women from other classes as well. Widow halls not only provided residents with a place to live but also protected them from abduction. Wealthy widows also founded charitable estates to support less fortunate women who wanted to remain chaste. The spread of widow halls made it easier for women from modest backgrounds to decline remarriage, further increasing the number of faithful widows.

The cult of widowhood became so intense that people began to laud all forms of chastity as a side effect. Some reasoned that if sex was bad for a widow, ideally a woman might try to avoid it altogether. This line of thinking led to the emergence of the so-called faithful maiden (*zhennü*) cult in the sixteenth century, a social phenomenon that continued through the Qing. Faithful maidens were women betrothed to a fiancé who died before the wedding took place.[63] Although they had never married, they nevertheless remained faithful to their deceased fiancés and took on a social identity akin to widowhood. Faithful maidens were always very young when they took on this role, so they expected to have a long chaste life ahead of them.

Although chaste widowhood had widespread support, no one expected a woman to forego marriage after the death of a fiancé. Those around a faithful maiden usually regarded her sacrifice as unnecessary and obsessive. Parents did not encourage their daughters to take on this role, as they hoped for them to become wives and mothers. During the Ming, some literati criticized faithful maidens for exceeding the bounds of ritual propriety, but these determined women found more support from the Qing intellectual elite. While some Qing writers condemned faithful maidenhood as an unnecessary sacrifice, others praised it as an exceptional commitment to chastity. The fact that their voluntary martyrdom was not just difficult but also unnecessary made it seem even more exemplary. By taking the ethics of chastity to an extreme, faithful maidens hoped to demonstrate their consummate dedication to moral purity.

Although society regarded faithful maidens as zealots, it seems that some young women chose this option for practical reasons. Sometimes the parents of a deceased man agreed to treat his fiancée as his widow, and they gave her control of their son's estate. Through this sort of arrangement, a woman could win financial security without having to get married and bear children.

In the late imperial era, thinkers reassessed the nature of filial piety, affecting attitudes toward fidelity. Qing gazetteers describe women expressing filial piety in various ways.[64] A filial woman respected her parents, cared for them when sick, protected them from harm, conducted proper funerals, and observed full mourning. People were extremely interested in how women managed to fulfill such demanding obligations. Popular literature and performances often took the filial piety of daughters as a theme. Many operas centered on the difficulty of upholding filial virtue.[65]

As female manifestations of filial piety rose in visibility, women found themselves confronted with a disturbing quandary. They had been taught to regard filial piety toward parents as a key virtue. The ancient sage Mencius even lauded it as the foundation of ethics.[66] However, a daughter left home when she married, making it impossible for her to fully carry out her filial obligations after she wed. Some married women felt uneasy that they could not fulfill their obligations toward their parents. A poem by Lin Yining (1655–after 1730) summed up her feelings of guilt and shame due to this failure.[67]

> Who said giving birth to daughters is good?
> Child and adult, I have rarely seen my parent's face.
> Is it right not to care for one's parents?
> Yet how can I serve him in his later years?

Women had been taught to regard filial piety as the wellspring of virtue, but marriage seemed to prevent them from fulfilling this duty. Thinkers had traditionally addressed this apparent contradiction by envisioning female ethics as a series of obligations that shifted over the course of the life trajectory. According to this model, a woman should emphasize filial piety toward her parents when young, then transfer her primary allegiance to her husband.[68] Ancient ritualists even considered marriage an expression of filiality, as it fulfilled the expectations of the couple's parents and helped guarantee the continuation of the husband's family line.[69]

Over time, the rubric of parenthood gradually expanded to encompass a wider range of social roles, embracing parents-in-law as well as biological parents.[70] Wives started to consider their parents-in-law as surrogate parents, hence deserving of filial devotion. Alterations to female kinship status facilitated this shift. In antiquity a woman's primary identity and loyalty rested with her natal family, even after her marriage.[71] If she had to choose between supporting her husband or father, she put the blood bond first. Thereafter a woman's relationship with her parents fluctuated somewhat in each period. The Tang dynasty saw a major transition. At that time a woman's relationship with her natal family noticeably weakened and the law began to treat the wife as an integral member of her husband's family.[72] Relations between wives and their mothers-in-law had famously been fraught, so as wives drew closer to their husband's family, they were encouraged to treat their parents-in-law with filial regard to defuse tensions and foster harmony.[73]

During the Yuan and Ming eras, chaste widows began citing filial loyalty to parents-in-law as a justification for refusing to remarry.[74] Some reasoned that because a wife belonged to her husband's family, she owed his parents lifelong service. This belief imbued chastity with a powerful new motivation. Chaste widows were not just loyal to a deceased husband but exemplars of filial piety as well. This reinterpretation of chastity influenced the portrayal of this virtue. The *Classic of Filial Piety for Women* (*Nü xiaojing*), which had been highly admired during the Song and Yuan dynasties, lost popularity during the Qing, as it highlighted a woman's duty to her parents. Likewise, the Qing state apparatus downplayed women's devotion to parents and instead promoted attention to parents-in-law as a primary female virtue.[75]

As the cult of chastity intensified, practitioners demonstrated their commitment to virtue in increasingly extreme ways. It became common for women to mutilate themselves to preserve their chastity or demonstrate their filial piety. Although ancient writings mention men and women occasionally harming their bodies in the name of virtue, this was an extremely marginal practice. Subsequent developments convinced people to look upon certain types of mutilation in an increasingly favorable light.

Medieval records contain many mutilation stories. According to the Chinese pharmacopoeia, human flesh has highly efficacious medical value, so occasionally someone cut off a piece of their own body to brew an exotic potion.[76] Buddhist tales describe holy figures cutting off flesh from their bodies to feed to sick parents, portraying mutilation as an extravagant expression of filial devotion.[77] And Tang dynasty accounts include many descriptions of women who mutilated themselves to resist rape or forced remarriage.[78] Thereafter female self-mutilation became increasingly common. The *Complete Collection of Illustrations and Writings from the Earliest to Current Times* (*Gujin tushu jicheng*) lists 2,470 case of women and men who mutilated themselves to obtain medical material.[79] Although both sexes initially made this sort of sacrifice, over time virtuous self-mutilation became a stereotypically female practice.[80] During the Song dynasty, mutilation narratives usually describe a filial woman who cuts off some of her own flesh to brew medicine for a sick parent, most often her mother.[81]

During the Yuan and Ming eras, expressions of female virtue took a violent turn, as seen in the popularity of mutilation stories. About 60 percent of Ming dynasty narratives of filial women involve self-mutilation.[82] As before, usually an exemplar of filial devotion would cut off flesh to treat a sick parent. However, a rising number of stories describe dutiful women who mutilated themselves to heal an ailing parent-in-law, a reflection of the increasing integration of wives into their husbands' families.[83]

As virtuous self-mutilation became increasingly common, many observers expressed concern. From the Confucian perspective, this practice could seem perplexingly contradictory. A woman might justify self-mutilation as an expression of filial piety, but she nevertheless violated the ancient injunction that a child who damages her body is blatantly unfilial. The *Classic of Filial Piety* (*Xiaojing*) is unambiguous in this regard: "Your physical person with its hair and skin are received from your parents. Vigilance in not allowing anything to do injury to your person is where family reverence begins."[84] Authorities became concerned that self-mutilation was unfilial, and they sometimes tried to discourage or prohibit this practice.[85]

Despite these objections, virtuous self-mutilation became increasingly common during the Qing dynasty. Of a sample of 342 filial women, 245 demonstrated their resolve by cutting off part of their body to brew medicine for a sick elder, either a parent or parent-in-law.[86] As with other manifestations of female virtue, the popularity of filial mutilation varied by region. This practice was particularly popular in northern Anhui.[87] The gazetteer of Yingzhou county in Anhui, published in the late eighteenth century, lists thirty-one filial women. Twenty-two of them (74 percent) mutilated themselves to procure medicinal material. Likewise, the early nineteenth-century gazetteer of Fuyang county in Anhui lists thirty-four filial women, of which twenty-three (68 percent) mutilated themselves. People in this area seem to have been unusually superstitious, making them more likely to believe that exotic draughts made of human flesh could have amazing healing properties. Northern Anhui also experienced numerous uprisings and endemic banditry during the Qing, resulting in the premature deaths of many local men. In consequence, filial responsibilities fell more heavily on female survivors. They came under intense pressure to carry out their filial obligations, and some resorted to extreme measures to prove themselves worthy. Overall, however, fewer thinkers and officials expressed qualms about self-mutilation.[88] Literati tended to assume that these women were motivated by sincere sentiments (*zhiqing*), so they usually overlooked the unfilial aspects of self-harm.

Female suicide for the sake of virtue also increased during the late imperial era. Of the hundreds of female suicides documented in the *Complete Collection of Illustrations and Writings from the Earliest to Current Times*, 71.47 percent date to the Ming and 23.37 percent to the Qing.[89] However, this compendium was completed in 1725 and the Qing dynasty lasted for almost two more centuries, so the rate of documented virtuous female suicides seems to have exceeded that of the previous dynasty. Of the biographical narratives of exemplary women in the *Draft History of the Qing Dynasty* (*Qingshi gao*), about 60 percent either committed suicide or were killed.[90] These women died for various reasons. Most frequently they killed themselves to preserve their chastity when threatened with rape. Others committed suicide after the death of a husband or occasionally a parent. Widows sometimes committed suicide to avoid forced remarriage. Overall the suicides recorded in gazetteers and national records had a moral motivation. Women died because of their commitment to chastity, loyalty, or integrity.

From the beginning of the dynasty, female suicide won a prominent place in the popular imagination. During the Manchu invasion, 160 women are recorded as having been martyred during the Rape of Yangzhou. Some committed suicide in groups to avoid rape. However, not all of them died willingly. Adult women sometimes dispatched their daughters before killing themselves. Numerous poems and documentary accounts described these deaths. Authors praised martyrs who died during the chaos or who killed themselves and often blamed the women who survived and suffered rape.[91] This infamous incident raised the profile of female suicide.

Subsequent records mention many women who imitated the Yangzhou martyrs. Suicides constitute a considerable proportion of virtuous female acts described in Qing gazetteers. The late nineteenth-century gazetteer of Jimo county in Shandong records five hundred virtuous women.[92] Of these, 167 (33.4 percent) died for the sake of virtue. A few were killed while resisting rape, but most committed suicide. Similarly, a gazetteer for Tongren in Qinghai prefecture lists 112 exemplary women from the Qing dynasty, of whom 71 (63 percent) committed suicide.[93] In most cases a woman would either drown herself or jump off a cliff. Female suicide was also particularly common in Huizhou, as people there judged a woman's integrity mainly by the strength of her commitment to chastity.[94] It seems that a significant proportion of Huizhou widows killed themselves. Likewise, Fuqing county in Fujian also stands out for having a particularly large number of female martyrs.

The particulars and implications of Qing suicide were influenced by Jurchen customs, so these differed from Ming dynasty practices.[95] Traditionally, Jurchen suicide was a mortuary practice unassociated with heroism or martyrdom. A deceased Altaic khan was interred with a range of possessions for use in the afterlife. Wives, minor consorts, retainers, and servants might commit suicide to be buried with their lord so that they could continue to serve him, a custom called "following in death" (*dahame bucembi*). These customs influenced Manchu attitudes toward suicide at the beginning of the Qing dynasty. However, during the eighteenth century, the influence of these traditional ideas diminished. Instead of regarding suicide as a funerary practice, Manchus embraced Chinese views of the matter.

Today people consider suicide an intimate act. But during the Qing, women often tried to commit suicide in ways calculated to gain maximum exposure. Some even killed themselves in public. Qing female suicide did not have a single cause. Women killed themselves for various reasons depending on the individual's mindset and situation. In fact contradictory ethical priorities often pulled women in different directions.[96] When contemplating suicide, a woman had to weigh the value of posthumous accolades against responsibility to her family. She might want to kill herself to follow a husband or father to the grave but decide to remain alive to care for an elderly mother or parent-in-law. Similarly, a mother might decide against suicide because she did not want to orphan her children. Sometimes a woman decided to commit suicide but postponed the act until after she had carried out pressing family duties. A widow might remain chaste and faithfully care for her parents-in-law, then commit suicide after they died to belatedly demonstrate her loyalty to her deceased husband.

The purported motivation of suicide determined its moral significance. If a woman killed herself because she felt depressed or could not bear her mother-in-law's bullying, people regarded her death as merely pathetic. But if she ended her life for the sake of a moral principle such as chastity, loyalty, or filial piety, the community would judge the act praiseworthy. A proper suicide done for the right reason was considered a good death (*hao si*). Because women spent their lives secluded, they had few ways to gain public approbation. Suicide allowed them to win acclaim, albeit posthumously.[97] Parents or in-laws might even encourage a widow to commit suicide so that they could bask in the glory of her martyrdom.[98]

Virtuous suicide had various motivations. A woman might martyr herself to express loyalty to a husband or parent (*xunqin*). Many accounts stress that a woman killed herself not for the sake of personal glory but to safeguard her husband's honor (*wei fu shou zhen*). Otherwise, women committed suicide or died while struggling to avoid rape, most often during the chaos of war, uprisings, and natural disasters. Of seventy-one women in the Tongren county gazetteer, sixty-one killed themselves to avoid being violated.[99]

A woman might even kill herself if she felt that she had been publicly humiliated. In the eighteenth century the government set down laws to punish any man who insulted a woman who subsequently committed suicide.[100] A man's punishment varied according to the seriousness of the insult. If the verbal abuse involved sexual innuendo, the slanderer could be sentenced to death. Otherwise he might suffer exile. This law highlights the fragility of a woman's reputation. A public insult could instantly ruin a woman's good name. Because verbal abuse had such serious consequences for women, the government tried to shield them from public insults. If the judicial process failed to bring justice, a woman who had been insulted could commit suicide as a form of revenge. Her suicide would publicly embarrass her harasser and might even see him executed.

Given the number of factors at play, the motivations for a particular suicide were often ambiguous. Maybe a widow killed herself to show wifely loyalty, but perhaps she did it out of love. For a woman trapped in an abusive arranged marriage with no possibility of escape, suicide might have seemed like a reasonable option. Women also killed themselves to protest mistreatment. But if neighbors believed that a wife had committed suicide in response to unbearable abuse from in-laws, her husband's family would be disgraced.

Because suicide had many potential causes, women and their families went to great lengths to manage public perceptions. If a widow killed herself due to mistreatment, her in-laws might take pains to laud her as a selfless martyr, thereby turning potential disgrace into honor. Doubtless some allegedly virtuous suicides were committed not to express a high ideal but out of despair. To avoid being misunderstood, some women wrote an explanatory poem to explain and justify their decision to die.[101] They often stressed that they were acting of their own accord, portraying their death as an expression of individual agency.

Household dynamics also gave rise to suicide.[102] People living under the same roof often had opposing interests despite their proximity. A widow competed with her brothers-in-law for limited family resources, so they might treat her as an enemy. A young widow living among her husband's male kinsmen might even have to fend off sexual harassment. And a family faced with downward mobility might try to force their women into concubinage or prostitution or bully widows to remarry against their will. When faced with dire circumstances, women might consider suicide the best possible alternative.

Emperors, government ministers, literati, and ordinary people had conflicting attitudes toward the disturbing frequency of female suicide. The Qing government had to somehow harmonize the very different traditions of suicide among Manchus and Han.[103] When the Jurchens entered China, they initially considered suicide unproblematic, as it had been a traditional funerary custom in their culture. However, as emperors became acculturated to Han values, they began to regard Altaic-style suicide as embarrassing and even barbaric.[104] Even so, Manchus had conflicting views toward Chinese-style suicide. Although the emperors Kangxi, Yongzheng, and Qianlong all detested widow suicide, many Manchus took pride in the virtuous suicides of their own widows, as these demonstrated their commitment to Chinese ethics.

Initially, the Qing commendation system followed Ming precedent and awarded posthumous awards to women who committed suicide or were killed resisting rape.[105] However, emperors began to have qualms about encouraging their subjects to kill themselves. In 1688 the Kangxi emperor demonstrated his benevolence by banning widow suicide.[106] However, this prohibition only applied to women who killed themselves recklessly for no good reason. It was still acceptable for a woman to commit suicide for the sake of principle. In other words, Kangxi rejected female suicide motivated by emotion but sanctioned it when done in the name of morals.

The Yongzheng emperor also felt troubled by the frequency of female suicide.[107] Some of his officials even suspected that women were killing themselves to evade onerous family responsibilities. To prevent meaningless loss of life, in 1728 Yongzheng issued an edict forbidding women from committing suicide to evade family duties, such as caring for parents-in-law or young children. This expression of displeasure seems to have affected official attitudes. Most suicide cases in the *Draft History of the Qing* occurred either prior to Yongzheng's reign or during the late nineteenth century. At the end of the dynasty, the government became more amenable to extreme expressions of virtue, so authorities once again celebrated virtuous female suicide. The rulers of the Qing regarded suicide as a socially disruptive act, so they tried to regulate it.[108] Most importantly, they distinguished between women who committed suicide for the sake of principle and those deemed irresponsible or overwrought. When a woman killed herself, local officials had to assess her state of mind. Their conclusions determined how the state apparatus would react.

To reduce the number of suicides, the government strongly encouraged women to devote themselves to pacific forms of virtue such as filial piety. Increasing the sense of obligation to care for elders probably kept many widows alive. State functionaries also endorsed the cult of chaste widowhood as an alternative to martyrdom. This decision helps explain the notable rise in the number of chaste widows during the Qing. In part this practice gained popularity because the government considered it a benign alternative to widow suicide.

Qing society debated the merits and drawbacks of virtuous suicide.[109] A woman's death could strike a blow to her family. If authorities deemed a woman's death virtuous, she would require a particularly grand and expensive funeral, perhaps impoverishing the survivors. Moreover, the premature death of widows further exacerbated the gender imbalance. And many opposed the suicide of family members for practical reasons. Vulnerable parents-in-law often feared that a widow would kill herself, depriving them of care and support. Having already lost a son, the suicide of a daughter-in-law could bring added hardship. They might encourage her to remain alive as a chaste widow so that they would have a dedicated caregiver in their old age.

Despite these drawbacks, many people continued to laud virtuous suicide as a heroic act of martyrdom. During the Ming dynasty, many commentators believed that suicidal women were carrying out the injunctions of the ancient classics and Confucian ethical works. They began to see righteous suicide as an expression of loyalty to Chinese civilization.[110] Although opinions hardened during the Qing, a lingering respect for female martyrs remained. Popular fiction often described suicidal women as steadfast and determined.[111]

During the twilight of the Qing, views toward ethical questions rapidly shifted, and people reassessed virtuous suicide. Self-consciously modern thinkers strongly condemned this practice. During the May Fourth Movement of the 1920s, both reformers and radicals denounced the frequency of suicide as emblematic of the oppression of women by a cruel patriarchal society.[112] Instead of seeing suicidal woman as martyrs, society began to regard them as pathetic and misguided victims. This viewpoint has continued down to the present. People today bemoan the countless thousands of women who killed themselves for ideals that now seem hard to comprehend.

7

Image

During the Qing dynasty, the basic nature of womanhood came under intense discussion. As part of this ferment, the images used to represent normative and exceptional womanhood underwent significant changes. This was not a move toward objectivity and literalism. Art, literature, and historical writing did not necessarily aim to describe actual women, as these documents were usually products of the male gaze. In every era, male creators invented images of women, whether visual or written, to serve their own purposes.[1] During the Qing era, male-dominated media continued to interpret aspects of womanhood to fit them into the shifting gendered context of ideas, objects, and behavior.[2] Not all of these cultural products were new. Many standard female tropes had a long history, so they represented views that had been common centuries earlier. For example, the authors of Tang fiction created many stock female characters such as fox spirits, female knights errant, beautiful palace ladies, and lovelorn beauties.[3] Qing authors inserted these time-tested tropes into their own plots, which were also often borrowed from prior works. Many Qing images of women thus consisted of established stereotypes grafted onto newer ideas.

  As before, people understood gender within the binary framework constituting the substrate of Chinese thought. Since antiquity, Chinese thinkers tended to conceptualize reality as a single principle divided into two contrasting and interacting parts, such as yin/yang, Heaven/Earth, and the *qian/kun* trigrams of the *Classic of Changes* (*Yijing*).[4] They saw man and woman as comparable to dualistic metaphysical templates. According to this way of thinking, binary gender constitutes just one of several fundamental duos underlying the visible world of experience.[5]

People regarded male and female identity as dynamic and interactive. This view of gender is readily apparent in *Dream of the Red Chamber*. The novel's protagonist Jia Baoyu implicitly challenges the idea of static and discrete gender identity by exhibiting many androgynous characteristics. Despite his male gender, he often behaves in a way that readers considered typically feminine.[6] Significantly, the novel does not portray Jia as abnormal or a failure. To the contrary, the author holds him up as a generally positive fusion of male and female characteristics. By willingly embracing both masculine and feminine, Jia Baoyu embodies a complete and perfected human being.

Rejection of a simplistic model of masculinity shaped mainstream Qing assumptions about ideal manhood.[7] Portraits of elite men often depicted them as willowy, delicate, and passive.[8] Artists did not see these stereotypically feminine characteristics as negative. After all, they were painting respected men, so artists wanted to depict them in positive terms. Androgynous portraiture implied that when a man embraces the best aspects of femininity, he becomes a better person.

Society held complex and contradictory perceptions of women as well. The authors of fiction often portrayed them as almost divine creatures who fascinated the men around them. The character Jia Baoyu fetishizes anything feminine, and his worshipful fascination constitutes a major theme of *Dream of the Red Chamber*.[9] Yet the feminine did not always seem so immediate or positive. Because writing and the visual arts almost always depicted women from a male standpoint, femininity could seem distant, marginal, and exotic. Men could even see womanhood as barbaric. Cartographers filled remote blank spaces with fantastical kingdoms ruled by women. Similarly, accounts of foreign and minority peoples inhabiting China's southern border regions, often described them as having womanly customs or being dominated by powerful matriarchs.[10]

Views toward women's emotions were widely reassessed during the late imperial era. Starting in the Ming dynasty, many thinkers reacted against restrictive Song Neo-Confucian dogma. In particular, they challenged Neo-Confucian views of emotion. That school's adherents regarded emotion as inherently amoral and feared that it might lead us astray. Ming thinkers reassessed emotionalism, and their innovative ideas affected popular culture.[11] Authors became fascinated with the range of human emotion, and Late Ming fiction explored human feelings in detail. This trend continued into the Qing. Much of the literature written by Qing women, from poetry to ballad lyrics, dealt with emotional themes. The early Qing also saw a revival of interest in the fifth-century compilation *A New Account of Tales of the World* (*Shishuo xinyu*), which emphasizes the strong and authentic feelings of notable women.[12] Many later authors wrote imitations of this work, and these epigones spurred readers to ponder the inner workings of female psychology.

Some fiction writers portrayed gender identity as potentially unstable. In 1769 Wang Yun (1749–1815) wrote the script to "A Dream of Glory" (*Fanhua meng*), one of the few plays of the anomaly (*chuanqi*) genre written by a woman.[13] Wang interrogated gender stereotypes by imagining what it would be like for a woman to become male. The plot centers on a woman who dreams that the bodhisattva Guanyin has turned her into a man. After this sex change, he immediately seeks to satisfy typical male ambitions by becoming a student and falling in love with beautiful women. Eventually the protagonist passes the civil service examinations, serves as a high official, marries, and takes concubines. In other words, the woman at the center of the story dreams of becoming a man so that she can gain the standard emblems of male success. In the end, the protagonist wakes up and realizes that she had been dreaming. The audience finds this awkward realization amusing, allowing them to accept the previous transgression of gender norms.

Although the comic tone renders the play benign in the eyes of the audience, this drama nevertheless raises profound questions regarding gender relations. Prior to her dream, the main character wonders why she had been born a woman. She chafes at the limitations that she faces because of her sex, which bars her from the most important and respected endeavors. However, once she becomes a man, she immediately feels overwhelmed by the responsibilities she faces and doubts that she is up to the challenge. The play thus not only emphasizes the limitations faced by women but also reminds female audience members of the daunting expectations confronting men. Despite the frivolous tone, this clever story of gender inversion presents a profound critique of the challenges faced by both sexes.

Although people in this era often regarded human beings as fundamentally androgynous to a degree, they nevertheless saw gender difference as objectively grounded in physical characteristics. The female and male bodies were considered very different. People assumed that the female body was more fragile than that of men. Also, women were alleged to have more intense emotions than men, and these were believed to give rise to illness, so it was assumed that women tended to be sickly.[14] Emphasis on physical difference between the sexes had a major impact on gynecology and obstetrics. Ideas regarding female physiology and ailments became increasingly sophisticated in the late imperial era.[15] The rapid rate of population increase led doctors to improve techniques for contraception and abortion. Most importantly, Qing scholars also turned toward empiricism and practical learning, which led inquisitive doctors to cast doubt on the numerous unsubstantiated assertions in medical texts. Qing physicians embraced a more analytical and pragmatic view of the female body. Empirical medicine resulted in a reassessment of aspects of fertility, childbirth, and postpartum care. Due to this shift, the treatment of certain conditions such as breast maladies improved.[16]

Different types of people practiced medicine. Herbalists, shamans, and amateur healers all competed with professional physicians who had studied standard medical texts. During the late imperial era, many literati who failed the official examinations ended up as physicians and herbalists, and their training in the ancient classics informed their assumptions.[17] They frequently drew conclusions about medical conditions based on abstract metaphysical principles. Accordingly, some physicians considered childbirth healthy for women, as it fulfilled their yin nature and thus helped them overcome their allegedly frail constitution.[18] In the nineteenth century, Western medicine began to influence Chinese gynecology. Missionary physicians introduced Western medical techniques, and Chinese began to import new medicines, affecting the treatment of female illnesses.

Some male physicians specialized in gynecology. The monks of the Bamboo Grove Monastery (Zhulin si) in Zhejiang were perhaps the most unusual gynecological experts.[19] These clerics dedicated themselves to healing the sick as an expression of Buddhist compassion and focused their attentions on female disorders. But for monks to take up gynecology seemed morally questionable. Even ordinary men had to keep apart from women, and monks were expected to observe even stricter separation, as they were sworn to chastity. To complicate matters, the lascivious monk was a stock comic character in popular stories. Some skeptics assumed that the Bamboo Grove monks specialized in gynecology as an excuse to view women's private parts. Others cast doubt on the medical qualifications of these monks and accused them of being greedy quacks. Yet in spite of these suspicions, their books on gynecology were widely distributed. Women who did not want to expose their genitalia to a male physician could use these specialized medical texts to diagnose and treat gynecological problems themselves.

The female pudendum was associated with the yin element, lending it negative connotations. Traditionally the yin element was closely associated with death.[20] Accordingly, mortuary ritual included many feminine features. As in many other cultures, blood emanating from the vagina was considered highly polluting, so people looked on menstruation, pregnancy, and delivery as unclean.[21] They regarded vaginal discharge with horror, and contact was strictly tabooed. Menstruating women were forbidden from entering sacred spaces and sometimes physically isolated from men. After giving birth, a woman had to undergo a period of strict seclusion until the taint of the pollution had receded. Men tried to avoid contact with any woman polluted by menstruation or postpartum fluid. Any man who willingly exposed himself to this substance was the target of criticism.[22]

Female pollution provided a physical justification for women's exclusion from public life and isolation within the home. However, the polluting power of female blood also imbued women with certain powers.[23] Men even harnessed it as a military weapon.[24] In the late sixteenth century, rebels defending besieged cities forced naked women, usually prostitutes or pregnant mothers, to stand on the ramparts and wave winnowing baskets or pig heads at government troops. Rebels believed that vaginal pollution was so potent that it could ward off cannon fire. They considered these women a military unit and called them the "vaginal orifice formation" (*yinmen zhen*). The militarization of the vagina continued up to the end of the nineteenth century. During the Boxer Rebellion, militias put many restrictions on female movement to contain and perhaps harness female pollution.

A woman could manipulate and ornament her body, influencing how she presented herself to the world and how society received her. The Qing was a large multiethnic empire, so women dressed differently depending on background and region.[25] At the beginning of the dynasty, Han and Manchu women wore distinct types of clothing. Unlike the complicated Chinese combinations of blouses and skirts, Manchu women wore a long loose-fitting robe with two slits, one on each side. Over the course of the dynasty, Han and Manchu clothing merged, giving rise to a fusion style.[26] Manchu-style gowns contracted, creating a straight silhouette. Collars narrowed and sleeves widened. Intricate Chinese-style embroidery featuring animals, flowers, butterflies, clouds, and auspicious symbols ornamented these new types of robes.

During the late Qing, women became increasingly fashion conscious, and they often changed their clothing and hair to appear à la mode.[27] Some women adopted new fashions to express a modern image or implicitly support social reform. The integration of Western items into a woman's wardrobe conveyed subtle ideological messages about the relationship between China and the outside world. In the early twentieth century, demand for new and modern fashions caused the Manchu robe to contract even further, turning it into the form-fitting *qipao* (*cheongsam*). People today consider this garment the iconic traditional Chinese dress, despite its Manchu origins.

Women wore their hair in a dazzling variety of styles that revealed information about ethnicity, place of residence, and social station. A woman's appearance linked her to group identities. Whereas Han women usually tied their hair into a bun, Manchus wrapped their hair around a framework made of wood, metal, or ivory.[28] The frame could be very large, rising high above the head and extending far to each side, plaiting the hair onto a flat surface. A woman would then decorate the sheet of hair with silk tassels, ornate hairpins, and artificial flowers made of jade, pearl, coral, ornamental stones, precious metal, and fabric. Clothing, hairstyle, and other types of personal ornamentation allowed women to materialize their identities. Arranging carefully chosen objects on the body made personal image seem concrete.[29] Although a woman's appearance had to broadly conform to the collective identity of her social group, she still had a degree of agency to express her individual character.

Footbinding stands out as the most distinctive aspect of female appearance (figure 7.1).[30] Unnaturally small feet heightened physical gender difference, distinguishing women from men. Even educated women were proud of their dainty feet, as they saw them as an important emblem of the ideal feminine persona.[31] As the Qing declined, this custom became highly contentious. Both reformers and revolutionaries condemned footbinding as a depraved custom that exemplified the negative side of traditional society, even as conservatives strove to uphold this tradition.

Mutilating the feet to make them smaller began as a marginal erotic practice in the medieval era. Bound feet gained popularity gradually, became widespread during the Ming dynasty, and remained common through the Qing. Footbinding had a close association with Han culture. Most minority peoples either did not bind women's feet or else they adopted this custom relatively late. Notably, although the Qing emperors allowed their Han subjects to bind their daughters' feet, they forbade Manchus from following suit. They saw natural feet as an ethnic marker that distinguished Manchu from Han and help their people maintain a distinct identity.[32] Even so, some Manchu women yearned for smaller feet, as they considered natural feet unattractive. Some wrapped their feet in cloth and wore ungainly shoes that gave them a gait similar to that of Han women with bound feet.[33]

Although footbinding began as an aesthetic practice, it gained popularity for financial reasons.[34] Some groups, such as Hakkas, considered it acceptable for women to work outside the home in full view of strangers. There was no economic incentive for Hakkas to bind their feet, as it would prevent them from carrying out their traditional work in the fields.[35] However, it was far more common for Han women to seclude themselves inside the home. Instead of laboring in the fields or walking long distances, cloistered women would spin, weave, and embroider. Young women excelled at textile work due to their dexterity and good eyesight, so they could bring in a significant income for their families. However, youth also made them energetic, and many girls would rather play than

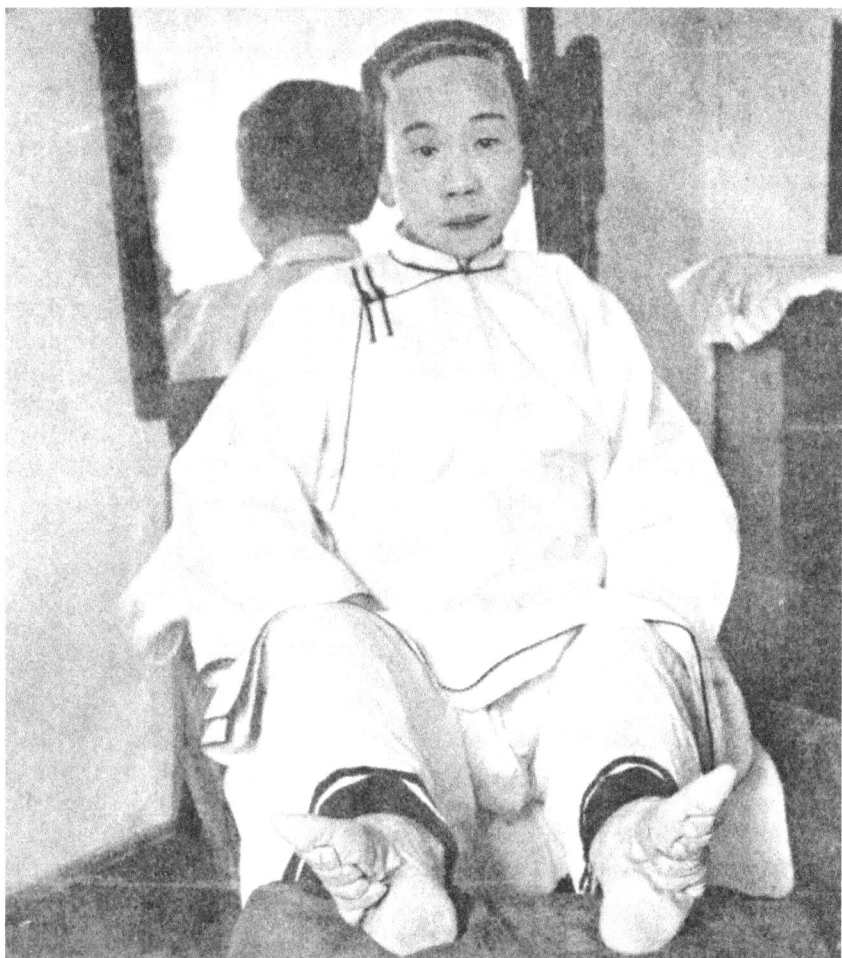

Figure 7.1. Bound Feet
Wikimedia Commons

sit still and work. If parents bound a daughter's feet, she would have to be relatively stationary, making her well suited for sedentary textile work. Footbinding thus allowed parents to increase the productivity of their daughters. Because binding a secluded woman's feet tended to raise her productive output, she would make a more valuable marriage partner than a woman with natural feet. In addition to these practical functions, footbinding also accrued secondary associations such as beauty and social prestige, giving families more reasons to bind a daughter's feet.

In the late nineteenth century, footbinding attracted fierce criticism. Foreigners regarded this custom with disgust. Christian missionaries vigorously campaigned against footbinding, seeing it as a sign of pagan darkness, while Western physicians pathologized bound feet and treated it as a malady.[36] Progressive Chinese were embarrassed that visitors from other countries considered footbinding strange and inhumane.[37] When Chinese started to examine their own country through foreign eyes, they were appalled to realize that others considered them cruel barbarians.

The antifootbinding movement attracted support from various quarters.[38] Most participants were men, as women usually kept a low profile and did not dare participate in public debates. At first, writers criticized footbinding in print. Then missionaries established formal organizations dedicated to the eradication of bound feet. After China's defeat by Japan in 1895, this movement gained momentum, and many reformers joined the cause. Some appealed to modernization and liberation to justify unbinding women's feet. Others used Confucian rhetoric of filial piety to condemn footbinding as the cruel torment of the nation's mothers. A poem by Xu Zihua (1873–1935) harnessed traditional imagery to issue a stern critique.[39]

> That two hooked feet are bewitching is such nonsense:
> A beautiful golden lotus left behind at each step!
> I hate so much the last ruler of the Southern Tang:
> He originated an evil to plague a thousand years.

Opponents of footbinding established numerous organizations of local, regional, and national scope to agitate against the custom. Modern schools and the emerging mass media also disseminated critiques of footbinding. In addition, economic shifts did away with the financial rationale for this custom. As industrialization flooded the market with inexpensive mass market cloth, it was no longer profitable for families to bind their daughters' feet to keep them seated before a loom.[40] Circumstances in each place affected the rate of decline in footbinding. Taiwanese abandoned footbinding relatively early.[41] Japanese colonial officials encouraged families to unbind women's feet as a way to modernize Taiwanese society and assimilate with Japan. In 1915 Taiwan's colonial government outlawed footbinding entirely. Footbinding did not remain common much longer on the Chinese mainland and disappeared not long after the end of the Qing dynasty.

Art and literature offer idealized images of women that reveal Qing standards of beauty. Most paintings of women were characters dreamed up by the artist. Few depictions of actual women survive. Even if a woman had her portrait painted, her family would not have displayed it in public and it would have been destroyed after her death to prevent strangers from seeing it. Because surviving images of actual women are so few, paintings and descriptions of idealized women exerted an oversized impact on perceptions of normative womanhood. Men created these images to serve their own purposes, so the ideal woman in painting was unrealistic and exaggerated.

Some painters, such as Gai Qi (1774–1829), specialized in genre paintings of female beauties (shinü) (figure 7.2).[42] He tried to capture the quintessence of feminine attractiveness, portraying his subjects as serene and gorgeous. Gai and other talented artists tried to depict the woman's physical form in ways that would reveal aspects of her inner spirit. Due to their efforts, these genre paintings often disclose deeper and more complex traces of their subjects' personalities, and female figures sometimes appear pensive or even sad.

The ideal Qing woman had a thin and frail physique. This differed from the standards of some previous eras. Tang dynasty society absorbed considerable influence from nomadic cultures, leading artists to depict women with sturdy bodies and willful expressions. Although the ancestors of the Manchus were nomads, they did not impose their ideas about normative femininity on Chinese. In Qing China, even educated men cultivated a soft and gentle image, so women felt compelled to appear even softer and weaker in comparison.[43] Also, footbinding prevented women from exercising and discouraged them even from walking short distances, affecting their constitution. *Dream of the Red Chamber* features the anemic character Lin Daiyu, who stands out as the classic Qing dynasty beauty (figure 7.3). The novel describes her as exceptionally thin and frail almost to the point of illness. At that time, a delicate constitution became a feminine ideal. To be beautiful, a woman had to look thin and weak. Sickly beauty was not limited to the elite. Popular images, such as New Year prints, also feature exceptionally thin women.

Although images of women most often portrayed them as beautiful by the standards of the time, literature also includes female characters that writers described as ugly.[44] Most often, fiction writers gave a character an unattractive body to visually express inner flaws, so the stereotypical evil woman often had an ugly appearance. Some bad women were not just ugly but bestial or demonic. However, occasionally an ugly appearance did not connote evil. Ordinary and even virtuous women in literature could also have a plain appearance to express hardships that they had endured. A good woman might become unattractive due to adversity, illness, grief, or anxiety, evoking the reader's empathy.

It seems that many women did not like their appearance. Most often, they complained that they were so thin and bony that they looked emaciated (*qiaocui*). Xi Peilan (1760–after 1829) described herself this way in a verse inscription of a portrait that shows her standing next to flowers.[45]

Figure 7.2. Stereotypical Beauty Painted by Gai Qi
Wikimedia Commons

Figure 7.3. Lin Daiyu
Wikimedia Commons

She used the poem to rue the contrast between the floral beauty and her own wasted looks.

> On the jade steps, heavenly fragrance prevails.
> Pearl curtain, the precious incense is slanting.
> Knowing about my emaciated shadow,
> I dare not to look at those flowers directly.

People thought that the ideal female body should be extremely thin, but Xi had taken this look to an alarming extreme. Her gaunt appearance revealed mental suffering of such intensity that it had affected her health and made her look ugly and unwell. Rather than blending in with the beautiful background of her portrait, she stands out as a strangely unappealing anomaly within a scene of natural beauty.

Other women who disliked their appearance did not blame themselves but instead faulted a society that held them to unrealistic standards of beauty and restricted their autonomy. The talented poet Gu Zhenli (1623–1699) described her appearance in unflattering terms. But rather than fault herself for her physical shortcomings, she condemned her failed marriage.[46]

> Hairdo resembling after falling from a horse, makeup imitating weeping,
> I just won't learn
> These manners of the boudoir.
> I'm used to being careless and lazy,
> Chewing petals and blowing leaves,
> Discarding powder and rouge.
> I have too many illnesses to be able to manage household chores;
> Although I'm not talented, I dare dislike my husband who is not my match.
> Looking at every strand on my temples,
> How long can they remain black?
> Don't make vain attempts.

Gu blamed her plain looks on an unhappy life. She considered herself an innocent victim. Although intelligent and talented, she had to waste her days toiling at domestic tasks. The poem concludes with a rejection of the expectations of conventional womanhood. Gu had no interest in household duties and did not feel the need to look beautiful or fashionable. Railing against society's unfairness provided her with a measure of solace.

The early Qing Chan (Zen) poet Chaoyi took the critique of stereotypical femininity even further. Although Chaoyi married, her husband passed away soon after the wedding. She became a Buddhist nun to maintain her chastity in widowhood and died just three years after entering a monastery. Although Chaoyi did not write much, critics hold her few surviving poems in high regard. In one poem, she describes herself laboring in the temple garden. As she toils, she gradually begins to take on the identity of the flowers around her.[47]

> Using soil to irrigate them, using water to plant them in—
> This topsy-turvy way of working allows me to do as I please.
> In the garden full of spring breezes, the flowers chatter to themselves;
> They do not feel the need to show off their colors to anyone else.

Chaoyi evokes floral imagery to capture the Buddhist renunciant's satisfaction at having repudiated vanity. She does not want to present herself to the world as a beautiful woman who embodies feminine stereotypes. Her faith has allowed her to transcend gender expectations and feel content merely to be herself, an ordinary woman. She has become an authentic individual who no longer feels obliged to put up a façade and pretend that she is someone else. By casting away the hackneyed female image, she discovered her true self.

8

The Late Qing

Historians refer to the eighteenth century as the High Qing. At that time, the empire enjoyed a long era of competent government, economic growth, and cultural effervescence. The White Lotus Rebellion of 1796 marked the end of this golden age. Thereafter the dynasty went into gradual decline. Even so, the situation did not immediately seem ominous. On the surface, China still seemed to be flourishing. Nevertheless, long-term problems were taking a toll. Most importantly, an unprecedented population explosion resulted in widespread downward mobility, and the economy went into a prolonged slump. Severe deflation pushed down the prices of agricultural products and manufactured goods, and wages decreased in tandem. As this economic crisis coincided with the reign of the Daoguang emperor (1820–1850), economic historians refer to this period of hardship as the Daoguang Depression.[1]

Not only did China's economy regress from its former heights, but it also fell far behind Europe. In the year 1600, China's per capita GDP stood at about 40 percent that of Great Britain. By 1840 this had declined to less than 20 percent.[2] The Industrial Revolution amplified the productive power of the West, and Europeans used their rising manufacturing capacity and technological innovations to build formidable militaries. European armies had modern weapons that could easily defeat Chinese forces armed with swords and spears. It was only a matter of time before the dynasty had to either undertake comprehensive reforms or be swept away.

Even as China faced daunting problems, the ruling elite remained blithely convinced of their country's innate superiority. Rulers tried to keep trade with the outside world to a minimum, as they believed that they had little to gain from interacting with their cultural inferiors. Spectacular defeats in the two Opium Wars (1839–1842, 1856–1860) shattered this self-assurance. These wars showcased China's weakness, evoking widespread dismay. Astute officials and intellectuals realized that the old order had failed, and they debated what changes the dynasty had to undertake to survive. The obvious military and economic superiority of Western aggressors cast doubt on Chinese values, beliefs, and system of government. Unfamiliar ideas from the West conflicted directly with Confucian verities and the ancient classics, forcing Chinese to assess the validity of their entire cultural legacy.

In the second half of the nineteenth century, foreign merchants and diplomats took up residence in China, mostly in coastal cities engaged in international trade. Large numbers of missionaries settled in China as well. Initially missionaries could not venture beyond the treaty ports, but after 1860 they began to travel across China. Missionaries found it difficult to convince self-assured literati to embrace a foreign religion, so they usually targeted the poor and marginal. Many ended up living in small towns in the interior, where they hoped to find a receptive audience. The local missionary was the only foreigner that most Chinese ever saw. To people in rural China, these proselytizers represented not just their religion but Western civilization in general. Many Western ideas and values filtered into China through Christian teaching, sermons, and tracts. Female missionaries had a high profile. In 1890, of the 1,296 active Protestant missionaries, 707 were women.[3] These foreign women, confident and energetic, challenged Chinese gender norms and agitated for wide-reaching changes in relations between the sexes. They opposed female seclusion, widow chastity, suicide and self-mutilation, prostitution, concubinage, and footbinding.

In this era, the West exerted a multifaceted influence on China, both negative and positive. The so-called declension model promoted by some theorists asserts that imperialism usually causes female status to decline.[4] However, historians of China have recently cast doubt on this simplistic assertion. Although Western incursions brought chaos, Chinese women took advantage of this upheaval to gain more autonomy and rights.

Chinese recoiled from the realization that their country was being integrated into a global economic system that served the interests of European colonial powers.[5] Rising dismay at the nation's predicament, compounded with mounting economic and military pressures, caused the social fabric to fray. Age-old ideas about proper governance had little relevance to new circumstances, reducing the effectiveness of the administrative system. As the dynasty declined, disaffected peasants rose up in rebellion.

The leaders of the massive Taiping Rebellion (1850–1864) promoted far-reaching policies aimed at reordering gender relations. Because this uprising began among the Hakka, their relatively egalitarian gender relations affected Taiping policies toward women.[6] The rebels outlawed prostitution and adultery. They expanded female inheritance rights, and daughters received the same amount of land as sons. The Taiping leadership also opposed footbinding. Not only did this practice contravene Hakka custom, but they believed that it weakened society by crippling half of the workforce. Women in rebel areas started to behave differently. Most strikingly, they no longer hid themselves from view. To the contrary, they dressed in colorful clothes to attract attention from passersby. The rebels expected women to work outside the home and declared their intention to allow women to take special civil service examinations and become government officials. One woman even became a high-ranking minister in the Taiping government.

The Taipings also tried to alter marriage and family life. In the cities, rebels broke up families and forced men and women to live and work in separate communal camps. Initially the rebels promoted celibacy, even within marriage, but they soon lifted the ban on marital intercourse and even encouraged couples to marry. The Taiping government banned concubinage for all men except their self-proclaimed king, Hong Xiuquan. He reportedly surrounded himself with more than two hundred wives and thousands of concubines and female servants. Yet in spite of some progressive measures, overall the Taiping Heavenly Kingdom had a negative impact on women. This episode stands out as perhaps the most violent rebellion in Chinese history, and millions perished in consequence. During the ensuing chaos, untold numbers of women suffered sexual violence, exploitation, kidnapping, robbery, and starvation.

As word of the Taiping social experiments spread, men in other regions expressed shock and disgust. However, these novel arrangements also sparked discussion. Progressive thinkers realized that China's traditional social organization was doomed, and they started to imagine what sort of system ought to replace it. They promoted reforms of every aspect of society, including gender notions. Reformers may have advocated a range of ideologies and policies, but they had the same goal. All of them wanted to strengthen China so that the nation could fend off the threat of foreign domination. To this end, some social critics condemned old-fashioned gender roles and female ethics, declaring them backward beliefs that weakened the nation. They realized that unleashing women's pent-up dynamism would empower China.

As the Qing dynasty fell into decline, visionaries put forward increasingly radical blueprints for national renovation. Liang Qichao (1873–1929) pointed out a long list of shortcomings that needed to be addressed, including the unjust circumstances facing women.[7] He argued that women should receive practical education that would prepare them to work outside the home. Liang reasoned that because China hid away half of its population and banned women from working in most professions, a potential asset had become a liability that pulled down the economy. He wanted to turn women from consumers into producers, boosting economic output and revitalizing the nation.

Kang Youwei (1858–1927) envisioned a far more comprehensive reordering of gender relations.[8] Kang considered the hierarchy and inequality of Chinese society a major problem and believed that social distinctions should be reduced. In the resulting egalitarian utopia, the divisions between men and women would disappear. Kang advocated the dissolution of traditional marriage and family life. Marriage would no longer be a permanent relationship, and couples would be bound together by a temporary marriage contract. Rather than maintaining separate families, people would live in dormitories and eat in communal dining halls. Children would be raised by the community rather than their families. Although Kang wrote a book describing these ideas in 1905, he did not dare publish it, and his utopian vision only came to light after his death. Even so, the fact that progressive thinkers were contemplating such radical ideas attests to the spirit of creative destruction that arose at the end of the Qing dynasty. A sense of national crisis led influential visionaries to question the most basic assumptions underpinning gender relations.

Some female intellectuals also demanded far-reaching changes. The anarchist He-Yin Zhen (ca. 1884–ca. 1920) published several essays in the final years of the Qing that called for an end to male domination of women.[9] He-Yin considered men the enemy of women and sought to liberate women from male exploitation. She believed that the debased social status of women was the result of economic inequality. She pointed out that since antiquity, women had not controlled the fruits of their labor. Men seized the wealth that women created and used it to empower themselves and maintain their domination. He-Yin did not believe that Western models offered solutions for Chinese women's plight. To the contrary, she believed that the entry of China into the system of global capitalism had only exacerbated women's problems. Although He-Yin did not achieve prominence, her impassioned writings reveal the diversity of ideals circulating at the end of the dynasty and the radical views of that some women had begun to embrace.

Many reformers singled out education as the best way to improve women's standing in society. Liang Qichao hoped to raise women's educational level so that they could contribute to national development.[10] He lamented women's general ignorance, as he believed that it made them conservative, passive, and quarrelsome. Not knowing any better, they passed false beliefs down to their children, corrupting the next generation. Uneducated women also produced too little, dragging down the national economy. Even if they were free to leave the home and seek work outside, a lack of education and training limited their prospects. Liang considered female education an essential prerequisite for national renewal.

Foreign missionaries also prioritized education. They considered education both a way to uplift ordinary people and also a useful vehicle for evangelizing. During the nineteenth century, most Chinese Protestant women came from poor or middling backgrounds, so they were usually illiterate.[11] Joining a congregation often gave them their first opportunity to receive an education. Missionaries encouraged converts to educate their daughters to make them better wives and mothers and also to enable them to read the Bible and participate in church activities. Many Christian families heeded these calls and sent their daughters to mission schools. Missionaries also took in female orphans and educated them.

Missionaries did not limit their ambitions to proselytizing. They believed themselves to be engaged in a civilizing mission.[12] Most missionaries despised Chinese culture and wanted to elevate believers by inculcating Western values and customs. Although missionaries did not consider the sexes equal, they opposed the most onerous constraints that Chinese women endured. Mission schools taught female pupils to reject arranged marriages, lifelong seclusion, widow chastity, and footbinding. They even tried to alter the Chinese lifestyle. American missionaries considered China appallingly dirty, so their mission schools emphasized the importance of cleanliness and taught American-style hygiene practices.

Christian schools introduced athletics to the educational curriculum.[13] Chinese had never associated exercise and sports with education, so the sight of female students exercising at school shocked onlookers. Not only did this seem strange, but they also considered it extremely immodest. Even some female missionaries considered exercise unfeminine. Mission schools introduced sports for boys very early, but girls' athletics developed much more slowly. In 1888 a school for girls first required students to exercise, and physical education gradually became a standard part of the mission school curriculum. However, girls' schools usually limited exercise to calisthenics instead of the team sports played by male students. Bound feet precluded participation in athletics, so many schools required girls to unbind their feet as a prerequisite for admission.

Although foreign missionaries introduced many new ideas, ultimately the greatest changes resulted from shifting opinions among the Chinese elite. Men and women often had different perspectives on the rapid changes taking place around them. While men called for social reforms out of a sense of despair, the emergence of unprecedented opportunities made women increasingly optimistic about the future. The nation's defeat by Japan gave rise to a sense of severe crisis, spurring the government to action. During the reform movement of 1898, leading intellectuals advocated improvements intended to turn China into a modern nation state.[14] As before, reformers saw female education as a pragmatic means to bolster the nation's economic and military strength.

In 1897 the first school for girls outside the missionary framework was established.[15] To fend off accusations of improper mixing of the sexes, this school had a completely female staff. Even so, reactionaries subjected the school's teachers and students to withering criticism, forcing it to close after a short time. But with the dynasty clearly failing, authorities had no choice but to embrace change. At the beginning of the twentieth century, the Empress Dowager Cixi introduced a series of reforms referred to as the New Policies. These included the abolition of the civil service examinations and establishment of a school system with a modern curriculum. At first, state schools only taught male students, and the court encouraged families to continue teaching girls at home. Then in 1907 the government began to open elementary schools for girls and institutes to train female teachers. The curriculum for girls remained far less comprehensive than that for boy students. Their studies stressed traditional ethics and needlework. The system also limited women's education to eight years and did not allow them to go beyond elementary school. Women did not have a chance to receive a full education up through the university level until after the fall of the Qing dynasty.

As girls began to study outside the home, the content of textbooks became a topic of contention. Prominent late Qing reformers had conflicting priorities. They wanted schools to prepare female students to thrive in a rapidly modernizing nation, yet many also wanted to inculcate girls with traditional values.[16] Generally speaking, most male reformers wanted to maintain the Confucian curriculum. Only a minority of progressive male thinkers took a critical view of traditional female ethics.

Progressives argued that old-style female education had in fact limited women's intellectual potential. Women had previously spent much of their time learning how to write poetry, which reformers dismissed as frivolous. They also complained that Confucian ethics encouraged women to be idle and kept them tied to the home. The nationalistic project required women to become productive members of society. Progressives demanded that female students study contemporary writings and learn about the modern world. They should become acquainted with politics, economics, and events beyond China's borders. This knowledge would allow them to participate in building a strong China capable of competing in the international arena.

Textbooks for female students changed gradually.[17] For centuries, women had studied didactic biographies of role models. Late Qing textbooks continued to employ this format. Some schools simply used time-honored texts, such as the Han dynasty *Biographies of Women* (*Lienü zhuan*). Reformers introduced new teaching material, such as biographies of foreign women. However, when a textbook included stories about foreign women, the author often chose narratives that illustrated conventional Confucian virtues. Simply adding the biographies of Western women to the curriculum did not necessarily alter the underlying ideological content. Some textbooks even criticized foreign ideas about gender and disparaged these arrangements as inappropriate for China. Gradually, however, textbooks for girls came to stress nationalism, science, and progressive values. The overall goal was to direct women's energies toward strengthening China. By combining traditional and modern visions of the feminine, reformers gradually created a new model of womanhood more appropriate to new conditions.

The transition from traditional to modern ideas of the feminine did not constitute a sudden rupture. Women often reinterpreted familiar virtues in new ways suitable to contemporary conditions. During the late Qing, some women used filial piety to justify pursuing achievements in the public realm.[18] They argued that the best way to honor their parents and ancestors was to use their talents and become a success. Even Christian education directed classical female ethics toward new ends.[19] Protestants mined the contents of the *Four Books for Women* for moral lessons congruent with their faith. By combining Protestant beliefs with Confucian ethics, they sought to create a new kind of Chinese woman who used her culture's native values to strengthen her Christian convictions and maintain a high standard of conduct.

Many female graduates took an interest in current affairs. Initially, educated women had to read publications aimed at a male readership. But after the 1898 Reform Movement, about thirty-seven new magazines appeared catering specifically to a female readership.[20] Most were published in Shanghai or Tokyo and were aimed at student activists. Because Qing censors had no authority over these areas, writers could use these publications to freely criticize the dynasty and its policies. Most women's magazines only had a single staff member and little capital, so they rarely lasted for more than a few issues. Even so, these periodicals provided women with valuable insights on a changing world. Women wrote most of the content, so they provided female writers a forum for sharing their ideas with sympathetic readers.

Articles and essays discussed current events and introduced women to ongoing debates about social, political, and intellectual issues. The earliest generation of magazines embraced the nationalistic priorities of nineteenth-century reformers, relegating women's issues to second place. They did not see the uplifting of women as an end in itself but as a step toward the overriding goal of national rejuvenation. Magazine writers frequently urged their readers to imitate energetic female role models in Europe and America and contribute to their society.

The earliest women's magazines catered to a small elite of the most highly educated and politically engaged women. Publishers soon began to put out lowbrow pictorial magazines aimed at women with less education and little disposable income.[21] Periodicals for educated women were written in a difficult style and had few illustrations. In contrast, pictorials featured compelling illustrations to spark interest and help readers understand the content. The editors used simple language and pictures to introduce current events and new ideas. This accessibility soon gave pictorial magazines a large readership. The content may have been simplistic, but these magazines nevertheless served as an important source of information for less educated women.

Female authors also started to write long format works. Chinese were becoming increasingly interested in the outside world, and some women wrote about matters beyond China's borders. Previous accounts of foreign countries had usually been highly condescending. The novel *Humble Words of a Rustic Elder* (*Yesou puyan*), written during the High Qing by Xia Jingqu (1705–1787), describes Europe as strange and depraved.[22] But during the late Qing, both men and women began to write about foreign countries in a more positive tone.[23]

During the final years of the dynasty, women started to enjoy far more freedom of movement. It became acceptable for a woman with a male escort to travel across China and even go abroad for pleasure. Previously, women had almost never written travelogues or novels. If they wanted to share their impressions of travel, they used poetry rather than prose. But toward the end of the Qing, women began to write detailed accounts of their travels and novels about foreign places. However, as novels were still considered vulgar, female authors approached the genre cautiously.

Female travelers recorded their impressions of the outside world. These works did not just entertain but also sought to inform female readers about how they might use unfamiliar new opportunities. Late Qing women felt disoriented by the rapid pace of social change. They were uncertain of their proper place in the world and often doubted their ability to handle unfamiliar situations. Female authors of travelogues and novels tried to reassure their readers. They encouraged women whose feet had been unbound to exercise and travel. These books also taught female readers about world geography, expanding their horizons.

As modern education spread, many women became interested in politics. Many were inspired by nationalistic rhetoric, and they participated in the debates over current affairs. Some expressed political opinions in an old-fashioned style. During the First Opium War, some women wrote poetry lauding China's military and populace for resisting foreign invasion. A poem by Shen Shanbao (1808–1862) typifies these optimistic expressions of burgeoning nationalism.[24]

> I hear it told that covering the seas is a poison vapor [opium],
> Along the river a deadly miasma
> [British] ships of war line the Guabu harbor [across the river from Nanjing].
> Guns and ships may be fierce and swift
> But do we lack river guards and archers?
> Stalwart angry braves, hair on end, caps atop;
> Students casting down their brushes [to take up arms],
> Laughing while they attack the enemy.

When foreigners unexpectedly crushed the Qing army, this sort of naïve conceit dissipated. Moreover, in the aftermath of China's defeats, opium poured into China, giving rise to serious social problems.[25] Some women became addicts. Others were sold into prostitution by a family elder who used the proceeds to purchase the drug. A growing sense of national crisis evoked a new round of patriotic sentiments.

During the late Qing, the "fragrant and bedazzling" (*xiangyan*) poetry movement changed its orientation to become a medium for expressing nationalism. Some writers believed that they could redeploy romanticism and classical lyricism to encourage national reform.[26] The performing arts also addressed the rising tide of nationalism. The Empress Dowager Cixi ordered playwrights to come up with a new version of "The Generals of the Yang Family" (*Yangjia jiang*), a popular drama about a martial family that defended China from foreign invasion during the Song dynasty.[27] Cixi enjoyed the *kunju* version, performed in a southern dialect, as it included women warriors. She had court writers create a similar script in the language used in the capital. Nationalistic content made this opera extremely popular, and it is still frequently performed.

Charity had long been considered a permissible activity for women, and during the chaos of the late Qing many women directed their philanthropy toward nationalistic causes. Benevolent women worried that the government could no longer cope with repeated uprisings, military defeats, and natural disasters, so they threw themselves into charity work to take on some of the burden.[28] Although female philanthropy had a long history in China, these women had a novel motivation. Instead of Confucian benevolence or Buddhist compassion, many felt inspired by nationalistic ideologies.

During the late Qing, women participated in numerous charities, ranging from the support of chaste widows to disaster relief. Because women could now move about in public, they began to establish larger charities. Some organizations became national in scope. Initially, wealthy women financed charities themselves, but in the early twentieth century they became adept at fundraising. Female leaders saw high-profile charity work as a sign of women's progress, and many self-consciously modern women devoted themselves to philanthropic activities.

Although men led the reform process, educated women also debated social issues, particularly those directly pertaining to women's lives.[29] Emerging mass media provided talented female essayists and reporters with platforms to air their opinions to a wide audience. Like their male counterparts, women took a wide range of positions toward the problems of the day. Whereas most politically engaged women had moderate views, some extremists began to advocate revolution. Radicals attracted attention out of proportion to their numbers, as they were most likely to act on their beliefs. The Shining Red Lanterns, teenaged female soldiers who participated in the Boxer Uprising, displayed a new kind of radical female spirit.[30] However, in many respects these passionate women displayed traditional traits as well. They claimed magical powers and posed as deities, gaining charisma by associating themselves with beliefs from Daoism and folk religion. These female militants harnessed traditional religious beliefs to push a nationalistic political agenda.

The colorful revolutionary Qiu Jin (1875–1907) exemplified late Qing radicalism (figure 8.1).[31] Born into a wealthy family, she received a cutting-edge education that exposed her to Western and Japanese ideas. Her parents arranged for her to wed a merchant, but the marriage soon failed and in 1904 she went to Tokyo to continue her studies. There Qiu fell in with a community of Chinese student radicals and published a journal that advocated revolution.

Qiu Jin's writings reveal her exhilaration at newfound intellectual liberation. She realized how lucky she was. Unlike women who had come of age a few decades earlier, Qiu no longer had to stay secluded in the home and devote herself to domestic chores. She could walk about in public, meet with politically engaged men, and speak out on controversial issues of the day.[32] Qiu often wrote in a poetic format, as this was still the most conventional mode of female discourse. However, she used this traditional medium to express novel ideas.

> To read a book, I toss aside my
> embroidery needle.
> Laughing, you and I then play critics,
> you challenging my views and I yours.

Figure 8.1. Qui Jin
Wikimedia Commons

In spite of her exhilarating freedoms, Qiu remained frustrated by the remaining restrictions that women faced. She realized that even though women were free to talk, it was much harder for them to take meaningful action and implement their ideas.[33]

> In vain I worry about my country;
> It's hard to trade kerchief and dress for a helmet.

Qiu felt that men had failed the nation. They had not been able to overthrow the decayed Qing regime or create a strong and modern society. She believed that because men had not realized national rejuvenation, women had to step up and assume leadership. Qiu assumed that women had a pure and lofty character that would allow them to quickly bring about major changes.[34]

> In this filthy world,
> How many men are heroic and wise?
> I reckon only among women
> Are there paragons.

After returning to China in 1906, Qiu Jin found a job teaching at a school for girls, but her vocal anti-Qing views led to her dismissal. She then became the principal of another school, where she had the female students do military drills in preparation for combat. It seems that she envisioned women participating in the battles of an upcoming revolution. Qiu also founded a magazine devoted to the twin causes of nationalism and women's liberation. Finally, in 1907 Qiu Jin tried to act on her ideals. She joined a group planning to overthrow the dynasty by force. The plot failed, and she was beheaded.

Qiu Jin remains a controversial figure. Feminists and revolutionaries have lauded her as a hero. However, she also had an impractical dramatic streak. She enjoyed dressing up in attention-grabbing uniforms and costumes, and some of her statements and actions seem very naïve in retrospect. In many ways, Qiu Jin was a typical product of her generation. Like many educated women, she espoused progressive ideas. Yet she went beyond most of her peers in advocating violent political action as a necessary prelude to women's liberation. Combining feminism with revolution seemed unusual at the time. However, Qiu Jin presaged China's future. During the twentieth century, China would experience repeated revolutions. Qiu Jin's life and death portended women's participation in the tumultuous events yet to come.

Conclusion

Up until the final decades of the Qing dynasty, Chinese women looked to the past for guidance on what to think and how to behave. In doing so, they used inherited culture as the raw material for what the anthropologist Claude Lévi-Strauss called bricolage.¹ In his studies of how people come up with their ideas, Lévi-Strauss noted that each culture provides people with an extensive repertoire of time-tested concepts and behaviors. When someone wants to address an issue at hand, she rarely acts in a completely novel manner. Instead, she will probably piece together beliefs and opinions from the rich body of existing beliefs. Due to this process, the corpus of ideas ends up being repurposed over the centuries. The result is not stagnation. As people apply the common cultural legacy to resolve new problems, their inherited resources take on new meanings and functions.

Over the centuries, Chinese gender practices developed through repeated rounds of bricolage. Sometimes this occurred at the community level. Huizhou merchants took existing values, such as widow chastity, and made a show of revering them. In this way they hoped to appear respectable in spite of their embarrassing association with the murky world of commerce. Similarly, individual women used agency to deploy the cultural legacy for their own benefit. No one expected a woman to remain permanently chaste if her fiancé died before the wedding. But by taking the concept of fidelity from the trove of common values and accentuating it to an unusual degree, she could claim to be extremely good and pure. She would likely gain approbation for her exceptional behavior.

When the Qing dynasty began in the seventeenth century, Chinese had access to a rich trove of accumulated cultural resources that stretched back to the Bronze Age. China's extraordinarily long stretch of cultural continuity presented people with a far greater range of potential options than those in societies with a shorter cultural memory. As in previous eras, government officials, influential gentry, members of different professions, lineages, families, and individuals all borrowed from the accumulated storehouse of ideas to construct ideas about femininity appropriate to their own circumstances. While they rarely had a completely novel understanding of womanhood, neither were their views identical to those of previous eras.

The Qing holds a unique place in Chinese history. During the twilight of the imperial era, foreign ideas challenged the legitimacy of traditional culture. As before, when confronted with a daunting challenge, the gentry and officialdom reacted by putting even more emphasis on inherited values, including stereotypical gender notions. Confucian doctrine held that in times of crisis, society could be renewed by elevating the ethical level to restore order. Even as late Qing reformers questioned the aptness of traditional female ethics, the number of chaste widows receiving official commendations skyrocketed.

Nineteenth century Chinese faced the unprecedented challenge of modernization. As society, economy, and politics realigned to conform with unfamiliar foreign patterns, many traditional assumptions became irrelevant or even problematic. When scrutinized from the standpoint of the new cultural context, widow chastity appeared wasteful and retrograde. If a woman dedicated her life to displaying fidelity to a deceased husband, some people no longer regarded her as a heroic martyr. Instead, they began to see her as a deluded victim of an unjust social order. Society similarly reassessed almost every other aspect of female identity. The Qing thus stands out as both the culmination and the conclusion of many traditional gender norms.

The Qing was a multiethnic state, and this diversity had a significant impact on views of womanhood. Chinese often understood their gender values by contrasting themselves with people living outside their cultural sphere. In this way, they came to identify nation with culture. Some previous dynasties, such as Song and Ming, had tried to define national identity by associating it with a restrictive vision of ethnic orthodoxy centered on a particular interpretation of Chinese culture.[2] Ethnic nationalists contrasted the supposedly pure and civilized culture of China (called Han or Hua) with the savagery of other peoples, particularly those who posed a military threat. They frequently mentioned gender customs as a way of contrasting Chinese and foreign practices. This juxtaposition portrayed the two sides as not just different, but as a hierarchy. A culture that diverged from the Chinese model was barbaric, while adherence to the classical rites and Confucian ethics attested to civilization. Chinese writers often pointed to foreigners' gender customs as proof of their backwardness. They made normative Chinese womanhood emblematic of civilization.

The expansive nature of the Qing state conflicted with the restrictive Ming view of the Chinese nation. The Manchus conquered an empire that included lands far beyond China's historic borders. These vast regions compassed numerous ethnicities, languages, religions, and cultures. While many Chinese hoped to Sinicize their neighbors, the Qing state never saw cultural fusion as a goal. In consequence, government functionaries had to reconcile very different views of womanhood held by different peoples. Whereas Jurchens customarily practiced levirate, Han Chinese stressed widow chastity. Likewise, the gender customs of Tibetans, Mongols, Uighurs, Dai, Pingpu, and myriad other peoples all had distinctive ideas about how women should behave. The cultural diversity of the Qing posed interminable problems when designing law and policy.

Because the overwhelming majority of the emperor's subjects were Han, the Manchus sought to gain their respect. To do so, Manchu monarchs associated themselves with stringent Confucian ethics to prove themselves moral and cultured. This project led the Manchus to patronize extreme iterations of Chinese gender ethics, such as widow chastity. The subsequent Republic of China and People's Republic of China inherited the ethnic mélange of the Qing empire, so contemporary gender politics arose from a similarly complicated cultural context. Although most people in China adhere to Han values, a significant minority have other opinions. Yet despite this diversity, PRC authorities have tended to promote uniform gender ideas as a way to strengthen national unity.

The Qing also stands out for the ways in which that era's economic and social trends influenced gender practices. Innovations in technology and business practices caused the economy to become increasingly sophisticated. The resulting commercial mindset affected people's thinking, values, and quotidian behavior. Moreover, markets overflowed with a cornucopia of goods, allowing women to pick and choose among them to express their personality and taste. They manipulated their clothing and the objects that surrounded them to create a respectable social image.

The impact of commercialization went even deeper, affecting how people measured the value of those around them. When marrying off a daughter or son, a family no longer put greatest stress on the genealogy of the prospective partner. Instead, they pragmatically sought maximum financial gain. By the Qing, marriage had come to resemble a business transaction. The families of wives paid out a generous dowry to ally with a son-in-law who appeared to have good prospects. Moreover, the decline in female dowry and inheritance rights made wives far more financially dependent on their husbands. When a man died, his widow would lose her dowry if she remarried. Changing laws and social norms forced many widows to decline remarriage just so that they could keep their dowries and avoid destitution.

The Qing may have had an enormous economy, but it suffered from severe inequality. A poor man could not afford a betrothal gift, and it would be difficult for him to find a woman willing to marry so low. To make matters worse, the skewed sex ratio, together with the custom of concubinage, made it impossible for many men to wed simply due to a shortage of women. Lifelong bachelors, derisively referred to as bare sticks, threatened China's social stability. They had no stake in the prevailing order and did not feel obligated to maintain it. Poor men resorted to expedient measures to procreate. Some temporarily rented a wife (*dianqi*) to bear a son who could care for them in old age. Unattached men also threatened women with sexual violence. Many were kidnapped and sold into marriage, concubinage, and prostitution. In response, women secluded themselves within the home to stay safe.

A series of daunting challenges in the nineteenth century plunged established institutions into crisis. Economic problems culminating in the Daoguang Depression intensified hardship among the poor and vulnerable. The White Lotus Rebellion marked the beginning of a series of uprisings that culminated in the catastrophic Taiping Rebellion, an event that laid waste to a large swath of southern China and took perhaps twenty million lives. China also had to contend with intensifying aggression from abroad. The two Opium Wars exposed China's backwardness compared to the rising powers of the industrial world.

These disasters gave rise to disorientation and trauma, evoking contrary responses. Reactionaries doubled down on traditional values. They claimed that China's failures stemmed from insufficient commitment to the foundational ethics and institutions that had sustained their nation since antiquity. This reassertion of orthodoxy focused heavily on female ethics. Conservatives regarded female behavior as symbolic of the national character, so they considered women's sexual probity essential for the country's success. During the late Qing, even as ancient Confucian principles came under attack from reformers, the government expanded the commendation system rewarding female virtue to an unprecedented scale. Tens of thousands of widows received recognition for remaining faithful to their deceased spouses.

Yet even as some traditional values intensified, others went into decline. Foreigners and Chinese reformers criticized established ways of thinking and acting, arguing that stagnant traditions were holding China back. Japan's shocking victory over Chinese forces in 1895 validated the reformist position. The Manchu court saw the need for rapid reform and undertook a thorough renovation of society and government.

The final decades of the Qing dynasty witnessed the most rapid and far-reaching changes to gender norms that had ever occurred in China's long history. Schools for girls were established, allowing them to study outside the home for the first time. They could exercise and learn about science, mathematics, world geography and current affairs. This modernized curriculum was intended to produce a new kind of woman, and it succeeded. Confucian education had instilling female students with restrictive values that made them conformist, passive, and reclusive. The new curriculum had the opposite effect. Graduates tended to be bold and ambitious. Women began to leave the domestic sphere and sought ways to use their talents, voice their opinions, and chart their own course in life.

At first, society resisted women's most audacious demands, and the male establishment shut them out of most jobs. They were usually limited to menial and low status work. Women from middle class families refused to seek employment because they considered the available jobs beneath their station.[3] Even if men had been willing to hire female employees, women still lacked specialized learning and training to qualify them for good jobs.

Although women's opportunities did not meet their rising expectations, they nevertheless expressed optimism and continued to hope for more. At the very least, they could freely express their opinions in public. Educated women wrote for magazines and newspapers and agitated for positive change. The most engaged women joined political organizations and actively worked to improve the nation. After the fall of the Qing dynasty, discussions about women's roles in a rapidly changing China intensified. Women made their voices heard in the reformist and revolutionary debates of the late Qing and early Republican periods.

During the late Qing, Chinese were buffeted by a confusing array of alien ideologies. Confronted with capitalism, socialism, democracy, egalitarianism, constitutionalism, militarism and many other possibilities, people engaged in anxious debates. Society changed so rapidly that not long after the dynasty's fall, the Qing era had already begun to seem distant and alien. This rapidity of the transition to modernity resulted in a stark rupture in ideas about womanhood.

During the twentieth century, as Chinese sought to comprehend the tumultuous changes around them, they reassessed the past. People in the Republican era compared their own lives with the Qing to understand the disorienting rift between China's past and present. When they looked back on the imperial era, they were usually thinking about the Qing, as that period was closest to them and had the most impact on their own society. For many people, the final dynasty came to represent the entire imperial legacy. Twentieth century women thus used Qing gender relations as a yardstick to measure progress. Significantly, important twentieth-century thinkers of every stripe condemned the Qing society as backward. Marxists branded it as "feudal" and fundamentally oppressive, and they condemned the treatment of women under the old society.

Yet even as progressives rejected traditional gender values in the name of modernity, old ideas lingered. Since antiquity, historians had blamed the collapse of each dynasty on the malfeasance of an evil ruler together with an equally wicked woman. Academics and the populace at large used this hoary stereotype to account for the fall of the Qing. The enduring acceptance of this ancient historical model explains why Empress Dowager Cixi has such a poor reputation. Cixi had to face daunting problems while contending with stubborn reactionaries and rival factions. With the exception of her ruinous support for the Boxer Rebellion, she was basically a moderate reformer. Yet strangely, most Chinese today regard her as one of history's greatest villains. They blame her not just for decades of humiliation culminating in the collapse of the Qing, but for the destruction of the age-old imperial system. According to popular myth, the entire edifice of traditional politics, society, and culture was destroyed by a woman. The legend of an evil dragon empress leading China toward destruction shows how gender concepts from imperial era continue to influence contemporary China. Even though the Qing dynasty has come to an end, it continues to exert a powerful hold on the Chinese imagination.

Glossary

Bailian 白蓮
Ban Zhao 班昭
baojuan 寶卷
Cai Runshi 蔡潤石
cainü 才女
chaguan 茶館
Chai Jingyi 柴靜儀
Chan 禪
Chaoyi 超一
Chen Hongmou 陳宏謀
Chen Susu 陳素素
Chongqing (empress) 重慶
chuanqi 傳奇
ci 詞
Cixi 慈禧
Dai 傣
daniu 大妞
Daoguang 道光

Dong	侗
efu	額駙
Fanhua meng	繁華夢
fengjiao	風教
Fuqing	福清
furen	夫人
Fuyang	阜陽
Gai Qi	改琦
Gong (prince)	恭
gongzhu	公主
Gu Chun	顧春
Gu Taiqing	顧太清
Gu Yanwu	顧炎武
Gu Zhenli	顧貞立
guanggun	光棍
Guanyin	觀音
gui	閨
guiyin	閨隱
Gujin tushu jicheng	古今圖書集成
Haitang shishe	海棠詩社
Hao Yixing	郝懿行
He Shuangqing	賀雙卿
Hong Xiuquan	洪秀全
Honglou meng	紅樓夢
huangdi	皇帝
Huizhou	徽州
Jia Baoyu	賈寶玉
jian	賤
Jiaoyuan shishe	蕉園詩社
Jiaqing	嘉慶
Jimo	即墨

jinshi	進士
Kang Youwei	康有為
Kangxi	康熙
Kangxi zidian	康熙字典
keguan	客館
kun	坤
kunju	崑劇
Langao	蘭皋
Li Hongzhang	李鴻章
Li Zicheng	李自成
Lian	連
liang	良
Liang Hongyu	梁紅玉
Liang Qichao	梁啟超
lianyin changhe	聯吟唱和
Lin	林
Lin Daiyu	林黛玉
Lin Yining	林以寧
Lingao	臨高
Liu Xiang	劉向
Longyu	隆裕
Luo Qilan	駱綺蘭
Mabingying	馬兵營
Miao	苗
Miaoshan	妙善
mingyuan	名媛
Nü lunyu	女論語
Nü sishu	女四書
Nü xiaojing	女孝經
nüxia	女俠
Pang Buyan	龐不燕

Pingpu	平埔
Puyi	溥儀
qian	乾
Qian Fenglun	錢鳳綸
Qianlong	乾隆
qiaocui	憔悴
Qin Shihuang	秦始皇
qing (emotion)	情
qing (purity)	清
Qingshi gao	清史稿
qipao	旗袍
Qiu Jin	秋瑾
Sanshui	三水
Shen Shanbao	沈善寶
shilü	詩侶
shinü	仕女
Shun (dynasty)	順
Shunzhi	順治
Siku quanshu	四庫全書
sui	歲
Taiping Tianguo	太平天國
tanci	彈詞
Tongcheng	桐城
Tongren	銅仁
Wang Duan	汪端
Wang Duanshu	王端淑
Wang Xiuchu	王秀楚
Wang Yun	王筠
Wang Zhaoyuan	王照圓
wei fu shou zhen	為夫守貞
Wei Yizhen	韋懿貞

woyou	臥遊
Wu Jiaji	吳嘉紀
Wu Qi	吳琪
Wu Sangui	吳三桂
Wu Xun	吳巽
Wu Zetian	武則天
Wufeng	霧峰
Wusheng Laomu	無生老母
Wushengmu	無生母
Xi Peilan	席佩蘭
xiake	俠客
Xia Jingqu	夏敬渠
Xianfeng	咸豐
xianfu	賢婦
Xiangshan	香山
xiangyan	香豔
xiao	孝
Xiaojing	孝經
Xiaosheng	孝聖
Xiaozhuangwen	孝莊文
Xu Zihua	徐自華
xunqin	殉親
Xuzhou	徐州
ya	雅
"Yangjia jiang"	楊家將
Yangzhou	揚州
Yangzhou baguai	揚州八怪
Yangzhou shiri ji	揚州十日記
Yesou puyan	野叟曝言
Yi	彝
Yi Xin	奕訢

yifu	義夫
Yihetuan	義和團
Yijing	易經
yinfu	淫婦
yingqie	媵妾
Yingzhou	潁州
yinji	隱疾
yinmen zhen	陰門陣
Yongzheng	雍正
yu ying tang	育嬰堂
Yuan Mei	袁枚
Yuanduan	元端
Zhang Xuecheng	章學誠
zhang zhong zhu	掌中珠
zhao fu yang fu	招夫養夫
zhennü	貞女
zhiqing	至情
Zhu Xi	朱熹
Zhu Yuanzhang	朱元璋
Zhulin si	竹林寺
zongren fu	宗人府
zunzhang	尊長
Zuo Xixuan	左錫璇

Notes

1. Li, *Women's Poetry of Late Imperial China*, 131.

INTRODUCTION

1. Bernhardt, "A Ming-Qing Transition," 29–50, provides a cogent overview of these issues.
2. He, *Mingchu yijiang renkou*, 316, 328–30.
3. Von Glahn, *The Economic History of China*, 352.
4. Elvin, "Blood and Statistics," 144.
5. Rowe, *China's Last Empire* gives an insightful overview of the era.
6. A quotation from *A Record of Ten Days at Yangzhou* (*Yangzhou shiri ji*) by Wang Xiuchu, translated in Struve, *Voices from the Ming-Qing Cataclysm*, 36.
7. Li, *Women and National Trauma*, 391. See also pp. 392–93, 485–86.
8. Li, *Women and National Trauma*, 517.
9. Von Glahn, *The Economic History of China*, 316–29.
10. Von Glahn, *The Economic History of China*, 358.
11. Ni, *Zuijia nüxing miaoxie cidian* defines a large number of terms traditionally used in relation to women. Chen, *Zaotou guowei* presents documents regarding the lives of ordinary Qing women.
12. Liu, "Mingdai qingxing sichao," 31; Carlitz, "Lovers, Talkers, Monsters," 185.
13. Kuhn, *The Age of Confucian Rule*, 146. Birge, *Women, Property and Confucian Reaction*, 229–79, describes changes in policies toward women over the course of the Yuan.

14. Rowe, "Women and the Family," 2–5. Bernhardt, "A Ming-Qing Transition," 43–45, notes that these sorts of critical ideas were largely limited to the Jiangnan region.
15. Liu and Zeng, "Qingdai Taiwan tuzhu funü de richang shenghuo," 85–92.
16. Zurndorfer, "Women in Chinese Learned Culture," 27.
17. Madsen, "Ethics and the Family," 285.
18. Paderni, "Between Constraints and Opportunities," 258.
19. Ebrey, "Women, Money, and Class," 13.
20. Cahill, "Resenting the Silk Robes that Hide Their Poems," 521.
21. Naquin and Rawski, *Chinese Society in the Eighteenth Century*, 35.
22. Scott, "Gender: A Useful Category of Historical Analysis," 1053–75.
23. Sweely, "Introduction," 1.
24. Ponterotto, "Brief Note," 538–49.

CHAPTER 1

1. Watson, "The Named and the Nameless," 120, 124, 127.
2. Ochs and Taylor. "The 'Father Knows Best' Dynamic," 97.
3. Chen, *Ming Qing qiyue wenshu*, 30.
4. Bian, "Ming Qing shiqi hunyin lifa," 116.
5. Guo, *Lunli yu shenghuo*, 28–35.
6. Guo, *Lunli yu shenghuo*, 52–57.
7. Guo, *Lunli yu shenghuo*, 36–46.
8. Naquin and Rawski, *Chinese Society in the Eighteenth Century*, 34.
9. Ma, "Cong chilu lüli," 43. A sample of 3,455 nineteenth-century men with *jinshi* degrees had a total of 5,470 sons and 3,625 daughters. The author suspects that the births of daughters were not always recorded, so the actual birth rate was higher.
10. Chow, *The Rise of Confucian Ritualism*, 3.
11. Johnson and Earle, *The Evolution of Human Societies*, 6–7.
12. Zhang, *Jiating shihua*, 122.
13. Chen, *Ming Qing qiyue wenshu*, 202. Qing law followed Ming precedent in this regard. Jiang, "Legislating Hierarchical Yet Harmonious Gender Relations," 33–34.
14. Jiang, "Qingdai cainü zaozu xianxiang kaolun," 203, 211–32.
15. The ages in this section are given in *sui*, which differed from the Western system of reckoning age. For a description of the various ways that Chinese calculated *sui*, see Elvin, "Blood and Statistics," 178–83; Chen, "'Age Inflation and Deflation,'" 527–33.
16. Zhang, *Jiating shihua*, 122–13; Jiang, "Qingdai cainü zaozu," 14.
17. Coale, "Age Patterns of Marriage," 193–214.
18. Telford, "Covariates of Men's Age at First Marriage," 29. Data are from genealogies of families in Tongcheng county, Anhui. The residents of Tongcheng county compiled and preserved unusually comprehensive genealogies. This

study analyzes data about 10,512 married men and their 11,804 wives and concubines, born between 1520 and 1661. Statistics from other places likely differed.

19. Telford, "Covariates of Men's Age at First Marriage," 27.
20. Huang, "Ming Qing shiqi Huizhou nüzi," 151–53.
21. Mann, "Grooming a Daughter for Marriage," 206.
22. Guo and Ding, *Qingdai minjian hunshu yanjiu*, 104–46.
23. Ma, "Cong chilu lüli," 42.
24. Hsiung, *A Tender Voyage*, 199–200; Lu, "'A Pearl in the Palm,'" 62–97.
25. Wu, "Qingdai Hunan hunyin liyi xiaofei ji tedian," 132–36.
26. Hu, "Maishen hunshu," 3.
27. Hu, "Maishen hunshu," 9–11; Zhang, *Qingdai diceng shehui*, 62–91.
28. Zhang, *Qingdai diceng shehui*, 49–59.
29. For marriage law, see Jones, *The Great Qing Code*, 123–36. For variations in marriage practices, see Wolf, "The Origins and Explanation of Variation," 241–60.
30. Zhou, *Manzu funü shenghuo*, 17.
31. Zhang, *Jinshi lungao*, 145–47.
32. Birge, "Levirate Marriage," 107–46.
33. Ma and Ren, "Lun Zhongguo gudai shouji hunzhi," 124–25.
34. Li and Shi, "Lun Qingdai shoujihun lousu," 133–34.
35. Harris, "The Evolution of Human Gender Hierarchies," 67–68.
36. Baker, *Chinese Family and Kinship*, 45.
37. For example, there is copious evidence of this practice from the Tang dynasty. Chen, *Tangdai de funü wenhua*, 74–94.
38. Waltner, *Getting an Heir*, 107, 120; Guo and Ding, *Qingdai minjian hunshu yanjiu*, 147–79; Li, "Qingdai 'zhaofu yangzi,'" 17–18.
39. Lu, "'A Pearl in the Palm,'" 73–74.
40. Zhang, *Jiating shihua*, 127; Guo and Ding, *Qingdai minjian hunshu yanjiu*, 180–96; Guo, *Lunli yu shenghuo*, 251–58; Lu, "Qingdai Taiwan yangnü zhidu," 70–74.
41. Brown, *Is Taiwan Chinese?*, 136.
42. Wolf, *The House of Lim*, 75–76.
43. Stockard, *Daughters of the Canton Delta*, 31–32, 37.
44. Stockard, *Daughters of the Canton Delta*, 4–5, 148. For the definition and origins of this term, see Mencher, "Changing Familial Roles," 231n7.
45. Stockard, *Daughters of the Canton Delta*, 90–92; Jordan, "Two Forms of Spirit Marriage in Rural Taiwan," 181–89.
46. Wang, Zhang, and Yang, "Shilun Yinxu wuhao mu de Fu Hao," 19–20, discuss a case of posthumous marriage during the Shang dynasty. Zhao, "Tangdai hunyin fengsu," 58, notes fluctuations in the popularity of posthumous marriage during the Tang dynasty.
47. Wolf, *Women and the Family in Rural Taiwan*, 33.
48. Wu, "Through the Prism of Male Writing," 9–12, 27.
49. Holzman, "The Place of Filial Piety in Ancient China," 1–15.
50. Liu, "Han Wei liuchao Daojiao de xiaodao," 39–41; Liao, *Tangdai de muzi guanxi*, 125–32.
51. Kindall, "The Paintings of Huang Xiangjian's Filial Journey," 297–357.

52. Hsiung, "Constructed Emotions," 102–10; Epstein, *Orthodox Passions*. Gu, "Qingdai jielie nüzi," 44–51, cites biographies of famous men that attribute their success to their mothers.
53. Sommer, "Abortion in Late Imperial China," 97–165.
54. Bai and Zhou, "Ming Qing nibi zinü xianxiang fenxi," 126–41.
55. Fuma, "Seidai zenki no ikuei jigyou," 143–50, 186–98, 270–318, 547–55.
56. Hershatter, *Women and China's Revolutions*, 38–39.
57. Zhang, *Jiating shihua*, 132.
58. Hsiung, "Constructed Emotions," 88–93.
59. Lau, "Changes to Women's Legal Rights," 707.
60. Rowe, *China's Last Empire*, 116, 118.
61. Grafflin, "Social Order in the Early Southern Dynasties," 49; Watson, "Chinese Kinship Reconsidered," 594.
62. Chang, "Theories about the Formation of Lineage System since the Song and Ming Dynasties," 41–77, introduces several theories often used to explain the rise of lineages.
63. Telford, "Family and State in Qing China," 921.
64. Chow, *The Rise of Confucian Ritualism*, 84, 119.
65. Von Glahn, *The Economic History of China*, 301–2.
66. Watson, "Anthropological Overview," 283.
67. Chow, *The Rise of Confucian*, 211–12.
68. Telford, "Covariates of Men's Age at First Marriage," 24; Mann, *Gender and Sexuality*, 4.
69. He, *Mingchu yijiang renkou*, 67–68, 81.
70. Naquin and Rawski, *Chinese Society in the Eighteenth Century*, 39.
71. Mann, *Gender and Sexuality*, 13; Zhang, "Renshen anquan zhi you," 109–11; Osburg, "Corruption, Masculinity, and *Jianghu* Ideology," 160.
72. He Xiang, "'Ning ke bao xiangzhi toulao,'" 6–8.
73. Stockard, *Daughters of the Canton Delta*, 92–3.
74. Feng, "Qingdai Huizhou xianyuan," 23.
75. Menegon, "Child Bodies, Blessed Bodies," 108, 112–13, 126–27, 129.
76. Tiedemann, "A Necessary Evil," 93, 96, 99–100.
77. Feng, "Qingdai Huizhou xianyuan," 28.
78. For women's place in the Huizhou market for tokens of high culture, see Yao, "Qingdai Huizhou mengyuan lüelun," 80–82.
79. Topley, "Marriage Resistance in Rural Kwangtung," 67–87; Stockard, *Daughters of the Canton Delta*, 70–71, 85–87, 159–60.

CHAPTER 2

1. Ebrey, *Chu Hsi's* Family Rituals.
2. Wang and Zhao, "'Wu sihuo' yu 'xu sicai,'" 163.
3. Skinner, "Conjugal Power in Tokugawa Japanese Families," 247–48.
4. Qian, *Qingdai "jiating baoli" yanjiu*, 31–49.
5. Zhang Zhijuan, "Ming Qing Jin shang jiazu," 47–49.

6. Epstein, "Reflections of Desire," 69–71; Huang, *Desire and Fictional Narrative*, 20, 26–27, 33–34, 39, summarizes various Ming era views toward *qing*.
7. Ko, *Teachers of the Inner Chambers*, 179–85.
8. Huang, *Intimate Memory*, 18–21, 37.
9. Xu, "Domesticating Romantic Love," 244.
10. Xu, "Domesticating Romantic Love," 262–63.
11. Lin, "Xunzhao Qingdai Hainan cainü Pang Buyan," 74–77.
12. Liu, *Ming Qing nüxing zuojia*, 90, 94–95.
13. Chang and Saussy, *Women Writers of Traditional China*, 457.
14. Li, *Women's Poetry of Late Imperial China*, 94–95.
15. Huang, *Intimate Memory*, 157, 164.
16. Qian, *Qingdai "jiating baoli" yanjiu*, 31–49, 63–93, 109–20.
17. Guo and Ding, *Qingdai minjian hunshu yanjiu*, 284–320.
18. Huang, *Civil Justice in China*, 29, 193.
19. Lai and Zhu, "Funü, jiating yu shehui," 1–40.
20. Divale and Harris, "Population, Warfare," 523.
21. Majumdar, *Himalayan Polyandry*, 75.
22. Sommer, *Polyandry and Wife-Selling*; Sommer, "Making Sex Work," 32–38, 43–47, 51; Zhang, *Qingdai diceng shehui "yi qi duo fu."* Zhang, "'Mai mou shao tou zui,'" 81–130, documents wife selling and renting among the lower strata of Taiwan society during the Qing dynasty and Japanese colonial eras. Polyandry often emerges as a strategy to overcome intense economic pressure. Peter, *A Study of Polyandry*, 54.
23. Polyandry among the Caribou Inuit of Hudson Bay had similar motivations. That society also had a high rate of female infanticide that led to a shortage of marriageable women. To overcome this problem, sometimes two men shared one wife. Both men were considered fathers of all of her children. Flannery and Marcus, *The Creation of Inequality*, 23, 25.
24. Zhang, *Songdai hunyin jiazu shilun*, 142–43.
25. Sommer, "Making Sex Work," 29–30.
26. Katkov, "The Domestication of Concubinage in Imperial China," 275, 277–78, 373.
27. Guo and Ding, *Qingdai minjian hunshu yanjiu*, 197–223; Hsieh, "The Market in Concubines," 273–77.
28. Hsieh, "The Market in Concubines," 262.
29. Lewis, *China's Cosmopolitan Empire*, 187.
30. Guo, *Lunli yu shenghuo*, 337–85, provides an overview of Qing concubinage.
31. Guo, *Lunli yu shenghuo*, 368.
32. Elliott, *The Manchu Way*, 255.
33. Ma, "Cong chilu lüli kan Qingdai jinshi juren," 43.
34. Wu, "Qingdai Taiwan 'qie' diwei zhi yanjiu," 22–59.
35. Huang, *Intimate Memory*, 113–33.
36. White and Burton, "Causes of Polygyny," 884.
37. Hsieh, *Concubinage and Servitude*, 11.
38. Hsieh, *Concubinage and Servitude*, 13, 15.
39. Wang, *Shiji binü shengcun zhuangtai yanjiu*, 16–18.

CHAPTER 3

1. Altenburger, *The Sword or the Needle*; Wang and Feng, "Ming Qing xiaoshuo nüxing," 1–4.
2. Dong, *Mulan's Legend*; Goyama, *Ming Qing shidai de nüxing yu wenxue*, 460–91.
3. Wu, "Liang Hongyu," 238–39.
4. Chang and Saussy, *Women Writers of Traditional China*, 391.
5. Chang, *Empress Dowager Cixi*, 215–16; Idema and West, *The Generals of the Yang Family*.
6. For biographies of Qing empresses and major consorts, see Ju, *Zhongguo huanghou quanzhuan*, 915–1003; Wang and Li, *Qingdai houfei*; Peng, "Empresses and Qing Court Politics," 128–41. Wang, *Qingdai houfei*, 391–406, conveniently summarizes basic information about these women into a long table.
7. Erler and Kowaleski, "Introduction," 3.
8. Miyawaki-Okada, "The Role of Women in the Imperial Succession," 147.
9. Rawski, "Qing Empresses and Their Place in History," 34–35.
10. Pozzi, "Manchu Women of the Early Stage," 192–94; Ying-Chen Peng, "Empresses and Qing Court Politics," 129.
11. McMahon, *Celestial Women*, xvii.
12. Han, "Wu Zetian gushi."
13. McMahon, "The Polyandrous Empress," 47, 50.
14. McMahon, "Women Rulers in Imperial China," 212.
15. Rawski, "Ch'ing Imperial Marriage and Problems of Rulership," 171.
16. McMahon, "The Institution of Polygamy," 918–19, 921.
17. Torbert, *The Ch'ing Imperial Household Department*, 74.
18. Torbert, *The Ch'ing Imperial Household Department*, 76–77.
19. Holmgren, "Imperial Marriage," 76, 88–89.
20. Zhu, "Qingdai hougong zhidu lunshu," 323–24; Rawski, "Qing Empresses and Their Place in History," 38.
21. Hummel, *Eminent Chinese of the Ch'ing Period*, 451; Pang, "The Destiny of Qing Taizu Nurhaci's Second Wife Gundai," 183–87.
22. Qiu, "Mingdai gonzen de rong yu ru," 91–125.
23. Qiu, "Yongren zirao," 421–57.
24. Zhan, "Qingdai 'Bai Miao tu,'" 6–15.
25. Qing empresses often had multiple titles that changed over time. This woman was also titled Empress Xiaosheng. Zhao, *Qingshi gao*, 214: 8914–15; Peng, "Empresses and Qing Court Politics," 129–30.
26. Teng, "Qingdai gongzhu de zhuanglian," 196–202.
27. Throughout this book, all ages are given in *sui*.
28. Lü Wenli, "Man Meng lianhun yu Qingdai bianjiang," 65–73.
29. Chung, "The Much Maligned Empress Dowager," 177–96.
30. Chang, *Empress Dowager Cixi* is the most complete and insightful biography of Cixi in English. However, the author wrote this book with revisionist intentions and deliberately tries to salvage Cixi's reputation, so this representation of Cixi remains controversial. The many Chinese language biographies of Cixi tend to be far more negative.

31. Dale, *Inside the World of the Eunuch*, 4, 26, 59, 74–75.
32. Lei, *Liwan kuanglan*, describes the struggle between Cixi and Kang in detail.

CHAPTER 4

1. Wu, *Shechi de nüren*.
2. Shiga, "Family Property and the Law of Inheritance," 109–10; Bernhardt, *Women and Property in China*, 9–10; Sasaki, "An Overview of Shiga Shūzō's *Principles of Chinese Family Law*," 173–83.
3. Meskill, *A Chinese Pioneer Family*, 245.
4. Wu, "Qingdai funü minshi susong," 153–62; Yao, "Qingdai funü baogao tanxi," 63–66.
5. Li, "Ming Qing Huizhou funü zai tudi," 53–56, describes women's land transactions in Huizhou. Liu, *Ming Qing diyu shehui*, 101–69, documents the use of contracts by women in rural Guangdong, mostly for buying and selling land.
6. Chen and Lin, "Fu/Mu ming nan wei?," 1–50.
7. Lau, "Changes to Women's Legal Rights," 707; Birge, *Women, Property and Confucian Reaction*, 76, 91, 97–98, 217, 220–21.
8. Dennerline, "Marriage, Adoption, and Charity," 202; Bernhardt, *Women and Property in China*, 4–5, 47–48, 52–53.
9. Lai and Xu, "Qingdai qiren funü caichan zhi qianxi," 3–33; Elliott, *The Manchu Way*, 250.
10. Silberstein, *A Fashionable Century*, 44.
11. Lü, "Qingdai guafu lisi wenti tanxi," 34–42; Lü, *Qingdai lisi jicheng zhidu*, 175, 177, 186–94.
12. A Feng, *Ming Qing shidai funü*, 174–81; Li, "Qingdai 'zhaofu yangzi' yu 'daichan ruzhui,'" 17–18.
13. Dennerline, "Marriage, Adoption, and Charity," 186, 188, 190, 193–94, 204.
14. Guo Songyi, *Lunli yu shenghuo*, 103–8.
15. Mann, "Grooming a Daughter for Marriage," 204.
16. A Feng, *Ming Qing shidai funü*, 31–35, transcribes dowry provisions of marriage contracts from Huizhou.
17. Mao, *Qingdai jiazhuang yanjiu*, 11–13, 15, 25–29, 147–58.
18. Wu, "Qingdai Hunan hunyin liyi," 132.
19. Mao, "Lun Qingdai 'liantian,'" 54–63.
20. Mann, "Grooming a Daughter for Marriage," 205.
21. Xiao, "Qingdai Jiangxi ninü fengsu," 53–56; Wang, "Qingdai Fujian de ninü," 137–44.
22. Birge, *Women, Property*, 163, 263, 277; Zhang, "Songdai funü lianchan," 88.
23. Birge, *Women, Property*, 151.
24. Mann, "Dowry Wealth and Wifely Virtue," 65.
25. Li, "Cong 'fufu bingzuo,'" 101–9; Li, "'Nan geng nü zhi,'" 10–22.
26. Wu, "Cong qiyue wenshu," 155–61.
27. Huang, *The Peasant Family and Rural Development*, 64, 74, 85, 111.
28. Von Glahn, *The Economic History of China*, 352.

29. Huang, *The Peasant Family and Rural Development*, 49–50.
30. Huang, *The Peasant Family and Rural Development*, 51.
31. Constable, "Introduction," 25–27; Liu and Qiao, "Ming Qing kejia nüxing," 47.
32. Pomeranz, *The Great Divergence*, 99.
33. Bray, *Technology and Gender*, 205–6, 233.
34. Von Glahn, *The Economic History of China*, 352.
35. Mann, *Precious Records*, 144; Zurndorfer, "Cotton Textile Production," 72, 80; Von Glahn, *The Economic History of China*, 353.
36. Pomeranz, *The Great Divergence*, 100–102.
37. Hinsch, "Textiles and Female Virtue," 170–202.
38. Bray, *Technology and Gender*, 243–44.
39. Fong, "Female Hands," 1–58; Zhang, "Gui zhong hanmo."
40. Huang, *The Peasant Family and Rural Development*, 91, 110.
41. Rawski, "Economic and Social Foundations," 18, 25.
42. Sutton, "From Credulity to Scorn," 1–39; Liu, "Lun 'Nishan Saman zhuan,'" 16–23; Zhang, "Ming Qing Wanbei funü gegu," 106–7.
43. Wu, *Reproducing Women*.
44. Luo Xinquan, "Ming Qing nüxing wenxue xinbian," 77–81.
45. Gronewold, *Beautiful Merchandise*, 4–5; Yan, *Zhongguo mingji*, 126–29, 131; Sommer, *Sex, Law, and Society*, 9–10, 12, 260–64.
46. Rawski, "Economic and Social Foundations," 12; Remick, *Regulating Prostitution*, 24.
47. Gronewold, *Beautiful Merchandise*, 5–6; Henriot, *Prostitution and Sexuality*, 79–80.
48. Mackerras, *The Rise of the Peking Opera*, 46–47.
49. Remick, *Regulating Prostitution*, 23, 26–27.
50. Yan, *Zhongguo mingji*, 130; Zurndorfer, "Prostitutes and Courtesans," 214–15.
51. Zeitlin, "The Gift of Song," 1–46.
52. Mann, *Precious Records*, 123; Zurndorfer, "Prostitutes and Courtesans," 214–15.
53. Yeh, "Reinventing Ritual," 1–63; Henriot, *Prostitution and Sexuality*, 26–32; Yeh, *Shanghai Love*, 21, 22, 26, 94–95.

CHAPTER 5

1. Ko, "Pursuing Talent and Virtue," 9.
2. Mann, "Talented Women in Local Gazetteers," 123–41.
3. Mao, *Qingdai jiazhuang yanjiu*, 41–42.
4. Mann, "The Education of Daughters," 24–25.
5. Birge, "Chu Hsi and Women's Education," 356; Ko, "Pursuing Talent," 9.
6. Ko, *Teachers of the Inner Chambers*, 158–69.
7. Shi, "Qingdai shishen jiazu," 35–37.
8. Jiang, "Qingdai cainü zaozu xianxiang kaolun," 13–14.

9. Widmer, "The Epistolary World of Female Talent," 29–30.
10. Mann, *The Talented Women of the Zhang Family*.
11. Xu, "Domesticating Romantic Love," 224.
12. Wang, "Qingdai 'xianfu' yu keju," 41–46.
13. Yao, "Qingdai Huizhou mengyuan lüelun," 80–82.
14. Chang and Saussy, *Women Writers of Traditional China*, 372–73.
15. Mann, "The Education of Daughters," 28–35.
16. Lemert, *Social Things*, 5.
17. Rawski, *Education and Popular Literacy*, 6–7.
18. Johnson, "Communication, Class, and Consciousness," 70.
19. Mann, "Grooming a Daughter for Marriage," 213.
20. Ko, "Pursuing Talent and Virtue," 19; Wang, "Qingdai 'xianfu' yu keju," 41–46.
21. Mann, "Grooming a Daughter for Marriage," 214–15; Mann, "The Education of Daughters," 20; Wang, "Ming Qing mushi jiaoyu," 77–80.
22. Fong, *Herself an Author*, 54–84.
23. Ko, "Pursuing Talent and Virtue," 12; Li, *Nüzi zhi buxiu*.
24. Ko, "Pursuing Talent and Virtue," 23.
25. Mann, "Grooming a Daughter for Marriage," 213–14.
26. Sun, "*Nü sishu* de bianzuan yu liuchuan," 156–57.
27. Wang and Li, "Ming Qing shiqi *Nü lunyu*," 46–55.
28. Liu, "Zuo wei Mengxue yu nüjiao duben," 1–64.
29. Murray, *Mirror of Morality*, 12.
30. Chang and Saussy, *Women Writers of Traditional China*, 418.
31. Johnson, "Communication, Class, and Consciousness," 62; Lemert, *Social Things*, 81, 176.
32. Widmer, *The Beauty and the Book*, 130–31.
33. Rolston, *Traditional Chinese Fiction*, 130.
34. Song, *Qingdai Jiangnan nüxing wenxue shilun*; Ko, *Teachers of the Inner Chambers*, 29; Mann, "Talented Women in Local Gazetteers," 123–41; Zurndorfer, "Women in Chinese Learned Culture," 28.
35. Hu, *Lidai funü zhuzuo kao*; Goyama, "Ming Qing nüzi tibi shi kao," 53.
36. Wang, *Songdai wenxue jiazu*, 376, estimates that 53.8 percent of known female authors in the imperial era lived during the Qing. Zurndorfer, "Women in Chinese Learned Culture," 28.
37. Zhong, *Qingdai nüshiren yanjiu*, 5–6, 15.
38. Rolston, *Traditional Chinese Fiction*, 19.
39. Chang and Saussy, *Women Writers of Traditional China*, 704.
40. Wang, *Reverie and Reality*, 3, 7–8.
41. Mann, *Precious Records*, 30–31, 83–90.
42. Yang, *Women's Poetry and Poetics in Late Imperial China*, 1–2, 4–5, 9–17.
43. Wang, *Ming Qing nüxing de wenxue piping*.
44. Mann, "'Fuxue,'" 43–44.
45. Li, "Qingdai nüxing ciguan," 112–15.
46. Hayes, "Specialists and Written Materials," 86; Widmer, "The Epistolary World," 17, 19; Widmer, "Letters as Windows," 747.

47. Hua, *Ming Qing funü zhi xiqu*, 151–52; Liu, *Ming Qing nüxing zuojia xiqu*, 5, 11.

48. Hayes, "Specialists and Written Materials," 89; Epstein, "Patrimonial Bonds," 1; Yu Zhang, *Interfamily Tanci Writing in Nineteenth-Century China*, xiii, xix, xx; Bao, *Qingdai nüzuojia tanci*, 83–94, introduces the major Qing dynasty collections of *tanci*. Wei, *Ming Qing nüzuojia tanci*, 1–66, gives basic information about female authors of *tanci* lyrics.

49. Epstein, "Patrimonial Bonds," 26–27; Wei, *Ming Qing nüzuojia tanci*, 76–96, 102–16.

50. He, *Danqing qipa*, 18–39, 41–48, 61–85; Wu, "Yangzhou baguai," 636–41, 645; Sheng, "Ming Qing mingji de bimo biaoqing," 42–47.

51. Mann, "The Education of Daughters," 22–23.

52. Li, *Women's Poetry of Late Imperial China*, 71.

53. Mann, *Precious Records*, 78.

54. Wang, "Ming Qing shiqi nüxing bixia," 119–22.

55. Xing, *Qingdai Yangxian lianhun jiazu wenxue huodong yanjiu*.

56. Duan, "Qingdai nüxing 'heyou shi' lun," 126–28.

57. Chang and Saussy, *Women Writers of Traditional China*, 579–80, 582–83.

58. Yan, "Qingdai nüxing shiren de lianyin changhe," 57–68.

59. Widmer, "The Epistolary World," 24; Zhong, *Qingdai nüshiren yanjiu*, 37–42, 173–257; Cheng, "Lun Ming Qing nüxing shishe," 76–80, 96.

60. Waley, *Yuan Mei*, 77, 179; Widmer, "The Epistolary World," 1; Mann, *Precious Records*, 92–3; Zhong, *Qingdai nüshiren yanjiu*, 173–257.

61. Mann, "'Fuxue,'" 41, 44.

62. Berg, *Women and the Literary World*, 222–43.

63. Ho, "Encouragement from the Opposite Gender," 308–53; Zhong, *Qingdai nüshiren yanjiu*, 128–53.

64. Fu and Zeng, "Lun Qingdai nüshiren," 69–75.

65. Yan, "Qingdai Zhuangzu nüwenren Wei Yizhen," 27–30.

66. Idema, *Two Centuries of Manchu Women Poets*.

67. Lü, "Lun Qingdai Beijing Manzu nüzuojia," 62–67; Ying, "Tanxi Qingdai Manzu," 22–25.

68. Cahill, "Resenting the Silk Robes," 521, offers five useful tools for interpreting the poetry of Chinese women.

69. Mann, "Learned Women in the Eighteenth Century," 44–46.

70. Lü, "Qingdai Huizhou nüxing shige," 81–84; Peng, "Shilun Qingdai lienü," 108–9; Luo, "Qingdai caiyuan," 1–7.

71. Ho, "History as Leisure Reading," 27–64.

72. Peng, "Shilun Qingdai lienü," 109–11; Luo, "Qingdai caiyuan," 5–6.

73. Goyama, "Ming Qing nüzi tibi," 53–57.

74. Li, *Women's Poetry of Late Imperial China*, 5–6, 53, 58.

75. Wang, "Nüxing shige," 108; He, "Lun Qingdai Jiangnan nüxing shi," 169–75.

76. Li, *Women's Poetry of Late Imperial China*, 121.

77. Wang, "Ming Qing chuanqi," 118–20.

78. Goossaert, "Irrepressible Female Piety," 212, 215–16.

79. Bray, *Technology and Gender*, 144; Song, "Ming Qing Jiangnan funü 'yeyou,'" 40–42.
80. Li, "Ming Qing nüxing canjia miaohui," 578–81.
81. Watson, "Standardization of the Gods," 293–94.
82. Li, "Ming Qing funü shenghuo," 47–51.
83. Pu Wenqi, "Nüxing jiazhi," 111–15.
84. Yuan, "Ming Qing yilai nianhua," 114–15.
85. Zhong, "Kejia funü yu shenming chongbai," 13–18.
86. Hong, "Qingdai minjian mimi zongjiao," 157, 191–98.
87. Susan, "The Transmission of White Lotus Sectarianism," 255–61.
88. Overmyer, "Values in Chinese Sectarian Literature," 219–54.
89. Wang, "Ming Qing nüxing baozhenshu muti," 42–47.
90. Grant, *Daughters of Emptiness*, 120.
91. Berg, "Cultural Discourse on Xue Susu," 185–86; Lou and Wu, "'Guiyin,'" 120–25; Yang, "The Female Recluse," 263–69; Yang, *Women's Poetry and Poetics*, 29–57.

CHAPTER 6

1. Elvin, "Female Virtue and the State in China," 135.
2. Hinsch, "The Origins of Separation of the Sexes," 595–616.
3. Hsiung, *A Tender Voyage*, 185–190.
4. Bray, *Technology and Gender*, 130, 143.
5. Gao, "'Kongjian' yu 'jia,'" 21–50; Mann, "The Virtue of Travel," 57, 59–61, 70–71.
6. Du, "Ming Qing yiliao," 74–79.
7. Zhang, "Nüxing bingzhe yu nanxing yijia," 188–200.
8. Chang and Saussy, *Women Writers of Traditional China*, 532.
9. Chang and Saussy, *Women Writers of Traditional China*, 422.
10. Sommer, "The Uses of Chastity," 84.
11. Paderni, "Fighting for Love," 46–47.
12. Sommer, *Sex, Law, and Society*, 67–68.
13. Ng, "Ideology and Sexuality," 56–57, 63.
14. Zhang, "Renshen anquan zhi you," 114.
15. Leung, "To Chasten Society," 6–7; Yan and An, "Qingdai shouliu mishi zinü lü," 133–36; Guo, "Qingdai jingshi guaimai funü," 80–87. When the treaty ports opened after the Opium Wars, many women from coastal regions of south China were kidnapped and sold overseas. Kaji, *Zhuhua*.
16. Mackerras, *The Rise of the Peking Opera*, 34. A late eighteenth-century edict banned women from attending theatrical performances in order to keep the sexes from mingling. Mackerras, 214–15, 217. Although this prohibition was observed in enclosed theaters in the cities, women in rural areas continued to watch outdoor performances.
17. Cummins, *The Travels and Controversies of Friar Domingo Navarrete*, vol. 2, 217. I have modernized the orthography.

18. Stevenson, "Wanton Women in Late-Imperial Chinese Literature," 3–26.
19. Wu, *The Lioness Roars*.
20. Theiss, "Explaining the Shrew," 45–46.
21. Liu, "Lun Ming Qing xiaoshuo," 59.
22. Lin, "Chastity in Chinese Eyes," 13–40, provides an overview of the development of the concept of chastity and its terminology.
23. Elvin, "Blood and Statistics," 135–222.
24. Telford, "Covariates of Men's Age at First Marriage," 27.
25. T'ien, *Male Anxiety and Female Chastity*, 126; Elliott, "Manchu Widows and Ethnicity," 35, 39, 56–57, 60–63; Elliott, *The Manchu Way*, 250–53.
26. Li Shizhong, "Lienü shuxie," 81–91.
27. Sommer, *Sex, Law, and Society*, 171.
28. Goyama, *Ming Qing shidai de nüxing*, 179–80.
29. Guo and Ding, *Qingdai minjian hunshu*, 112–46, discusses marriage contracts for remarried women.
30. Sommer, "The Uses of Chastity," 84.
31. Dong, "Lidai jielie funü de tongji," 111–17.
32. Mann, "Historical Change in Female Biography," 72–73.
33. Li, "Cong Xiangshan xianzhi," 34–41; Zhu, *Xinxiu Xiangshan xianzhi*.
34. Wang, "Jielie jingbiao," 61–64.
35. Gao Hua, "Cong *Jimo xianzhi lienü zhuan*," 18; Jimo shizhi bianzuan weiyuanhui, *Jimo shi xinbian difangzhi conshu*.
36. Lai, "Qingdai huangzu funü de jiating diwei," 15.
37. Giersch, *Asian Borderlands*, 189–90.
38. Shen, *Ming Qing Yunnan funü shenghuo*, 186, 189, 193; Shen, "Bianyuan wenhua zhuliuhua," 66–70. The career of the eighteenth-century Qing official Chen Hongmou provides a detailed case study of the Confucianization and Sinicization of Yunnan and other border regions. See Rowe, *Saving the World*.
39. Gao, "Cong *Jimo xianzhi lienü zhuan*," 19.
40. Li, "Cong *Xiangshan xianzhi*," 39.
41. Mann, "Widows in the Kinship, Class, and Community Structures," 37.
42. Theiss, *Disgraceful Matters*.
43. Wei, *Weishu*, 108D:2805, draws an explicit parallel between the relationship of lord and official and that of husband and wife. These roles were considered similar because both the official and wife share the key virtue of obedience. Also see Goldin, *The Culture of Sex*, 34–35, 40–42; Bossler, "Faithful Wives and Heroic Maidens," 761–62, 765.
44. Chow, *The Rise of Confucian Ritualism*, 3.
45. T'ien, *Male Anxiety and Female Chastity*, 70–89.
46. Mann, "Widows in the Kinship, Class, and Community Structures," 44–45.
47. Li, "Cong Ming Qing ni huaben xiaoshuo," 58–62.
48. Li, "Ming Qing xiaoshuo," 19–26.
49. Ko, "The Complicity of Women," 453–88.
50. Chang and Saussy, *Women Writers of Traditional China*, 430.
51. Wang, "Qingdai yichan sannan jingbiao zhengce," 715–18.
52. Na, "Qingdai yifu jiefu jingbiao zhi bijiao," 205–12, found only seventy-one examples of *yifu* from national Qing records and another forty from gazetteers.

53. Mann, "Widows in the Kinship, Class, and Community Structures," 50–51; Fei, *You dianfan dao guifan*, 67–128; Guo, "Qingdai funü de shoujie he zaijia," 124–32; Yang, "Gangchang yu xianshi," 62–68.

54. Wang, "Jielie jingbiao," 62–63, documents the procedures for *jingbiao* applications made in the Huizhou area.

55. Chow, *The Rise of Confucian Ritualism*, 208.

56. Wu, "Let People See and Be Moved," 117–63.

57. Yang, "Gangchang yu xianshi," 62–63.

58. Wang, "Ming Qing shiqi zhanluan," 37–41; Wang, "Ming Qing Huizhou funü jielie," 43; Wang, "On Variations in Huizhou Women's Chastity," 43–57.

59. Xu, "Bijiao shiye xia Qingdai Min Tai jiefu," 106, 108–10.

60. Yang, "Gangchang yu xianshi," 64–65; Chow, *The Rise of Confucian Ritualism*, 211–12.

61. Dennerline, "Marriage, Adoption, and Charity," 193–94, 204; Leung, "To Chasten Society," 1–32.

62. Chow, *The Rise of Confucian Ritualism*, 74.

63. Lu, *True to Her Word*; Wei, "Tamen keyi hui shi zhi bu yu?," 64–70.

64. Zhang, "Ming Qing shiqi Wanbei nüzi xiaoxing," 61–65.

65. Fan, "Ming Qing nüxiao xiqu chutan," 105–10.

66. Van Norden, *Mengzi*, 98, 101; Liu, "Filiality versus Sociality and Individuality," 234.

67. Chang and Saussy, *Women Writers of Traditional China*, 409.

68. Zhu, Li, Yao, and Long, "Tangdai funü xiaoxing tezheng," 112.

69. Kurihara, *Kodai Chūgoku koninsei*, 73–79.

70. Huang, "Tangdai sanfu bamu de falü diwei," 89–117.

71. Li, *The Readability of the Past*, 150–51; Zhou, *Festivals, Feasts, and Gender Relations*, 207–8.

72. Li, "Nüren de Zhongguo zhonggushi," 477–78. Sun, "Tangdai benjia dui nüxing hunyin," 104–7, attributes this change to the adoption of certain ritual concepts and the rise of the examination system.

73. Duan, *Tangdai funü diwei yanjiu*, 59; Luo, *Tongju gongcai*, 354–60, 380–88.

74. Carlitz, "Desire, Danger, and the Body," 105–6; Ge, "Yuandai Hanzu funü shoujie," 59; Goyama, *Ming Qing shidai de nüxing yu wenxue*, 198–200.

75. Du and Mann, "Competing Claims on Womanly Virtue," 233, 238.

76. Qiu, "Renyao yu xueqi," 67–116.

77. Knapp, "Chinese Filial Cannibalism," 135–49.

78. Lu, "Cong nanxing shuxie cailiao," 24–31, 36.

79. Qiu, "Bu xiao zhi xiao," 52.

80. Chong, *Cannibalism in China*, 95–96.

81. Fang, "Songdai nüxing gegu liaoqin wenti shixi," 210.

82. Lin, "Xiaodao yu fudao," 1–29; Chong, *Cannibalism in China*, 100–102.

83. Carlitz, "Desire, Danger, and the Body," 102.

84. Rosemont and Ames, *The Chinese Classic of Family Reverence*, 105. Also Qiu, "Bu xiao zhi xiao," 81–90.

85. Chong, *Cannibalism in China*, 97–98.

86. Li, "Zhongguo gudai funü xiaoxingshi," 73–82.

87. Zhang, "Ming Qing Wanbei funü gegu liaoqin," 105–6.

88. Qiu, "Bu xiao zhi xiao," 87–88.
89. Dong, "Lidai jielie funü de tongji."
90. Du and Mann, "Competing Claims on Womanly Virtue," 234; Zhang, "Bei kending de fouding," 40–49. Of the 599 exemplary women whose stories appear in the *Lienü zhuan* section of *Qingshi gao*, 294 committed suicide.
91. Li, *Women and National Trauma*, 392–93, 480–85, 498–519.
92. Gao, "Cong *Jimo xianzhi lienü zhuan*," 18, 20.
93. Li, "Qingdai Tongren nüxing zisha de tedian," 22–44; Jing, *Daoguang Tongren fuzhi*.
94. Wang, "Ming Qing Huizhou funü jielie xingwei," 43–46; Wang, "On Variations in Huizhou Women's Chastity Behaviors," 54.
95. Elliott, "Manchu Widows and Ethnicity," 38, 43, 50.
96. Wang, "On Variations in Huizhou Women's Chastity Behaviors," 46–47, 49, 51–52.
97. This dynamic was not unique to China. For example, a similar desire for posthumous respect motivated many early Christian martyrs. Nixey, *The Darkening Age*, 78.
98. Lu, *True to Her Word*, 12.
99. Li, "Qingdai Tongren nüxing zisha," 22–24.
100. Carlitz, "The Daughter, the Singing-Girl," 26; MacCormack, "Liability for Suicide," 103–4.
101. Fong, "Signifying Bodies," 112–13; Luo, "Qingdai caiyuan yong xiao, zhen," 5–6.
102. T'ien, *Male Anxiety and Female Chastity*, 126–48.
103. Theiss, "Managing Martyrdom," 47.
104. Elliott, "Manchu Widows and Ethnicity," 43, 45, 53.
105. Yang, "Gangchang yu xianshi," 63.
106. Theiss, "Managing Martyrdom," 53.
107. Du and Mann, "Competing Claims on Womanly Virtue," 234–35; Theiss, "Managing Martyrdom," 55–56.
108. Mann, "Historical Change in Female Biography," 71; Du and Mann, "Competing Claims on Womanly Virtue," 233; Wang, "Ming Qing Huizhou funü jielie," 43–44; Theiss, "Managing Martyrdom," 57, 68–69.
109. Mann, "Widows in the Kinship, Class, and Community Structures," 45, 47; Wang, "On Variations in Huizhou Women's Chastity," 55–56.
110. Carlitz, "Shrines, Governing-Class Identity," 622.
111. Paola, "Untamed Hearts," 77–104.
112. Ropp, "Passionate Women," 4.

CHAPTER 7

1. Mann, *Precious Records*, 3.
2. Ricoeur, "Narrative Identity," 73.
3. Kong, "Tangdai xiaoshuo nüxing xingxiang," 130–33.
4. Liu, "An Exploration of the Mode of Thinking," 387–97.

5. Hinsch, *Women in Early Imperial China*, 143–67.
6. Epstein, "Reflections of Desire," 89–90; Wu, "'Beautiful Boys,'" 19–40. Jia Baoyu's androgyny has generated a torrent of discussion in Chinese academia. Many scholars take a negative view of his behavior. For example, see Zheng, "Qianxi Jia Baoyu de shenjingzheng renge," 36–37.
7. Song, *The Fragile Scholar*, 45, 47.
8. Han, "Shou zuo yi lou hun," 54, 57.
9. Goyama, *Ming Qing shidai de nüxing*, 281–304.
10. Teng, *Taiwan's Imagined Geography*, 173, 181–84.
11. Eifring, "Introduction," 1–36; Bao, *Qingdai nüzuojia tanci*, 31–34.
12. Qian, "Milk and Scent," 189–90.
13. Tan, "A 'Glorious' Dream," 277–78, 293, 304.
14. Wu, "The Bamboo Grove Monastery," 62.
15. Wu, *Reproducing Women*; Chang, "Qingdai shehui yinsu," 65–67.
16. Wu, "Body, Gender, and Disease," 83–128.
17. Chu, "Family Instructions and the Moral Economy," 77–92.
18. Furth, "Concepts of Pregnancy," 28.
19. Wu, "The Bamboo Grove Monastery," 41–76.
20. Thompson, "Death, Food, and Fertility," 102–8.
21. Ahern, "The Power and Pollution of Chinese Women," 193–214; Furth, "Concepts of Pregnancy," 28–29.
22. Wu, "The Bamboo Grove Monastery," 47.
23. Perdue, *Cherokee Women*, 29–30, 37.
24. Jiang, "Nüti yu zhanzheng," 159–87.
25. Li, *Zhongguo lidai zhuangshi*, 135–61.
26. Sun, *Qingdai nüxing fushi wenhua*.
27. Finnane, "Yangzhou's 'Modernity,'" 401, 405.
28. Elliott, *The Manchu Way*, 249–50.
29. Earle and Kristiansen, "Introduction," 8, 14.
30. Bossen and Gates, *Bound Feet, Young Hands*, 6, 8–10.
31. Ko, *Teachers of the Inner Chambers*, 143–47, 158–69.
32. Shepherd, "The Qing, the Manchus, and Footbinding," 279–322.
33. Elliott, *The Manchu Way*, 247.
34. Gates, "Footloose in Fujian," 130–48.
35. Liu and Qiao, "Ming Qing kejia nüxing," 47.
36. Zito, "Secularizing the Pain of Footbinding," 1–24.
37. Drucker, "The Influence of Western Woman," 183; Wang, "Youguan xifang nüchuanjiaoshi," 237–52; Ebrey, "Gender and Sinology," 194–219.
38. Lin, "Qingji de funü buchanzu yundong," 139–80.
39. Chang and Saussy, *Women Writers of Traditional China*, 661.
40. Bossen et al., "Feet and Fabrication," 347–83.
41. Wu, "Riju shiqi Taiwan de fangzu duanfa yundong," 465–510.
42. He, *Gaiqi pingzhuan*, 198–99. Huang, *Shinühua de yanjiu yu jifa* describes the development of the *shinü* genre and introduces representative painters from the Qing and prior eras.
43. Han, "Shou zuo yi lou hun," 51–58.
44. Sun, "Ming Qing changpian shiqing xiaoshuo," 11–13.

45. Wang, "The Emaciated Soul," 57.
46. Li, *Women's Poetry of Late Imperial China*, 105–6.
47. Grant, *Daughters of Emptiness*, 69.

CHAPTER 8

1. Von Glahn, *The Economic History of China*, 348, 365.
2. Von Glahn, *The Economic History of China*, 358.
3. Drucker, "The Role of the YWCA," 421–40; Hershatter, *Women and China's Revolutions*, 44.
4. Perdue, *Cherokee Women*, 7.
5. Hopkins and Wallerstein, *World-Systems Analysis*.
6. Hershatter, *Women and China's Revolutions*, 32–33.
7. Orliski, "The Bourgeois Housewife as Laborer," 43–44.
8. Hershatter, *Women and China's Revolutions*, 62.
9. Zarrow, "He Zhen and Anarcho-Feminism," 796–813; Liu, "Feminism," 779–800; Bailey, "Chinese Women Go Global," 223; Hershatter, *Women and China's Revolutions*, 83.
10. Hershatter, *Women and China's Revolutions*, 61.
11. Dunch, "'Mothers to Our Country,'" 332–33.
12. Chin, "Beneficent Imperialists," 328, 334.
13. Graham, "Exercising Control," 23–48; Gimpel, "Freeing the Mind," 322–23.
14. Qian, *Politics, Poetics, and Gender*, 123, 125, 131.
15. Cheng, "Going Public Through Education," 117–18; Hershatter, *Women and China's Revolutions*, 73–74.
16. Cheng, "Going Public Through Education," 111, 114; Qian, *Politics, Poetics, and Gender*, 151, 153.
17. Judge, "Meng Mu Meets the Modern," 129–77; Judge, "Reforming the Feminine," 161–62, 167, 170; Judge, "Blended Wish Images," 102–35; Judge, "Mediated Imaginings," 147–66; Yang, "A Pictorial Autobiography," 297.
18. Hu, "'How Can a Daughter Glorify the Family Name?," 235.
19. Dunch, "Christianizing Confucian Didacticism," 65–101.
20. Qian, "The Mother *Nü Xuebao*," 257, 266–68; Bailey, "Chinese Women Go Global," 225–28.
21. Chen, "Male Gaze/Female Students," 315–47.
22. Bailey, "Chinese Women Go Global," 214–15.
23. Widmer, "Gentility in Transition," 21, 31, 33.
24. Hershatter, *Women and China's Revolutions*, 28. Zuo Xixuan (fl. mid-nineteenth century) wrote similar patriotic poems. Chang and Saussy, *Women Writers of Traditional China*, 617–18.
25. Hershatter, *Women and China's Revolutions*, 28–29.
26. Li, *The Poetics and Politics of Sensuality*.
27. Chang, *Empress Dowager Cixi*, 215–16.
28. Shi, *At Home in the World*, 19, 23, 42, 44–45.
29. Qian, *Politics, Poetics, and Gender*, 123–84.

30. Hershatter, *Women and China's Revolutions*, 52.
31. Rankin, "The Emergence of Women," 39–66; Rowe, *China's Last Empire*, 266; Hershatter, *Women and China's Revolutions*, 77–83.
32. Chang and Saussy, *Women Writers of Traditional China*, 634.
33. Chang and Saussy, *Women Writers of Traditional China*, 638.
34. Chang and Saussy, *Women Writers of Traditional China*, 653.

CONCLUSION

1. Lévi-Strauss, *The Savage Mind*, 24.
2. Tackett, *The Origins of the Chinese Nation*, 159–63.
3. Orliski, "The Bourgeois Housewife as Laborer," 59–61.

Bibliography

A Feng 阿風. *Ming Qing shidai funü de diwei yu quanli—yi Ming Qing qiyue wenshu, susong dang'an wei zhongxin* 明清時代婦女的地位與權利—以明清契約文書, 訴訟檔案為中心. Beijing: Shehui kexue wenxian, 2009.

Ahern, Emily M. "The Power and Pollution of Chinese Women." In *Women in Chinese Society*, edited by Margery Wolf and Roxanne Witke, 193–214. Stanford: Stanford University Press, 1975.

Altenburger, Roland. *The Sword or the Needle: The Female Knight-errant (xia) in Traditional Chinese Narrative*. Bern: Peter Lang, 2009.

Bai Hua 柏樺 and Zhou Youbin 周囿彬. "Ming Qing nibi zinü xianxiang fenxi" 明清溺斃子女現象分析. *Suzhou Daxue xuebao* 蘇州大學學報 2 (2014): 51–60.

Bailey, Paul J. "Chinese Women Go Global: Discursive and Visual Representations of the Foreign 'Other' in the Early Chinese Women's Press and Media." *Nan Nü* 19 (2017): 213–62.

Baker, Hugh D. R. *Chinese Family and Kinship*. New York: Columbia University Press, 1979.

Bao Zhenpei 鮑震培. *Qingdai nüzuojia tanci yanjiu* 清代女作家彈詞研究. Tianjin: Nankai Daxue, 2008.

Berg, Daria. "Cultural Discourse on Xue Susu, a Courtesan of Late Ming China." *International Journal of Asian Studies* 6, no. 2 (2009): 171–200.

———. *Women and the Literary World in Early Modern China, 1580–1700*. London: Routledge, 2013.

Bernhardt, Kathryn. "A Ming-Qing Transition in Chinese Women's History? The Perspective From Law." In *The History and Theory of Legal Practice in China: Toward a Historical-Social Jurisprudence*, edited by Philip C. C. Huang and Kathryn Bernhardt, 29–50. Leiden: Brill, 2014.

———. *Women and Property in China, 960–1949*. Stanford: Stanford University Press, 1999.

Bian Li 卞利. "Ming Qing shiqi hunyin lifa de tiaozheng yu jiceng shehui de wending" 明清時期婚姻立法的調整與基層社會的穩定. *Anhui Daxue xuebao* 安徽大學學報 6 (2005): 115–20.

Birge, Bettine. "Chu Hsi and Women's Education." In *Neo-Confucian Education: The Formative Stage*, edited by William Theodore de Bary and John Chaffee, 325–67. Berkeley: University of California Press, 1989.

———. "Levirate Marriage and the Revival of Widow Chastity in Yuan China." *Asia Major* (third series) 8, no. 2 (1995): 107–46.

———. *Women, Property and Confucian Reaction in Sung and Yüan China (960–1368)*. Cambridge: Cambridge University Press, 2002.

Bossen, Laurel, et al. "Feet and Fabrication: Footbinding and Early Twentieth-Century Rural Women's Labor in Shaanxi." *Modern China* 37, no. 4 (2011): 347–83.

Bossen, Laurel, and Hill Gates. *Bound Feet, Young Hands: Tracking the Demise of Footbinding in Village China*. Stanford: Stanford University Press, 2017.

Bossler, Beverly. "Faithful Wives and Heroic Maidens: Politics, Virtue, and Gender in Song China." In *Tang Song nüxing yu shehui* 唐宋女性與社會, edited by Deng Xiaonan 鄧小南, vol. 2, 751–84. Shanghai: Shanghai cishu, 2003.

Bray, Francesca. *Technology and Gender: Fabrics of Power in Late Imperial China*. Berkeley: University of California Press, 1997.

Brown, Melissa J. *Is Taiwan Chinese?: The Impact of Culture, Power, and Migration on Changing Identities*. Berkeley, CA: University of California Press, 2004.

Cahill, Suzanne. "Resenting the Silk Robes that Hide Their Poems: Female Voices in the Poetry of Tang Dynasty Nuns." In *Tang Song nüxing yu shehui* 唐宋女性與社會, edited by Deng Xiaonan 鄧小南, vol. 2, 519–66. Shanghai: Shanghai cishu, 2003.

Carlitz, Katherine. "The Daughter, the Singing-Girl, and the Seduction of Suicide." *Nan Nü* 3, no. 1 (2001): 22–46.

———. "Desire, Danger, and the Body: Stories of Women's Virtue in Late Ming China." In *Engendering China*, edited by Christina K. Gilmartin et al., 101–24. Cambridge, MA: Harvard University Press, 1994.

———. "Lovers, Talkers, Monsters, and Good Women: Competing Images in Mid-Ming Epitaphs and Fiction." In *Beyond Exemplar Tales: Women's Biography in Chinese History*, edited by Joan Judge and Hu Ying, 175–92. Berkeley: University of California Press, 2011.

———. "Shrines, Governing-Class Identity, and the Cult of Widow-Fidelity in Mid-Ming Jiangnan." *Journal of Asian Studies* 56, no. 3 (1997): 612–40.

Chang Jianhua. "Theories about the Formation of Lineage System since the Song and Ming Dynasties." *Frontiers of History in China* 3, no. 1 (2008): 41–77.

Chang Jiu 常久 et al. "Qingdai shehui yinsu dui fuchan kexue de yingxiang yanjiu" 清代社會因素對婦產科學的影響研究. *Zhongguo xing kexue* 中國性科學 8 (2014): 65–67.

Chang, Jung. *Empress Dowager Cixi*. London: Vintage Books, 2014.

Chang, Kang-i Sun, and Haun Saussy, eds. *Women Writers of Traditional China: An Anthology of Poetry and Criticism*. Stanford: Stanford University Press, 1999.

Chen Pingyuan. "Male Gaze/Female Students: Late Qing Education for Women as Portrayed in Beijing Pictorials, 1902–08," translated by Anne S. Chao. In *Dif-

ferent Worlds of Discourse: Transformations of Gender and Genre in Late Qing and Early Republican China, edited by Nanxiu Qian, Grace S. Fong, and Richard J. Smith, 315–47. Leiden: Brill, 2008.

Chen Ruoshui 陳弱水. *Tangdai de funü wenhua yu jiating shenghuo* 唐代的婦女文化與家庭生活. Taipei: Yunchen wenhua, 2007.

Chen, Sanping. "'Age Inflation and Deflation' in Medieval China." *Journal of the American Oriental Society* 133, no. 3 (2013): 527–33.

Chen Yingxun 陳瑛珣. *Ming Qing qiyue wenshu zhong de funü jingji huodong* 明清契約 文書中的婦女經濟活動. Taipei: Taiming wenhua, 2001.

———. *Zaotou guowei: Qingdai yilai minjian funü shenghuo shiliao de fajue yu yunyong* 灶頭鍋尾：清代以來民間婦女生活史料的發掘與運用. Sanchong: Licheng, 2009.

Chen Yunru 陳韻如 and Lin Yingyi 林映伊. "Fu／Mu ming nan wei?: Qingzhi Taiwan fenjia zhong zhi jiaoling yu yizhu" 父／母命難違?：清治臺灣分家中之教令與遺囑. *Taiwanshi yanjiu* 臺灣史研究 27, no. 1 (2020): 1–50.

Cheng Jun 程君. "Lun Ming Qing nüxing shishe de sanzhong leixing" 論明清女性詩社的三種類型. *Xiamen Guangbo Dianshi Daxue xuebao* 廈門廣播電視大學學報 2 (2017): 76–80, 96.

Cheng, Weikun. "Going Public Through Education: Female Reformers and Girls' Schools in Late Qing Beijing." *Late Imperial China* 21, no. 1 (2000): 107–44.

Chin, Carol C. "Beneficent Imperialists: American Women Missionaries in China at the Turn of the Twentieth Century." *Diplomatic History* 27, no. 3 (2003): 327–52.

Chong, Key Ray. *Cannibalism in China*. Wakefield, NH: Longwood Academic, 1990.

Chow, Kai-wing. *The Rise of Confucian Ritualism in Late Imperial China: Ethics, Classics, and Lineage Discourse*. Stanford: Stanford University Press, 1994.

Chu, Pingyi. "Family Instructions and the Moral Economy of Medicine in Late Imperial China." *The Chinese Historical Review* 24, no. 1 (2017): 77–92.

Chung, Sue Fawn. "The Much Maligned Empress Dowager: A Revisionist Study of the Empress Dowager Tz'u-Hsi (1835–1908)." *Modern Asian Studies* 13, no. 2 (1979): 177–96.

Coale, Ansley J. "Age Patterns of Marriage." *Population Studies* 25, no. 2 (1971): 193–214.

Constable, Nicole. "Introduction." In *Guest People: Hakka Identity in China and Abroad*, edited by Nicole Constable, 3–35. Seattle: University of Washington Press, 1996.

Cummins, J. S., ed. *The Travels and Controversies of Friar Domingo Navarrete, 1618–1686*. Cambridge: Cambridge University Press, 1962.

Dale, Melissa S. *Inside the World of the Eunuch: A Social History of the Emperor's Servants in Qing China*. Hong Kong: Hong Kong University Press, 2018.

Dennerline, Jerry. "Marriage, Adoption, and Charity in the Development of Lineages in Wu-hsi from Sung to Ch'ing." In *Kinship Organization in Late Imperial China 1000–1940*, edited by Patricia Buckley Ebrey and James L. Watson, 170–209. Berkeley and Los Angeles: University of California Press, 1986.

Divale, William Tulio, and Marvin Harris. "Population, Warfare, and the Male Supremacist Complex." *American Anthropologist*, New Series 78, no. 3 (1976): 521–38.

Dong Jiazun 董家遵. "Lidai jielie funü de tongji" 歷代節烈婦女的統計. In *Zhongguo funüshi lunji* 中國婦女史論集, edited by Bao Jialin 鮑家麟, 111–17. Taipei: Daoxiang, 1988.

Dong, Lan. *Mulan's Legend and Legacy in China and the United States*. Philadelphia: Temple University Press, 2011.

Drucker, Alison R. "The Influence of Western Woman on the Anti-Footbinding Movement 1840–1911." In *Women in China: Current Directions in Historical Scholarship*, edited by R. W. L. Guisso and Stanley Johannesen, 179–99. Youngstown, NY: Philo, 1981.

———. "The Role of the YWCA in the Development of the Chinese Women's Movement, 1890–1927." *Social Service Review* 53, no. 3 (1979): 421–40.

Du, Fangqin, and Susan Mann. "Competing Claims on Womanly Virtue in Late Imperial China." In *Women and Confucian Cultures in Premodern China, Korea, and Japan*, edited by Dorothy Ko, JaHyun Kim Haboush, and Joan R. Piggott, 219–47. Berkeley: University of California Press, 2003.

Du Jiaji 杜家驥. "Ming Qing yiliao zhong nüxing zhenbing de nannü zhi fang wenti—jian xi 'xuansi zhenmai' zhi shuo" 明清醫療中女性診病的男女之防問題—兼析"懸絲診脈"之說. *Lishi dang'an* 歷史檔案 1 (2018): 74–79.

Duan Jihong 段繼紅. "Qingdai nüxing 'heyou shi' lun" 清代女性"和友詩"論. *Wenxueyanjiu* 文學研究 6 (2011): 126–28.

Duan Tali 段塔麗. *Tangdai funü diwei yanjiu* 唐代婦女地位研究. Beijing: Renmin. 2000.

Dunch, Ryan. "Christianizing Confucian Didacticism: Protestant Publications for Women, 1832–1911." *Nan Nü* 11, no. 1 (2009): 65–101.

———. "'Mothers to Our Country': Conversion, Education, and Ideology among Chinese Protestant Women, 1870–1930." In *Pioneer Chinese Christian Women: Gender, Christianity, and Social Mobility*, edited by Jessie Gregory Lutz, 324–50. Bethlehem, PA: Lehigh University Press, 2010.

Earle, Timothy, and Kristian Kristiansen. "Introduction: Theory and Practice in the Late Prehistory of Europe." In *Organizing Bronze Age Societies: The Mediterranean, Central Europe, and Scandinavia Compared*, edited by Timothy Earle and Kristian Kristiansen, 1–33. Cambridge: Cambridge University Press, 2010.

Ebrey, Patricia Buckley. *Chu Hsi's Family Rituals: A Twelfth-Century Chinese Manual for the Performance of Cappings, Weddings, Funerals, and Ancestral Rites*. Princeton, NJ: Princeton University Press, 1990.

———. "Gender and Sinology: Shifting Western Interpretations of Footbinding, 1300–1890." In *Women and the Family in Chinese History*, 194–219. London: Routledge, 2003.

———. "Women, Money, and Class: Sima Guang and Song Neo-Confucian Views on Women." In *Women and the Family in Chinese History*, 10–38. London: Routledge, 2003.

Eifring, Halvor. "Introduction: Emotions and Conceptual History of Qing." In *Love and Emotions in Traditional Chinese Literature*, edited by Halvor Eifring, 1–36. Leiden: Brill, 2004.

Elliott, Mark C. *The Manchu Way: The Eight Banners and Ethnic Identity in Late Imperial China*. Stanford: Stanford University Press, 2001.

———. "Manchu Widows and Ethnicity in Qing China." *Comparative Studies in Society and History* 41, no. 1 (1999): 33–71.
Elvin, Mark. "Blood and Statistics: Reconstructing the Population Dynamics of Late Imperial China from the Biographies of Virtuous Women in Local Gazetteers." In *Chinese Women in the Imperial Past: New Perspectives*, edited by Harriet Zurndorfer, 135–222. Leiden: Brill, 1999.
———. "Female Virtue and the State in China." *Past & Present* 104 (1984): 111–52.
Epstein, Maram. *Orthodox Passions: Narrating Filial Love During the High Qing*. Cambridge, MA: Harvard University Asia Center, 2019.
———. "Patrimonial Bonds: Daughters, Fathers, and Power in Tianyuhua." *Late Imperial China* 32, no. 2 (2011): 1–33.
———. "Reflections of Desire: The Poetics of Gender in *Dream of the Red Chamber*." *Nan Nü* 1, no. 1 (1999): 64–106.
Erler, Mary C., and Maryanne Kowaleski. "Introduction: A New Economy of Power Relations: Female Agency in the Middle Ages." In *Gendering the Master Narrative: Women and Power in the Middle Ages*, edited by Mary C. Erler and Maryanne Kowaleski, 1–16. Ithaca: Cornell University Press, 2003.
Fan Hongjuan 范紅娟. "Ming Qing nüxiao xiqu chutan" 明清女孝戲曲初探. *Xinyang Shifan Xueyuan xuebao* 信陽師範學院學報 32, no. 3 (2012): 105–10.
Fang Yan 方燕. "Songdai nüxing gegu liaoqin wenti shixi" 宋代女性割股療親問題試析. *Qiusuo* 求索 11 (2007): 210–12.
Fei Siyan 費絲言. *You dianfan dao guifan: Cong Mingdai zhenjie lienü de bianshi yu liuchuan kan zhenjie guannian de yangehua* 由典範到規範：從明代貞節烈女的辨識與流傳看貞節觀念的嚴格化. Taipei: Guoli Taiwan Daxue Chubanshe, 1998.
Feng Erkang 馮爾康. "Qingdai Huizhou xianyuan de zhijia he shengcunshu" 清代徽州賢媛的治家和生存術. *Tianjin Shifan Daxue xuebao* 天津師範大學學報 4 (2015): 23–29.
Finnane, Antonia. "Yangzhou's 'Modernity': Fashion and Consumption in the Early Nineteenth Century." *positions* 11, no. 2 (2003): 395–425.
Flannery, Kent, and Joyce Marcus. *The Creation of Inequality: How Our Prehistoric Ancestors Set the Stage for Monarchy, Slavery, and Empire*. Cambridge, MA: Harvard University Press, 2012.
Fong, Grace S. "Female Hands: Embroidery as a Knowledge Field in Women's Everyday Life in Late Imperial and Early Republican China." *Late Imperial China* 25, no. 1 (2004): 1–58.
———. *Herself an Author: Gender, Agency, and Writing in Late Imperial China*. Honolulu: University of Hawaii Press, 2008.
———. "Signifying Bodies: The Cultural Significance of Suicide Writings by Women in Ming-Qing China." *Nan Nü* 3, no. 1 (2001): 105–42.
Fu Qiong 付瓊 and Zeng Xianfei 曾獻飛. "Lun Qingdai nüshiren de diyu fenbu—yi 'Guochao guixiu shi liuxu ji' suo shou shiren wei li" 論清代女詩人的地域分佈—以《國朝閨秀詩柳絮集》所收詩人為例. *Hainan Daxue xuebao* 海南大學學報 26, no. 1 (2008): 69–75.
Fuma Susumu 夫馬進. "Seidai zenki no ikuei jigyou" 清代前期の育嬰事業. In *Tō ajia seikai no seisei, hatten oyobi hoka bunmei to no kankei ni suite no kenkyū* 東アジア世界の生成、発展および他文明との関係についての研究, edited by Fuma Susumu 夫馬進, 5–42. Toyama: Toyama Daigaku Jinbun Gakubu, 1986.

Furth, Charlotte. "Concepts of Pregnancy, Childbirth, and Infancy in Ch'ing Dynasty China." *The Journal of Asian Studies* 46, no. 1 (1987): 7–35.
Gao Hua 高華. "Cong *Jimo xianzhi lienü zhuan* kan Ming Qing funü jingyu" 從 "即墨縣志列女傳" 看明清婦女境遇. *Dongfang luntan* 東方論壇 5 (2010): 17–21.
Gao Yanyi 高彥頤. "'Kongjian' yu 'jia'—lun Mingmo Qingchu funü de shenghuo kongjian" 空間與家—論明末清初婦女的生活空間. *Jindai Zhongguo funüshi yanjiu* 近代中國婦女史研究 8 (1995): 21–50.
Gates, Hill. "Footloose in Fujian: Economic Correlates of Footbinding." *Comparative Studies in Society and History* 43, no. 1 (2001): 130–48.
Ge Renkao 葛仁考. "Yuandai Hanzu funü shoujie wenti chutan" 元代漢族婦女守節問題初探. *Nei Menggu shehui kexue* 內蒙古社會科學 24, no. 3 (2003): 57–59.
Giersch, C. Patterson. *Asian Borderlands: The Transformation of Qing China's Yunnan Frontier*. Cambridge, MA: Harvard University Press, 2006.
Gimpel, Denise. "Freeing the Mind Through the Body: Women's Thoughts on Physical Education in Late Qing and Early Republican China." *Nan Nü* 8, no. 2 (2006): 316–58.
Goldin, Paul Rakita. *The Culture of Sex in Ancient China*. Honolulu: University of Hawaii Press, 2002.
Goossaert, Vincent. "Irrepressible Female Piety: Late Imperial Bans on Women Visiting Temples." *Nan Nü* 10, no. 2 (2008): 212–41.
Goyama Kiwamu 合山究. "Ming Qing nüzi tibi shi kao" 明清女子題壁詩考. *Hechi Shifan xuebao* 河池師專學報, translated by Li Yinsheng 李寅生, 1 (2004): 53–57.
———. *Ming Qing shidai de nüxing yu wenxue* 明清時代的女性與文學, translated by Xiao Yanwan 蕭燕婉. Taipei: Lianjing, 2016.
Grafflin, Dennis. "Social Order in the Early Southern Dynasties: The Formation of Eastern Chin." PhD dissertation, Harvard University, 1980.
Graham, Gael. "Exercising Control: Sports and Physical Education in American Protestant Mission Schools in China, 1880–1930." *Signs* 20, no. 1 (1994): 23–48.
Grant, Beata. *Daughters of Emptiness: Poems of Chinese Buddhist Nuns*. Somerville, MA: Wisdom Publications, 2003.
Gronewold, Sue. *Beautiful Merchandise: Prostitution in China, 1860–1936*. New York: Hawthorn Press, 1982.
Gu Zhen 顧真. "Qingdai jielie nüzi de jingshen shijie" 清代節烈女子的精神世界. *Lishi yuekan* 歷史月刊 135 (1999): 44–51.
Guo Songyi 郭松義. *Lunli yu shenghuo: Qingdai de hunyin guanxi* 倫理與生活: 清代的婚姻關係. Beijing: Shangwu yinshuguan, 2000.
———. "Qingdai funü de shoujie he zaijia" 清代婦女的守節和再嫁. *Zhejiang shehui kexue* 浙江社會科學 1 (2001): 124–32.
———. "Qingdai jingshi guaimai funü de fanzui huodong" 清代京師拐賣婦女的犯罪活. *Zhonghua Nüzi Xueyuan xuebao* 中華女子學院學報 5 (2012): 80–87.
Guo Songyi 郭松義 and Ding Yizhuang 定宜庄. *Qingdai minjian hunshu yanjiu* 清代民間婚書研究. Beijing: Renmin, 2005.
Han Lin 韓林. "Wu Zetian gushi de wenben yanbian yu wenhua neihan" 武則天故事的文本演變與文化內涵. PhD dissertation, Nankai University, 2012.
Han Zhiyang 韓織陽. "Shou zuo yi lou hun, yu yun xiang xiao qu—Qingdai nüxing shenmei xunzhen" 瘦作一縷魂, 玉隕香消去—清代女性審美尋真. *Wenshi tongshi* 文史通識 11 (2018): 51–58.

Harris, Marvin. "The Evolution of Human Gender Hierarchies: A Trial Formulation." In *Sex and Gender Hierarchies*, edited by Barbara Diane Miler, 57–79. Cambridge: Cambridge University Press, 1993.
Hayes, James. "Specialists and Written Materials in the Village World." In *Popular Culture in Late Imperial China*, edited by David Johnson et al., 75–111. Berkeley and Los Angeles: University of California Press, 1985.
He Bingdi 何炳棣. *Mingchu yijiang renkou ji qi xiangguan wenti, 1368–1953* 明初以降人口及其相關問題, 1368–1953. Beijing: Sanlian, 2000.
He Junhong 赫俊紅. *Danqing qipa: Wan Ming Qing chu de nüxing huihua* 丹青奇葩: 晚明清初的女性繪畫. Beijing: Wenwu Chubanshe, 2008.
He Xiang 何湘. "Lun Qingdai Jiangnan nüxing shi de fengyun zhi qi" 論清代江南女性詩的風雲之氣. *Suzhou Daxue xuebao* 蘇州大學學報 1 (2013): 169–75.
———. "'Ning ke bao xiangzhi toulao'—tan Qingdai xiaoshuo xiqu zhong de 'bu hun nü' xingxiang" "寧可抱香枝頭老"—談清代小說戲曲中的 "不婚女" 形象. *Mingzuo xinshang* 名作欣賞 17 (2012): 6–8.
He Yanzhe 何延喆. *Gaiqi pingzhuan: Qingdai shinü huajia* 改琦評傳: 清代仕女畫家. Tianjin: Tianjin renmin meishu, 1998.
Henriot, Christian. *Prostitution and Sexuality in Shanghai: A Social History, 1849–1949*, translated by Nöel Castelino. Cambridge: Cambridge University Press, 2001.
Hershatter, Gail. *Women and China's Revolutions*. Lanham, MD: Rowman & Littlefield, 2019.
Hinsch, Bret. "The Origins of Separation of the Sexes in China." *Journal of the American Oriental Society* 123, no. 3 (2003): 595–616.
———. "Textiles and Female Virtue in Early Chinese Historical Writing." *Nan Nü* 5, no. 2 (2003): 170–202.
———. *Women in Early Imperial China*, second edition. Lanham, MD: Rowman & Littlefield, 2011.
Ho, Clara Wing-chung. "Encouragement from the Opposite Gender: Male Scholars' Interests in Women's Publications in Ch'ing China: A Bibliographical Study." In *Chinese Women in the Imperial Past: New Perspectives*, edited by Harriet Zurndorfer, 308–53. Leiden: Brill, 1998.
———. "History as Leisure Reading for Ming-Qing Women Poets." *Hsiang Lectures on Chinese Poetry* 7 (2015): 27–64.
Holmgren, Jennifer. "Imperial Marriage in the Native Chinese and Non-Han State, Han to Ming." In *Marriage and Inequality in Chinese Society*, edited by Rubie S. Watson and Patricia Buckley Ebrey, 58–96. Berkeley: University of California Press, 1991.
Holzman, Donald. "The Place of Filial Piety in Ancient China." *Journal of the American Oriental Society* 118, no. 2 (1998): 1–15.
Hong Meihua 洪美華. "Qingdai minjian mimi zongjiao zhong de funü" 清代民間秘密宗教中的婦女. MA thesis, National Taiwan Normal University, 1992.
Hopkins, Terence K., and Immanuel Wallerstein et al. *World-Systems Analysis: Theory and Methodology*. Beverly Hills, CA: Sage Publications, 1982.
Hsieh Bao Hua. *Concubinage and Servitude in Late Imperial China*. Lanham, MD: Lexington Books, 2014.

———. "The Market in Concubines in Jiangnan during Ming-Qing China." *Journal of Family History* 33, no. 3 (2008): 262–90.

Hsiung Ping-chen. "Constructed Emotions: The Bond Between Mothers and Sons in Late Imperial China." *Late Imperial China* 15, no. 1 (1994): 102–10.

———. *A Tender Voyage: Children and Childhood in Late Imperial China*. Stanford: Stanford University Press, 2005.

Hu Wenkai. *Lidai funü zhuzuo kao* 歷代婦女著作考. Shanghai: Shangye yinshiguan, 1957.

Hu, Ying. "'How Can a Daughter Glorify the Family Name?' Filiality and Women's Rights in the Late Qing." *Nan Nü* 11, no. 2 (2009): 234–69.

Hu Zhongsheng 胡中生. "Maishen hunshu yu Ming Qing Huizhou xiaceng shehui de hunpei he renkou wenti" 賣身婚書與明清徽州下層社會的婚配和人口問題. In *Ming Qing renkou hunyin jiazu shilun—Chen Jiexian jiaoshou, Feng Erkang jiaoshou guxi jinian lunwenji* 明清人口婚姻家族史論—陳捷先教授, 馮爾康教授古稀紀念 論文集, edited by Ming Qing renkou hunyin jiazu shilun bianxie zu 明清人口婚姻 家族史論編寫組, 1–20. Tianjin: Tianjin guji, 2002.

Hua Wei 華瑋. *Ming Qing funü zhi xiqu chuangzuo yu piping* 明清婦女之戲曲創作與批評. Taipei: Zhongyang Yanjiuyuan Zhongguo Wenzhe Yanjiusuo, 2003.

Huang Jingjing 黃靜靜. "Ming Qing shiqi Huizhou nüzi de zeou biaozhun" 明清時期徽州女子的擇偶標準. *Jiamusi Daxue shehui kexue xuebao* 佳木斯大學社會科學學報 33, no. 2 (2015): 151–53.

Huang Jun 黃均. *Shinühua de yanjiu yu jifa* 仕女畫的研究與技法. Beijing: Beijing gongyi meishu, 1995.

Huang, Martin W. *Desire and Fictional Narrative in Late Imperial China*. Cambridge, MA: Harvard University Asia Center, 2001.

———. *Intimate Memory: Gender and Mourning in Late Imperial China*. Albany, NY: State University of New York Press, 2018.

Huang Meiyin 黃玫茵. "Tangdai sanfu bamu de falü diwei" 唐代三父八母的法律地位. In *Tangdai shenfen fazhi yanjiu—yi Tanglü minglilü wei zhongxin* 唐代身分法制研 究—以唐律名例律為中心, edited by Gao Mingshi 高明士, 89–117. Taipei: Wunan tushu, 2003.

Huang, Philip C. C. *Civil Justice in China: Representation and Practice in the Qing*. Stanford: Stanford University Press, 1996.

———. *The Peasant Family and Rural Development in the Lower Yangzi Region, 1350–1988*. Stanford: Stanford University Press, 1990.

Hummel, Arthur W., Sr. *Eminent Chinese of the Ch'ing Period, 1644–1912*. Washington, DC: United States Government Printing Office, 1943.

Idema, Wilt L. *Two Centuries of Manchu Women Poets: An Anthology*. Seattle: University of Washington Press, 2017.

Idema, Wilt L., and Stephen H. West. *The Generals of the Yang Family*. New Jersey: World Century/World Scientific, 2013.

Jiang Li 蔣麗. "Qingdai cainü zaozu xianxiang kaolun" 清代才女早卒現象考論. *Wenxue jiaoyu* 文學教育 2 (2014): 13–14.

Jiang, Yonglin. "Legislating Hierarchical Yet Harmonious Gender Relations in the Great Ming Code." *Ming Studies* 69 (2014): 27–45.

Jiang Zhushan 蔣竹山. "Nüti yu zhanzheng—Ming Qing yanpao zhi shu 'yinmen zhen' zaitan" 女體與戰爭—明清厭砲之術 "陰門陣" 再探. *Xin shixue* 新史學 9 (1999): 159–87.

Jimo shizhi bianzuan weiyuanhui 即墨市史志編纂委員會. *Jimo shi xinbian difangzhi congshu* 即墨市新編地方志叢書. Lanzhou: Lanzhou Daxue Chubanshe, 2003.

Jing Wen 敬文 et al. *Daoguang Tongren fuzhi* 道光銅仁府志. Changdu: Bashu, 2006.

Johnson, Allen W., and Timothy Earle. *The Evolution of Human Societies: From Foraging Group to Agrarian State*. Stanford: Stanford University Press, 1987.

Johnson, David. "Communication, Class, and Consciousness in Late Imperial China." In *Popular Culture in Late Imperial China*, edited by David Johnson et al., 34–72. Berkeley and Los Angeles: University of California Press, 1985.

Jones, William C., trans. *The Great Qing Code*. Oxford: Clarendon Press, 1994.

Jordan, David K. "Two Forms of Spirit Marriage in Rural Taiwan." *Bijdragen Tot De Taal-, Land- En Volkenkunde* 127, no. 1 (1971): 181–89.

Ju Jixin 車吉心 et al., eds. *Zhongguo huanghou quanzhuan* 中國皇后全傳. Jinan: Shandong Jiaoxi, 1997.

Judge, Joan. "Blended Wish Images: Chinese and Western Exemplary Women at the Turn of the Twentieth Century." *Nan Nü* 6, no. 1 (2004): 102–35.

———. "Mediated Imaginings: Biographies of Western Women and Their Japanese Sources in Late Qing China." In *Different Worlds of Discourse: Transformations of Gender and Genre in Late Qing and Early Republican China*, edited by Nanxiu Qian, Grace S. Fong, and Richard J. Smith, 147–66. Leiden: Brill, 2008.

———. "Meng Mu Meets the Modern: Female Exemplars in Early-Twentieth Century Textbooks for Girls and Women." *Jindai Zhongguo funüshi yanjiu* 近代中國婦女史研究 8 (2000): 129–77.

———. "Reforming the Feminine: Female Literacy and the Legacy of 1898." In *Rethinking the 1898 Reform Period: Political and Cultural Change in Late Qing China*, edited by Rebecca A. Karl and Peter Zarrow, 158–79. Cambridge, MA: Harvard University Asia Center, 2002.

Kaji Hiroaki 可儿弘明. *Zhuhua—bei fanmai haiwai de funü* 猪花—被販賣海外的婦女, translated by Sun Guoqun 孫國群 and Zhao Zongpo 趙宗頗. Zhengzhou: Henan Renmin, 1990.

Katkov, Neil Ennis. "The Domestication of Concubinage in Imperial China." PhD dissertation, Harvard University, 1997.

Kindall, Elizabeth. "The Paintings of Huang Xiangjian's Filial Journey to the Southwest." *Artibus Asiae* 67, no. 2 (2007): 297–357.

Knapp, Keith N. "Chinese Filial Cannibalism: A Silk Road Import?" In *China and Beyond in the Mediaeval Period: Cultural Crossings and Inter-Regional Connections*, edited by Dorothy C. Wong and Gustav Heldt, 135–49. New Delhi: Manohar Publishers, 2014.

Ko, Dorothy. "The Complicity of Women in the Qing Good Women Cult." In *Jinshi jiazu yu zhengzhi bijiao lishi lunwenji* 近世家族與政治比較歷史論文集, edited by Zhongyang Yanjiuyuan Jindaishi Yanjiusuo 中央研究院近代史研究所, 453–88. Taipei: Zhongyanyuan Jinshisuo, 1992.

———. "Pursuing Talent and Virtue: Education and Women's Culture in Seventeenth and Eighteenth Century China." *Late Imperial China* 13, no. 1 (1992): 9–39.

———. *Teachers of the Inner Chambers: Women and Culture in Seventeenth-Century China*. Stanford: Stanford University Press, 1994.

Kong Min 孔敏. "Tangdai xiaoshuo nüxing xingxiang dui Ming Qing wenxue zhi yingxiang" 唐代小說女性形象對明清文學之影響. *Mingzuo xinshang* 名作欣賞 2 (2016): 130–33.

Kuhn, Dieter. *The Age of Confucian Rule: The Song Transformation of China*. Cambridge, MA: The Belknap Press of Harvard University Press, 2009.

Kurihara Keisuke 栗原圭介. *Kodai Chūgoku koninsei no rei rinen to keitai* 古代中國婚姻制の禮理念と形態. Tokyo: Tōhō shoten, 1982.

Lai Huimin 賴惠敏. "Qingdai huangzu funü de jiating diwei" 清代皇族婦女的家庭地位. *Jindai Zhongguo funüshi yanjiu* 近代中國婦女史研究 6 (1994): 3–25.

Lai Huimin 賴惠敏 and Xu Siling 徐思泠. "Qingdai qiren funü caichan zhi qianxi" 清代旗人婦女財產權之淺析. *Jindai Zhongguo funüshi yanjiu* 近代中國婦女史研究 8 (1996): 3–33.

Lai Huimin 賴惠敏 and Zhu Qingwei 朱慶薇. "Funü, jiating yu shehui: Yong Qian shiqi guaitaoan de fenxi" 婦女, 家庭與社會: 雍乾時期拐逃案的分析. *Jindai Zhongguo funüshi yanjiu* 近代中國婦女史研究 6 (2000): 1–40.

Lau Nap-yin. "Changes to Women's Legal Rights in the Family from the Song to the Ming." In *Modern Chinese Religion I: Song-Liao-Jin-Yuan (960–1368 AD)*, edited by John Lagerwey and Pierre Marsone, vol. 1, 643–717. Leiden: Brill, 2015.

Lei Jiasheng 雷家聖. *Liwan kuanglan: wuxu zhengbian xintan* 力挽狂瀾: 戊戌政變新探. Taipei: Wanjuan lou, 2004.

Lemert, Charles. *Social Things: An Introduction to the Sociological Life*, fourth edition. Lanham, MD: Rowman & Littlefield, 2008.

Leung, Angela Ki Che. "To Chasten Society: The Development of Widow Homes in the Qing, 1773–1911." *Late Imperial China* 14, no. 2 (1993): 1–32.

Lévi-Strauss, Claude. *The Savage Mind*. Chicago: University of Chicago Press, 1966.

Lewis, Mark Edward. *China's Cosmopolitan Empire: The Tang Dynasty*. Cambridge, MA: The Belknap Press of Harvard University Press, 2009.

Li Bozhong 李伯重. "Cong 'fufu bingzuo' dao nan geng nü zhi—Ming Qing Jiangnan nongjia funü laodong wenti tantao zhi yi" 從 "夫婦並作" 到男耕女織—明清江南農家婦女勞動問題探討之一. *Zhongguo jingjishi yanjiu* 中國經濟史研究 3 (1996): 101–9.

———. "'Nan geng nü zhi' yu 'funü banbiantian' juese de xingcheng—Ming Qing Jiangnan nongjia funü laodong wenti tantao zhi er" "男耕女織" 與 "婦女半邊天" 角色的形成—明清江南農家婦女勞動問題探討之二. *Zhongguo jingjishi yanjiu* 中國經濟史研究 3 (1997): 10–22.

Li Fei 李飛. "Zhongguo gudai funü xiaoxingshi kaolun" 中國古代婦女孝行史考論. *Zhongguoshi yanjiu* 中國史研究 3 (1994): 73–82.

Li Fengjian 李奉戩. "Ming Qing xiaoshuo zhong de jinü yu aiqing zhenjie" 明清小說中的妓女與愛情貞節. *Ming Qing xiaoshuo yanjiu* 明清小說研究 2 (2005): 19–26.

Li Guotong 李國彤. *Nüzi zhi buxiu: Ming Qing shiqi de nüjiao guannian* 女子之不朽: 明清時期的女教觀念. Guilin: Guangxi Shifan Daxue Chubanshe, 2014.

Li Honghua 李洪華 and Shi Wei 石偉. "Lun Qingdai shoujihun lousu ji qi lüjin buzhi de yuanyin" 論清代收繼婚陋俗及其屢禁不止的原因. *Lanzhou xuekan* 蘭州學刊 9 (2008): 133–35.

Li Jiao 李姣. "Ming Qing Huizhou funü zai tudi maimai huodong zhong de tedian—yi Huizhou wenshu wei li" 明清徽州婦女在土地買賣活動中的特點—以徽州文書為例. *Chifeng Xueyuan xuebao* 赤峰學院學報 36, no. 9 (2015): 53–56.

Li Jinwei 李錦偉. "Qingdai Tongren nüxing zisha de tedian" 清代銅仁女性自殺的特點. *Baicheng Shifan Xueyuan xuebao* 百城師範學院學報 24, no. 4 (2010): 22–24.

Li Lanping 李蘭萍. "Cong *Xiangshan xianzhi* kan Qingdai funü de mingyun" 從香山縣志看清代婦女的命運. *Guangdong shizhi* 廣東史志 1 (2003): 34–41.

Li Shizhong 李世眾. "Lienü shuxie, fude guixun yu diyu zhixu—yi Ming Qing *Leqing xianzhi* wei zhongxin de kaocha" 列女書寫，婦德規訓與地域秩序—以明清樂清縣志為中心的考察. *Huadong Shifan Daxue xuebao* 華東師範大學學報 4 (2016): 81–91.

Li Tingting 李停停. "Cong Ming Qing ni huaben xiaoshuo zhenjie lienü xingxiang kan Ming Qing zhenjieguan de bianhua" 從明清擬話本小說貞節烈女形象看明清貞節觀的變化. *Hunan Renwen Kexue Xueyuan xuebao* 湖南人文科學學院學報 5 (2012): 58–62.

Li, Wai-yee. *The Readability of the Past in Early Chinese Historiography*. Cambridge, MA: Harvard University Asia Center, 2007.

———. *Women and National Trauma in Late Imperial Chinese Literature*. Cambridge, MA: Harvard University Asia Center, 2014.

Li Xiaoman 李小滿. "Qingdai nüxing ciguan de jindai zhuanxiang" 清代女性詞觀的近代轉向. *Xueshu tansuo* 學術探索 1 (2015): 112–17.

Li, Xiaorong. *The Poetics and Politics of Sensuality in China: The "Fragrant and Bedazzling" Movement (1600–1930)*. Amherst, NY: Cambria Press, 2019.

———. *Women's Poetry of Late Imperial China*. Seattle: University of Washington Press, 2012.

Li Ya 李芽. *Zhongguo lidai zhuangshi* 中國歷代妝飾. Beijing: Zhongguo fangzhi, 2004.

Li Yanfeng 李彥峰. "Qingdai 'zhaofu yangzi' yu 'daichan ruzhui' de liyi suqiu kaocha—yi 'Nanbu dang'an' hunqi wenyue wei li" 清代"招夫養子"與"待產入贅"的利益訴求 考察—以"南部檔案"婚契文約為例. *Chang'an Shifan Xueyuan xuebao* 長江師範學院學報 31, no. 5 (2015): 17–21.

Li Yongju 李永菊. "Ming Qing nüxing canjia miaohui de wanhua xuqiu fenxi" 明清女性參加廟會的文化需求分析. *Hubei Daxue xuebao* 湖北大學學報 31, no. 5 (2004): 578–81.

Li Zhende 李貞德. "Nüren de Zhongguo zhonggushi—xingbie yu Han Tang zhijian de lilü yanjiu" 女人的中國中古史—性別與漢唐之間的禮律研究, *Chūgoku no rekishi sekai—tōgō no shisutemu to takenteki hatsuten* 中國の歷史世界—統合のシステムと多元的發展, edited by Nihon Chūgokushi gakkai 日本中國史學會, 469–92. Tokyo: Kyūko, 2002.

Liao Yifang 廖宜方. *Tangdai de muzi guanxi* 唐代的母子關係. Taipei: Daoxiang, 2009.

Lin Liyue 林麗月. "Xiaodao yu fudao: Mingdai xiaofu de wenhuashi kaocha" 孝道與婦道：明代孝婦的文化史考察. *Jindai Zhongguo funüshi yanjiu* 近代中國婦女史研究 6 (1998): 1–29.

Lin Weihong 林維紅. "Qingji de funü buchanzu yundong (1894–1911)" 清季的婦女不纏足運動 (1894–1911). *Guoli Taiwan Daxue Lishixi xuebao* 國立臺灣大學歷史學系學報 8 (1991): 139–80.

Lin, Wei-hung. "Chastity in Chinese Eyes—Nan-Nu Yu-Pieh." *Hanxue yanjiu* 漢學研究 12 (1991): 13–40.

Lin Zhiqiang 林智強. "Xunzhao Qingdai Hainan cainü Pang Buyan shiluo de kuge" 尋找清代海南才女龐不燕失落的哭歌. *Shenzhou minsu* 神州民俗 2 (2014): 74–77.

Liu, Huiying. "Feminism: An Organic or an Extremist Position? On Tien Yee as Represented by He Zhen." *positions* 11, no. 3 (2003): 779–800.

Liu Jingshen. "An Exploration of the Mode of Thinking in Ancient China." *Philosophy East and West* 35, no. 4 (1985): 387–97.

Liu Junhua 劉軍華. *Ming Qing nüxing zuojia xiqu chuangzuo yanjiu* 明清女性作家戲曲創作研究. Beijing: Kexue Chubanshe, 2015.

Liu Lingdi 劉玲娣. "Han Wei liuchao Daojiao de xiaodao" 漢魏六朝道教的孝道. *Nandu xuetan* 南都學壇 27, no. 1 (2007): 39–41.

Liu Miaofen 呂妙芬. "Zuo wei Mengxue yu nüjiao duben de *Xiaojing*—jian lun qi wenben dingwei de lishi bianhua" 做為蒙學與女教讀本的"孝經"—兼論其文本定位的歷史變化. *Taida lishi xuebao* 台大歷史學報 6 (2008): 1–64.

Liu Min 劉敏. "Lun Ming Qing xiaoshuo zhong de nüxing handu wenhua—yi *Liaozhai zhiyi* zhong de 'handu fu' xingxiang wei li" 論明清小說中的女性悍妒文化—以"聊齋誌異"中的"悍妒婦"形象為例. *Shaanxi Xueqian Shifan Xueyuan xuebao* 陝西學前師範學院學報 31, no. 6 (2015): 57–60.

Liu, Qingping. "Filiality versus Sociality and Individuality: On Confucianism and Consanguinitism." *Philosophy East and West* 53, no. 2 (2003): 234–50.

Liu Shixun 劉世珣. "Lun 'Nishan Saman zhuan' zhong de Qingdai wuxi shining ji qi ta" 論"尼山薩滿傳"中的清代巫覡治病及其他. *Jilin Shifan Daxue xuebao* 吉林師範大學學報 4 (2014): 16–23.

Liu Shiyi 劉士義. "Mingdai qingxing sichao yu liangxing wenxue yanbian" 明代情性思潮與兩性文學演變. *Beifang luncong* 北方論叢 5 (2014): 29–34.

Liu Zhenggang 劉正剛. *Ming Qing diyu shehui bianqian zhong de Guangdong xiangcun funü yanjiu* 明清地域社會變遷中的廣東鄉村婦女研究. Beijing: Shehui Kexue Wenxian Chubanshe, 2016.

Liu Zhenggang 劉正剛 and Qiao Yuhong 喬玉紅. "Ming Qing kejia nüxing de shehui xingxiang: yi Longchuan wei li" 明清客家女性的社會形象: 以龍川為例. *Huanan Ligong Daxue xuebao* 華南理工大學學報 5 (2008): 46–52.

Liu Zhenggang 劉正剛 and Zeng Fanhua 曾繁花. "Qingdai Taiwan tuzhu funü de richang shenghuo" 清代台灣土著婦女的日常生活. *Xibei Minzu Daxue xuebao* 西北民族大學學報 2 (2010): 85–92.

Lou Hansong 樓含松 and Wu Lin 吳琳. "'Guiyin': Ming Qing zhi ji zhishi nüxing de shenfen xuanze yu jiazhi rentong" "閨陰": 明清之際知識女性的身分選擇與價值認同. *Zhejiang shehui kexue* 浙江社會科學 2 (2016): 120–25.

Lü Fei 呂菲. "Lun Qingdai Beijing Manzu nüzuojia Gu Chun de wenxue chuangzuo" 論清代北京滿族女作家顧春的文學創作. *Beijing shehui kexue* 北京社會科學 4 (2010): 62–67.

———. "Qingdai Huizhou nüxing shige zhong de nüde sixiang" 清代徽州女性詩歌中的女德思想. *Anhui Guangbo Dianshi Daxue xuebao* 安徽廣播電視大學學報 4 (2014): 81–84.

Lu Jianrong 盧建榮. "Cong nanxing shuxie cailiao kan san zhi qi shiji nüxing de shehui xingxiang suzao" 從男性書寫材料看三至七世紀女性的社會形象塑造.

Guoli Taiwan Shifan Daxue lishi xuebao 國立台灣師範大學歷史學報 26 (1998): 1–42.

Lü Kuanqing 呂寬慶. "Qingdai guafu lisi wenti tanxi" 清代寡婦立嗣問題探析. *Shixue yuekan* 史學月刊 6 (2007): 34–42.

———. *Qingdai lisi jicheng zhidu yanjiu* 清代立嗣繼承制度研究. Zhengzhou: Henan Renmin, 2008.

Lu, Weijing. "'A Pearl in the Palm': A Forgotten Symbol of the Father-Daughter Bond." *Late Imperial China* 31, no. 1 (2010): 62–97.

———. *True to Her Word: The Faithful Maiden Cult in Late Imperial China*. Stanford: Stanford University Press, 2008.

Lü Wenli 呂文利. "Man Meng lianhun yu Qingdai bianjiang—Man Meng lianhun yanjiu zongshu" 滿蒙聯婚與清代邊疆 - 滿蒙聯婚研究綜述. *Xidu Menggu luntan* 西都蒙古論壇 3 (2013): 65–73.

Lu Yanguang 盧彥光. "Qingdai Taiwan yangnü zhidu xingcheng de yuanyin" 清代台灣養女制度形成的原因. In *Lishi, yishu yu Taiwan renwen luncong* 歷史, 藝術與台灣人文論叢, edited by Xiao Baifang 蕭百芳 et al., 69–80. New Taipei: Bo Yang wenhua shiye, 2014.

Luo Tonghua 羅彤華. *Tongju gongcai: Tangdai jiating yanjiu* 同居共財: 唐代家庭研究. Taipei: Zhengda Chubanshe, 2015.

Luo Xinquan 駱新泉. "Ming Qing nüxing wenxue xinbian (er)—guixiu fu bi shici lungao" 明清女性文學新變 (二)—閨秀賦婢詩詞論稿. *Hengyang Shifan Xueyuan xuebao* 衡陽師範學院學報 1 (2016): 77–81.

———. "Qingdai caiyuan yong xiao, zhen, lienü shi lungao" 清代才媛咏孝, 貞, 烈女詩論稿. *Guangdong Jishu Shifan Xueyuan xuebao* 廣東技術師範學院學報 3 (2016): 1–7.

Ma Leiyin 馬蕾吟 and Ren Ruping 任汝平. "Lun Zhongguo gudai shouji hunzhi—yi Mingdai wei li" 論中國古代收繼婚制—以明代為例. *Fazhi yu jingji* 法制與經濟 7 (2014): 123–28.

Ma Yong 馬鏞. "Cong chilu lüli kan Qingdai jinshi juren de hunyin jiating yu zhuzhi" 從齒錄履歷看清代進士舉人的婚姻家庭與住址. *Kejuxue luncong* 科舉學論叢 2 (2013): 42–48.

MacCormack, Geoffrey. "Liability for Suicide in Qing Law on Account of Filthy Words." *Nan Nü* 12, no. 1 (2010): 103–41.

Mackerras, Colin P. *The Rise of the Peking Opera 1770–1870: Social Aspects of the Theatre in Manchu China*. Oxford: Clarendon Press, 1972.

Madsen, Richard. "Ethics and the Family: China/West." In *Chinese Ethics in Global Context: Moral Bases of Contemporary Societies*, edited by Karl-Heinz Pohl and Anselm W. Muller, 279–300. Leiden: Brill, 2002.

Majumdar, D. N. *Himalayan Polyandry: Structure, Functioning and Cultural Change, A Field-Study of Jaunsar-Bawar*. Bombay: Asia Publishing House, 1960.

Mann, Susan. "Dowry Wealth and Wifely Virtue in Mid-Qing Gentry Households." *Late Imperial China* 29, no. 1S (2008): 64–76.

———. "The Education of Daughters in the Mid-Ch'ing Period." In *Education and Society in Late Imperial China, 1600–1900*, edited by Benjamin Elman and Alexander Woodside, 19–49. Berkeley: University of California Press, 1994.

———. "'Fuxue' (Women's Learning) by Zhang Xuecheng (1738–1801): China's First History of Women's Culture." *Late Imperial China* 13, no. 1 (1992): 40–62.

———. *Gender and Sexuality in Modern Chinese History*. Cambridge: Cambridge University Press, 2011.

———. "Grooming a Daughter for Marriage: Brides and Wives in the Mid-Ch'ing Period." In *Marriage and Inequality in Chinese Society*, edited by Rubie S. Watson and Patricia B. Ebrey, 204–30. Berkeley: University of California Press, 1991.

———. "Historical Change in Female Biography from Song to Qing Times: The Case of Early Qing Jiangnan." *Transactions of the International Conference of Orientalists in Japan* 30 (1985): 65–77.

———. "Learned Women in the Eighteenth Century." In *Engendering China*, edited by Christina K. Gilmartin et al., 27–46. Cambridge, MA: Harvard University Press, 1994.

———. *Precious Records: Women in China's Long Eighteenth Century*. Stanford: Stanford University Press, 1997.

———. "Talented Women in Local Gazetteers of the Lingnan Region during the Eighteenth and Nineteenth Centuries." *Jindai Zhongguo funüshi yanjiu* 近代中國婦女史研究 3 (1995): 123–41.

———. *The Talented Women of the Zhang Family*. Berkeley: University of California Press, 2007.

———. "The Virtue of Travel for Women in the Late Empire." In *Gender in Motion: Divisions of Labor and Cultural Change in Late Imperial and Modern China*, edited by Bryan Goodman and Wendy Larson, 55–74. Lanham, MD: Rowman & Littlefield, 2005.

———. "Widows in the Kinship, Class, and Community Structures of Qing Dynasty China." *Journal of Asian Studies* 46, no. 1 (1987): 37–56.

Mao Liping 毛立平. "Lun Qingdai 'liantian'" 論清代 "奩田." *Zhongguo shehui jingji shi yanjiu* 中國社會經濟史研究 2 (2007): 54–63.

———. *Qingdai jiazhuang yanjiu* 清代嫁妝研究. Beijing: Renming Daxue Chubanshe, 2007.

McMahon, Keith. *Celestial Women: Imperial Wives and Concubines in China from Song to Qing*. Lanham, MD: Rowman & Littlefield, 2016.

———. "The Institution of Polygamy in the Chinese Imperial Palace." *The Journal of Asian Studies* 72, no. 4 (2013): 917–36.

———. "The Polyandrous Empress: Imperial Women and their Male Favorites." In *Wanton Women in Late-Imperial Chinese Literature: Models, Genres, Subversions and Traditions*, edited by Mark Stevenson and Wu Cuncun, 20–53. Leiden: Brill, 2017.

———. "Women Rulers in Imperial China." *Nan Nü* 15, no. 2 (2013): 179–218.

Mencher, Joan P. "Changing Familial Roles among South Malabar Nayars." *Southwestern Journal of Anthropology* 18, no. 3 (1962): 230–45.

Menegon, Eugenio. "Child Bodies, Blessed Bodies: The Contest Between Christian Virginity and Confucian Chastity." In *Pioneer Chinese Christian Women: Gender, Christianity, and Social Mobility*, edited by Jessie Gregory Lutz, 108–40. Bethlehem, PA: Lehigh University Press, 2010.

Meskill, Johanna. *A Chinese Pioneer Family: The Lins of Wu-feng, Taiwan, 1729–1895*. Princeton, NJ: Princeton University Press, 1979.

Miyawaki-Okada, Junko. "The Role of Women in the Imperial Succession of the Nomadic Empire." In *The Role of Women in the Altaic World*, edited by Veronica Veit, 143–49. Wiesbaden: Harrrassowitz Verlag, 2007.

Murray, Julia K. *Mirror of Morality: Chinese Narrative Illustration and Confucian Ideology*. Honolulu: University of Hawaii Press, 2007.

Na Xiaoling 那曉凌. "Qingdai yifu jiefu jingbiao zhi bijiao" 清代義夫節婦旌表之比較. *Xueshu jiaoliu* 學術交流 266, no. 5 (2016): 205–12.

Naquin, Susan. "The Transmission of White Lotus Sectarianism in Late Imperial China." In *Popular Culture in Late Imperial China*, edited by David Johnson et al., 255–91. Berkeley and Los Angeles: University of California Press, 1985.

Naquin, Susan, and Evelyn S. Rawski. *Chinese Society in the Eighteenth Century*. New Haven, CT: Yale University Press, 1987.

Ng, Vivian W. "Ideology and Sexuality: Rape Laws in Qing China." *Journal of Asian Studies* 46, no. 1 (1987): 57–70.

Ni Wenjie 倪文杰 et al. *Zuijia nüxing miaoxie cidian* 最佳女性描寫辭典. Beijing: Zhongguo guoji guangbo, 1990.

Nixey, Catherine. *The Darkening Age: The Christian Destruction of the Classical World*. Boston and New York: Houghton Mifflin Harcourt, 2018.

Ochs, Elinor, and Carolyn Taylor. "The 'Father Knows Best' Dynamic in Dinnertime Narratives." In *Gender Articulated: Language and the Socially Constructed Self*, edited by Kira Hall and Mary Bucholtz, 97–120. New York: Routledge, 1995.

Orliski, Constance. "The Bourgeois Housewife as Laborer in Late Qing and Early Republican Shanghai." *Nan Nü* 5, no. 2 (2003): 43–68.

Osburg, John. "Corruption, Masculinity, and *Jianghu* Ideology in the PRC." In *Changing Chinese Masculinities: From Imperial Pillars of State to Global Real Men*, edited by Kam Louie, 157–72. Hong Kong: Hong Kong University Press, 2016.

Overmyer, Daniel L. "Values in Chinese Sectarian Literature: Ming and Ch'ing *Pao-chüan*." In *Popular Culture in Late Imperial China*, edited by David Johnson et al., 219–54. Berkeley and Los Angeles: University of California Press, 1985.

Paderni, Paola. "Between Constraints and Opportunities: Widows, Witches, and Shrews in Eighteenth Century China." In *Chinese Women in the Imperial Past: New Perspectives*, edited by Harriet Zurndorfer, 258–85. Leiden: Brill, 1998.

———. "Fighting for Love: Male Jealousy in Eighteenth Century China." *Nan Nü* 4, no. 1 (2002): 35–69.

Pang, Tatiana A. "The Destiny of Qing Taizu Nurhaci's Second Wife Gundai." In *The Role of Women in the Altaic World*, edited by Veronica Veit, 183–87. Wiesbaden: Harrrassowitz Verlag, 2007.

Peng Guozhong 彭國忠. "Shilun Qingdai lienü de wenxue shijie—yi 'Qingshi gao—lienü zhuan' wei lun" 試論清代列女的文學世界—以清史稿—列女傳為論. *Beijing Daxue xuebao* 北京大學學報 52, no. 1 (2015): 106–15.

Peng, Ying-Chen. "Empresses and Qing Court Politics." In *Empresses of China's Forbidden City, 1644–1912*, edited by Daisy Yiyou Wang and Jan Stuart, 128–41. Salem, MA, and Washington, DC: Peabody Essex Museum and Freer/Sackler, Smithsonian Institution, 2018.

Perdue, Theda. *Cherokee Women: Gender and Cultural Change, 1700–1835*. Lincoln: University of Nebraska Press, 1998.

Peter, Prince of Greece and Denmark. *A Study of Polyandry*. The Hague: Mouton & Co., 1963.

Pomeranz, Kenneth. *The Great Divergence: China, Europe, and the Making of the Modern World Economy*. Princeton, NJ: Princeton University Press, 2000.

Ponterotto, Joseph G. "Brief Note on the Origins, Evolution, and Meaning of the Qualitative Research Concept 'Thick Description.'" *The Qualitative Report* 11, no. 3 (2006): 538–49.

Pozzi, Alessandra. "Manchu Women of the Early Stage: Fantasy and Reality." In *The Role of Women in the Altaic World*, edited by Veronica Veit, 189–98. Wiesbaden: Harrrassowitz Verlag, 2007.

Pu Wenqi 濮文起. "Nüxing jiazhi de zhangyang—Ming Qing shiqi minjian zongjiao zhong de funü" 女性價值的張揚—明清時期民間宗教中的婦女. *Lilun yu xiandaihua* 理論與現代化 5 (2006): 111–15.

Qian, Nanxiu. "Milk and Scent: Works About Women in the *Shishuo Xinyu* Genre." *Nan Nü* 1, no. 2 (1999): 187–236.

———. "The Mother *Nü Xuebao* versus the Daughter *Nü Xuebao*: Generational Differences Between 1898 and 1902 Women Reformers." In *Different Worlds of Discourse: Transformations of Gender and Genre in Late Qing and Early Republican China*, edited Nanxiu Qian, Grace S. Fong, and Richard J. Smith, 257–91. Leiden: Brill, 2008.

———. *Politics, Poetics, and Gender in Late Imperial China: Xue Shaohui and the Era of Reform*. Stanford: Stanford University Press, 2015.

Qian Yonghong 錢泳宏. *Qingdai "jiating baoli" yanjiu: fufu xiangfan de falü* 清代"家庭暴力"研究: 夫妻相犯的法律. Beijing: Shangwu yinshuguan, 2014.

Qiu Zhonglin 邱仲麟. "Bu xiao zhi xiao—Tang yilai gegu liaoqin xianxiang de shehuishi chutan" 不孝之孝—唐以來割股療親現象的社會史初探. *Xin shixue* 新史學 6, no. 1 (1995): 49–94.

———. "Mingdai gonzen de rong yu ru—cong zhiye funü yu shehui liudong de jiaodu qieru" 明代宮人的榮與辱—從職業婦女與社會流動的角度切入. *Gugong xuekan* 故宮學刊 2 (2014): 91–125.

———. "Renyao yu xueqi—'gegu' liaoqin xianxiang zhong de yiliao gainian" 人藥與血氣—"割股"療親現象中的醫療概念. *Xin shixue* 新史學 10, no. 4 (1999): 67–116.

———. "Yongren zirao—Qingdai caixuan xiunü de eyan yu shehui konghuang" 庸人自擾—清代採選秀女的訛言與社會恐慌. *Qinghua xuebao* 清華學報 44, no. 3 (2014): 421–57.

Rankin, Mary Backus. "The Emergence of Women at the End of the Ch'ing: The Case of Ch'iu Chin." In *Women in Chinese Society*, edited by Margery Wolf and Roxane Witke, 39–66. Stanford: Stanford University Press, 1975.

Rawski, Evelyn S. "Ch'ing Imperial Marriage and Problems of Rulership." In *Marriage and Inequality in Chinese Society*, edited by Rubie S. Watson and Patricia B. Ebrey, 170–203. Berkeley: University of California Press, 1991.

———. "Economic and Social Foundations of Late Imperial Culture." In *Popular Culture in Late Imperial China*, edited by David Johnson et al., 3–33. Berkeley and Los Angeles: University of California Press, 1985.

———. *Education and Popular Literacy in Ch'ing China*. Ann Arbor: University of Michigan Press, 1979.

———. "Qing Empresses and Their Place in History." I[n] *[The] Forbidden City, 1644–1912*, edited by Daisy Yiyou Wang [...] Salem, MA, and Washington, DC: Peabody Essex Museum [&] Smithsonian Institution, 2018.

Remick, Elizabeth J. *Regulating Prostitution in China: Gender and Loc[al States,] 1900–1937*. Stanford: Stanford University Press, 2014.

Ricoeur, Paul. "Narrative Identity." *Philosophy Today* 35, no. 1 (1991): 73–[81.]

Rolston, David L. *Traditional Chinese Fiction and Fiction Commentary: Read[ing and] Writing Between the Lines*. Stanford: Stanford University Press, 1997.

Ropp, Paul S. "Passionate Women: Female Suicide in Late Imperial China—Intr[o]duction." In *Passionate Women: Female Suicide in Late Imperial China*, edited by Paul S. Ropp et al., 3–21. Leiden: Brill, 2001.

Rosemont Jr., Henry, and Roger T. Ames. *The Chinese Classic of Family Reverence: A Philosophical Translation of the* Xiaojing. Honolulu: University of Hawaii Press, 2009.

Rowe, William T. *China's Last Empire: The Great Qing*. Cambridge, MA: The Belknap Press of Harvard University Press, 2009.

———. *Saving the World: Chen Hongmou and Elite Consciousness in Eighteenth-Century China*. Stanford: Stanford University Press, 2001.

———. "Women and the Family in Mid-Qing Social Thought: The Case of Chen Hongmou." *Late Imperial China* 13, no. 2 (1992): 1–41.

Sasaki Megumi. "An Overview of Shiga Shūzō's *Principles of Chinese Family Law*." In *Gender History in China*, edited by Masako Kohama and Linda Grove, 173–83. Kyoto and Tokyo: Kyoto University Press and Trans Pacific Press, 2021.

Scott, Joan Wallach. "Gender: A Useful Category of Historical Analysis." *American Historical Review* 91 (1986): 1053–75.

Shen Haimei 沈海梅. "Bianyuan wenhua zhuliuhua zhong de funü—Ming Qing shiqi de Yunnan lienüqun" 邊緣文化主流化中的婦女—明清時期的雲南列女群. *Sixiang zhanxian* 思想戰線 28 (2002): 66–70.

———. *Ming Qing Yunnan funü shenghuo yanjiu* 明清雲南婦女生活研究. Kunming: Yunnan Jiaoyu, 2001.

Sheng Shilan 盛詩瀾. "Ming Qing mingji de bimo biaoqing" 明清名妓的筆墨表情. *Shufa* 書法 3 (2014): 42–47.

Shepherd, John R. "The Qing, the Manchus, and Footbinding: Sources and Assumptions Under Scrutiny." *Frontiers of History in China* 11, no. 2 (2016): 279–322.

Shi, Xia. *At Home in the World: Women and Charity in Late Qing and Early Republican China*. New York: Columbia University Press, 2018.

Shi Xiaoling 石曉玲. "Qingdai shishen jiazu dui nüxing caihua de xingsu—yi Qingren wenji zhong de nüxing yizhuanwen wei zhongxin" 清代仕紳家族對女性才華的形塑—以清人文集中的女性憶傳文為中心. *Nanjing Shifan Daxue xuebao* 南京師範大學文學院學報 3 (2016): 34–40.

Shūzō Shiga. "Family Property and the Law of Inheritance in Traditional China." In *Chinese Family Law and Social Change in Historical and Comparative Perspective*, edited by David C. Buxbaum, 109–50. Seattle: University of Washington Press, 1978.

Silberstein, Rachel. *A Fashionable Century: Textile Artistry and Commerce in the Late Qing*. Seattle: University of Washington Press, 2020.

Sommer, G. William. "Conjugal Power in Tokugawa Japanese Families: A Matter of Life or Death." In *Sex and Gender Hierarchies*, edited by Barbara Diane Miler, 236–70. Cambridge: Cambridge University Press, 1993.

Sommer, Matthew H. "Abortion in Late Imperial China: Routine Birth Control or Crisis Intervention." *Late Imperial China* 31, no. 2 (2010): 97–165.

———. "Making Sex Work: Polyandry as a Survival Strategy in Qing Dynasty China." In *Gender in Motion: Divisions of Labor and Cultural Change in Later Imperial and Modern China*, edited by Bryan Goodman and Wendy Larson, 29–54. Lanham, MD: Rowman & Littlefield, 2005.

———. *Polyandry and Wife-Selling in Qing Dynasty China: Survival Strategies and Judicial Interventions*. Oakland, CA: University of California Press, 2015.

———. *Sex, Law, and Society in Late Imperial China*. Stanford: Stanford University Press, 2000.

———. "The Uses of Chastity: Sex, Law, and the Property of Widows in Qing China." *Late Imperial China* 17, no. 2 (1996): 77–130.

Song, Geng. *The Fragile Scholar: Power and Masculinity in Chinese Culture*. Hong Kong: Hong Kong University Press, 2004.

Song Lizhong 宋立中. "Ming Qing Jiangnan funü 'yeyou' yu fengjian lunli chongtu" 明清江南婦女冶游與封建倫理衝突. *Funü yanjiu luncong* 婦女研究論叢 1 (2010): 39–48.

Song Qingxiu 宋清秀. *Qingdai Jiangnan nüxing wenxue shilun* 清代江南女性文學史論. Shanghai: Shanghai guji, 2015.

Stevenson, Mark. "Wanton Women in Late-Imperial Chinese Literature: Models, Genres, Subversions and Traditions." In *Wanton Women in Late-Imperial Chinese Literature: Models, Genres, Subversions and Traditions*, edited by Mark Stevenson and Wu Cuncun, 3–26. Leiden: Brill, 2017.

Stockard, Janice E. *Daughters of the Canton Delta: Marriage Patterns and Economic Strategies in South China, 1860–1930*. Stanford: Stanford University Press, 1989.

Struve, Lynn A. *Voices from the Ming-Qing Cataclysm: China in Tiger's Jaws*. New Haven, CT: Yale University Press, 1993.

Sun Hongzhe 孫宏哲. "Ming Qing changpian shiqing xiaoshuo zhong nüxing de chouguai shenti" 明清長篇世情小說中女性的醜怪身體. *Jilin Shifan Daxue xuebao* 吉林師範大學學報 2 (2011): 11–13.

Sun Xinmei 孫新梅. "*Nü sishu* de bianzuan yu liuchuan" 女四書的編纂與流傳. *Lantai shijie* 蘭台世界 11 (2013): 156–57.

Sun Yanzhen 孫彥貞. *Qingdai nüxing fushi wenhua yanjiu* 清代女性服飾文化研究. Shanghai: Shanghai guji, 2008.

Sun Yurong 孫玉榮. "Tangdai benjia dui nüxing hunyin ganshequan de bianqian" 唐代本家對女性婚姻干涉權的變遷. *Zhonghua Nüzi Xueyuan xuebao* 中華女子學院學報 3 (2015): 104–7.

Sutton, Donald S. "From Credulity to Scorn: Confucians Confront the Spirit Mediums in Late Imperial China." *Late Imperial China* 21, no. 2 (2000): 1–39.

Sweely, Tracy L. "Introduction." In *Manifesting Power: Gender and the Interpretation of Power in Archaeology*, edited by Tracy L. Sweely, 1–14. London: Routledge, 1999.

Tackett, Nicolas. *The Origins of the Chinese Nation: Song China and the Forging of an East Asian World Order*. Cambridge: Cambridge University Press, 2017.

Tan, Yanbing. "A 'Glorious' Dream of Awkward Romance: Humor and Desire in Wang Yun's (1749–1819) *Fanhua meng*." *Nan Nü* 21, no. 2 (2019): 276–304.

Telford, Ted. A. "Covariates of Men's Age at First Marriage: The Historical Demography of Chinese Lineages." *Population Studies* 46, no. 1 (1992): 19–35.

———. "Family and State in Qing China: Marriage in the Tongcheng Lineages, 1650–1880." In *Jinshi jiazu yu zhengzhi bijiao lishi lunwenji* 近世家族與政治比較歷史論文集, edited by Zhongyang Yanjiuyuan Jindaishi Yanjiusuo, vol. 2, 921–42. Taipei: Zhongyang Yanjiuyuan Jindaishi Yanjiusuo and Department of History, University of California, Davis, 1992.

Teng Deyong 騰德永. "Qingdai gongzhu de zhuanglian" 清代公主的妝奩. *Ningxia shehui kexue* 寧夏社會科學 4 (2016): 196–202.

Teng, Emma Jinhua. *Taiwan's Imagined Geography: Chinese Colonial Travel Writing and Pictures, 1683–1895*. Cambridge, MA: Harvard University Asia Center, 2004.

Theiss, Janet. *Disgraceful Matters: The Politics of Chastity in Eighteenth-Century China*. Berkeley: University of California Press, 2005.

———. "Explaining the Shrew: Narratives of Spousal Violence and the Critique of Masculinity in Eighteenth-Century Criminal Cases." In *Writing and Law in Late Imperial China: Crime, Conflict, and Judgment*, edited by Robert E. Hegel and Katherine Carlitz, 44–63. Seattle: University of Washington Press, 2007.

———. "Managing Martyrdom: Female Suicide and Statecraft in Mid-Qing China." *Nan Nü* 3, no. 1 (2001): 47–76.

Thompson, Stuart E. "Death, Food, and Fertility." In *Death Ritual in Late Imperial and Modern China*, edited by James L. Watson and Evelyn S. Rawski, 71–108. Berkeley and Los Angeles: University of California Press, 1988.

Tiedemann, R. G. "A Necessary Evil: The Contribution of Chinese 'Virgins' to the Growth of the Catholic Church in Late Qing China." In *Pioneer Chinese Christian Women: Gender, Christianity, and Social Mobility*, edited by Jessie Gregory Lutz, 87–107. Bethlehem, PA: Lehigh University Press, 2010.

T'ien Ju-k'ang. *Male Anxiety and Female Chastity: A Comparative Study of Chinese Ethical Values in Ming-Ch'ing Times*. Leiden: Brill, 1988.

Topley, Marjorie. "Marriage Resistance in Rural Kwangtung." In *Women in Chinese Society*, edited by Margery Wolf and Roxane Witke, 67–87. Stanford: Stanford University Press, 1975.

Torbert, Preston M. *The Ch'ing Imperial Household Department: A Study of Its Organization and Principal Functions, 1662–1796*. Cambridge, MA: Council on East Asian Studies, Harvard University, 1977.

Van Norden, Bryan W., trans. *Mengzi: With Selections from Traditional Commentaries*. Indianapolis: Hackett Publishing, 2008.

Von Glahn, Richard. *The Economic History of China: From Antiquity to the Nineteenth Century*. Cambridge: Cambridge University Press, 2016.

Waley, Arthur. *Yuan Mei: Eighteenth Century Chinese Poet*. London: George Allen and Unwin Ltd., 1956.

Waltner, Ann. *Getting an Heir: Adoption and the Construction of Kinship in Late Imperial China*. Honolulu: University of Hawaii Press, 1990.

Wang Chuanman 王傳滿. "Ming Qing Huizhou funü jielie xingwei de yingxiang" 明清徽州婦女節烈行為的影響. *Nanyang Shifan Xueyuan xuebao* 南陽師範學院學報 8, no. 11 (2009): 43–46.

———. "Ming Qing shiqi zhanluan deng baoli yinsu yu Huizhou jielie funü" 明清時期戰亂等暴力因素與徽州節烈婦女. *Baoji Wenli Xueyuan xuebao* 寶雞文理學院學報 6 (2008): 37–41.

———. "On Variations in Huizhou Women's Chastity Behaviors during the Ming and Qing Dynasty." *Chinese Studies in History* 45, no. 4 (2012): 43–57.

Wang Danni 王丹妳 and Li Zhisheng 李志生. "Ming Qing shiqi *Nü lunyu* banben kaoshu" 明清時期 "女論語" 版本考述. *Shandong Nüzi Xueyuan xuebao* 山東女子學院學報 2 (2018): 46–55.

Wang Huaxu 王化旭. "Ming Qing chuanqi zhong nüni nüdao juese tedian tanwei" 明清傳奇中女尼女道角色特點探微. *Jiangsu Jiaoyu Xueyuan xuebao* 江蘇教育學院學報 29, no. 1 (2013): 18–120.

Wang Huiming 王禕茗 and Zhao Shaogeng 趙曉耕. "'Wu sihuo' yu 'xu sicai'—Songdai nüxing jiazhuang quanli de yizhong jiedu" "無私貨" 與 "蓄私財"—宋代女性嫁妝權利的一種解讀. *Jiangsu shehui kexue* 江蘇社會科學 2 (2013): 160–65.

Wang Ke 王珂. "Nüxing shige—yitiao jiankuan de heliu—Zhongguo nüxing shige gaiguan" 女性詩歌—一條漸寬的河流—中國女性詩歌概觀. *Mingzuo xinshang* 名作欣賞 4 (1997): 101–14.

Wang Li 王立. "Ming Qing nüxing baozhenshu muti ji qi Yindu wenhua suyuan" 明清女性保貞術母體及其印度文化溯源. *Ningxia Daxue xuebao* 寧夏大學學報 1 (2007): 42–47.

Wang Li 王立 and Feng Zhihua 馮智華. "Ming Qing xiaoshuo nüxing yi ji fuchou miaoxie yu shehui xinli" 明清小說女性以技復仇描寫與社會心理. *Dandong Shifan xuebao* 丹東師專學報 24, no. 3 (2002): 1–4.

Wang Liyu 王麗玉. *Ming Qing nüxing de wenxue piping* 明清女性的文學批評. Shanghai: Huadong Shilan Daxue Chubanshe, 2017.

Wang Meng 王萌. "Ming Qing shiqi nüxing bixia de jiemei qingyi" 明清時期女性筆下的姐妹情誼. *Henan Jiaoyu Xueyuan xuebao* 河南教育學院學報 4 (2005): 119–22.

Wang Peihuan 王佩環. *Qingdai houfei gongting shenghuo* 清代后妃宮廷生活. Beijing: Gugong Chubanshe, 2014.

Wang Weiman 王偉滿. "Jielie jingbiao—Ming Qing Huizhou jielie xianxiang de zhongyao yinsu" 節烈旌表—明清徽州節烈現象的重要因素. *Aba Shifan Gaodeng Zhuanke Xuexiao xuebao* 阿壩師範高等專科學校學報 26, no. 4 (2009): 61–64.

Wang Weiping 王偉萍. "Ming Qing mushi jiaoyu suyang shulun" 明清母氏教育素養述論. *Neijiang Shifan Xueyuan xuebao* 內江師範學院學報 7, no. 28 (2013): 77–80.

Wang Xiuyun 王秀雲. "Youguan xifang nüchuanjiaoshi yu Zhongguo funü de jige lishi wenti: cong wenxian tanqi" 有關西方女傳教士與中國婦女的幾個歷史問題:從文獻談起. *Jindai Zhongguo funüshi yanjiu* 近代中國婦女史研究 6 (2000): 237–52.

Wang Xueping 王雪萍. *16–18 Shiji binü shengcun zhuangtai yanjiu* 16–18 世紀婢女生存狀態研究. Harbin: Heilongjiang Daxue Chubanshe, 2008.

Wang Xueshen 王學深. "Qingdai 'xianfu' yu keju" 清代 "賢婦" 與科舉. *Shandong Nüzi Xueyuan xuebao* 山東女子學院學報 4 (2012): 41–46.

Wang Yanchun 王豔春 and Li Xianshu 李賢淑. *Qingdai houfei* 清代后妃. Shenyang: Liaoning Minzu, 2004.

Wang, Yanning. *Reverie and Reality: Poetry on Travel by Late Imperial China Women.* Lanham, MD: Lexington Books, 2014.

Wang Yanzhang 王彥章. "Qingdai yichan sannan jingbiao zhengce de liubian" 清代一產三男旌表政策的流變. *Anhui Shifan Daxue xuebao* 安徽師範大學學報 11 (2010): 715–18.

Wang Yi 王毅. *Songdai wenxue jiazu* 宋代文學家族. Changsha: Hunan Shifa Daxue Chubanshe, 2008.

Wang Yifu 汪毅夫. "Qingdai Fujian de ninü zhi feng yu tongyang hunsu" 清代福建的溺女之風與童養婚俗. *Dongnan xueshu* 東南學術 2 (2007): 137–44.

Wang, Yuanfei. "The Emaciated Soul: Four Women's Self-Inscriptions on Their Portraits in Late Imperial China." *Nan Nü* 22, no. 1 (2020): 36–69.

Wang Yuxin 王宇信, Zhang Yongshan 張永山, and Yang Shengnan 楊升南. "Shilun Yinxu wuhao mu de Fu Hao" 試論殷墟五號墓的婦好. *Kaogu xuebao* 考古學報 2 (1977): 19–20.

Watson, James L. "Anthropological Overview: The Development of Chinese Descent Groups." In *Kinship Organization in Late Imperial China 1000–1940*, edited by Patricia Buckley Ebrey and James L. Watson, 274–92. Berkeley and Los Angeles: University of California Press, 1986.

———. "Chinese Kinship Reconsidered: Anthropological Perspectives on Historical Research." *China Quarterly* 92 (1982): 589–622.

———. "Standardization of the Gods: The Promotion of Ti'en You ('Empress of Heaven') Along the South China Coast, 960–1960." In *Popular Culture in Late Imperial China*, edited by David Johnson et al., 292–324. Berkeley and Los Angeles: University of California Press, 1985.

Watson, Rubie S. "The Named and the Nameless: Gender and Person in Chinese Society." In *Gender in Cross Cultural Perspective*, edited by Caroline B. Brettell and Carolyn F. Sargent, 120–33. Englewood Cliffs, NJ: Prentice Hall, 1993.

Wei Bohe 魏伯河. "Tamen keyi hui shi zhi bu yu?—yi *Ningyang xianzhi* jizai de Ming Qing 8 wei zhennü wei li" 她們何以會矢志不渝？—以寧陽縣志記載的明清 8 位貞女為例. *Shandong Nüzi Xueyuan xuebao* 山東女子學院學報 5 (2016): 64–70.

Wei Shou 魏收. *Weishu* 魏書. Beijing: Zhonghua, 1974.

Wei Shuyun 魏淑寶. *Ming Qing nüzuojia tanci xiaoshuo yu Ming Qing shehui* 明清女作家彈詞小說與明清社會. Tianjin: Tianjin Shehui Kexueyuan Chubanshe, 2017.

White, Douglas R., and Michael L. Burton. "Causes of Polygyny: Ecology, Kinship, and Warfare." *American Anthropologist* 90 (1988): 871–87.

Widmer, Ellen. *The Beauty and the Book: Women and Fiction in Nineteenth Century China*. Cambridge, MA: Harvard University Asia Center, 2006.

———. "The Epistolary World of Female Talent in Seventeenth-Century China." *Late Imperial China* 10 (1989): 1–43.

———. "Gentility in Transition: Travels, Novels, and the New *Guixiu*." In *The Quest for Gentility in China: Negotiations Beyond Gender and Class*, edited by Daria Berg and Chloë Starr, 21–44. London: Routledge, 2007.

———. "Letters as Windows on Ming-Qing Women's Literary Culture." In *A History of Chinese Letters and Epistolary Culture*, edited by Antje Richter, 744–74. Leiden: Brill, 2015.

Wolf, Arthur P. "The Origins and Explanation of Variation in the Chinese Kinship System." In *Anthropological Studies of the Taiwan Area: Accomplishments and Pros-*

pects, edited by Kuang-chou Li, et al., 241–60. Taipei: Department of Anthropology, National Taiwan University, 1989.

Wolf, Margery. *The House of Lim: A Study of a Chinese Farm Family*. New York: Appleton Century Crofts, 1968.

———. *Women and the Family in Rural Taiwan*. Stanford: Stanford University Press, 1972.

Wu Caimao 吳才茂. "Cong qiyue wenshu kan Qingdai yilai Qingshui jiang xiayou Miao, Dongzu funü de quanli diwei" 從契約文書看清代以來清水江下游苗, 侗族婦女的權利地位. *Xinan Daxue xuebao* 西南大學學報 7 (2013): 155–61.

Wu, Cuncun. "'Beautiful Boys Made Up as Beautiful Girls': Anti-Masculine Taste in Qing China." In *Asian Masculinities: The Meaning and Practice of Manhood in China and Japan*, edited by Kam Louie and Morris Low, 19–40. London: Routledge, 2003.

Wu, H. Laura. "Through the Prism of Male Writing: Representation of Lesbian Love in Ming-Qing Literature." *Nan Nü* 4, no. 1 (2002): 1–34.

Wu, Pei-yi. "Liang Hongyu." In *Biographical Dictionary of Chinese Women, Volume II: Tang Through Ming 618–1644*, edited by Lily Xiao Hong Lee and Sue Wiles, 238–39. Armonk, NY: M. E. Sharpe, 2014.

Wu Qiongmei 吳琼媚. "Qingdai Taiwan 'qie' diwei zhi yanjiu" 清代臺灣"妾"地位之研究. MA thesis, National Taiwan Normal University, 2000.

Wu Renshu 巫仁恕. *Shechi de nüren: Ming Qing shiqi Jiangnan funü de xiaofei wenhua* 奢侈的女人: 明清時期江南婦女的消費文化. Taipei: Sanmin Shuju, 2005.

Wu Weichun 武維春. "Yangzhou baguai yu Ming Qing cainühua zhi yuanyuan" 揚州八怪與明清才女畫之淵源. *Weiyang Shifan Xueyuan xuebao* 淮陽師範學院學報 5 (2010): 636–41, 645.

Wu Wenxing 吳文星. "Riju shiqi Taiwan de fangzu duanfa yundong" 日據時期台灣的放足斷髮運動. In *Zhongguo funüshi lunwenji* 中國婦女史論文集, edited by Li Youning 李又寧 and Zhang Yufa 張玉法, 465–510. Taipei: Taiwan Shangwu, 1981–1988.

Wu Xin 吳欣. "Qingdai funü minshi susong quanli kaoxi—yi dang'an yu pandu ziliao wei yanjiu duixiang" 清代婦女民事訴訟權利考析—以檔案與判牘資料為研究對象. *Shehui kexue* 社會科學9 (2005): 153–62.

Wu, Yenna. *The Lioness Roars: Shrew Stories from Late Imperial China*. Ithaca, NY: East Asia Program, Cornell University, 1995.

Wu, Yi-Li. "The Bamboo Grove Monastery and Popular Gynecology in Qing China." *Late Imperial China* 21, no. 1 (2000): 41–76.

———. "Body, Gender, and Disease: The Female Breast in Late Imperial Chinese Medicine." *Late Imperial China* 32, no. 1 (2011): 83–128.

———. *Reproducing Women: Medicine, Metaphor, and Childbirth in Late Imperial China*. Berkeley and Los Angeles: University of California Press, 2010.

Wu, Yulian. "'Let People See and Be Moved': Stone Arches and the Chastity Cult in Huizhou during the High Qing Era." *Nan Nü* 17, no. 1 (2015): 117–63.

Wu Zhengdong 吳正東. "Qingdai Hunan hunyin liyi xiaofei ji tedian" 清代湖南婚姻禮儀消費及特點. *Jiangxi shehui kexue* 江西社會科學 2 (2012): 132–36.

Xiao Qian 肖倩. "Qingdai Jiangxi ninü fengsu zhong de 'shejia' wenti" 清代江西溺女風俗中的"奢嫁"問題. *Jiangnan Daxue xuebao* 江南大學學報 4 (2005): 53–56.

Xing Ruijie 刑蕊杰. *Qingdai Yangxian lianhun jiazu wenxue huodong yanjiu* 清代陽羨聯婚家族文學活動研究. Beijing: Zhongguo shehui kexue, 2015.

Xu, Sufeng. "Domesticating Romantic Love during the High Qing Classical Revival: The Poetic Exchanges between Wang Zhaoyuan (1763–1851) and Her Husband Hao Yixing (1757–1829)." *Nan Nü* 15, no. 2 (2013): 219–64.

Xu Wenbin 徐文彬. "Bijiao shiye xia Qingdai Min Tai jiefu qunti yanjiu" 比較視野下清代閩台節婦群體研究. *Zhonggong Fujian Sheng Weidangxiao xuebao* 中共福建省委黨校學報 11 (2014): 105–12.

Yan Cheng 嚴程. "Qingdai nüxing shiren de lianyin changhe yu cungao qingkuang lishuo" 清代女性詩人的聯吟唱和與存稿情況例說. *Qinghua Daxue xuebao* 清華大學學報 1 (2013): 57–68.

Yan Jianping 顏建萍 et al. "Qingdai Zhuangzu nüwenren Wei Yizhen yanjiu" 清代壯族女文人韋懿貞研究. *Yulin Shifan Xueyuan xuebao* 玉林師範學院學報 32, no. 3 (2011): 27–30.

Yan Ming 嚴明. *Zhongguo mingji yishu shi* 中國名妓藝術史. Taipei: Wenjin, 1992.

Yan Wenbo 閆文博 and An Yuanyuan 安媛媛. "Qingdai shouliu mishi zinü lü yu guaimai renkou zuifan" 清代收留迷失子女律與拐賣人口犯罪. *Lanzhou xuekan* 蘭州學刊 12 (2010): 133–36.

Yang, Binbin. "A Pictorial Autobiography by Zeng Jifen (1852–1942) and the Use of the 'Exemplary' in China's Modern Transformation." *Nan Nü* 19 (2017): 263–315.

Yang, Haihong. "The Female Recluse: The Trope of Withdrawal and Self-Representation in Poems by Two Late Ming/Early Qing Women Writers." *Nan Nü* 18, no. 2 (2016): 257–90.

———. *Women's Poetry and Poetics in Late Imperial China: A Dialogic Engagement*. Lanham, MD: Lexington Books, 2017.

Yang Yifeng 楊毅奉. "Gangchang yu xianshi: Qingdai zhongqi yingxiang funü zaihun de duochong yinsu" 網常與現實：清代中期影響婦女再婚的多重因素. *Yibin Xueyuan xuebao* 宜賓學院學報 8 (2015): 62–68.

Yao Xuemei 姚雪梅. "Qingdai Huizhou mengyuan lüelun" 清代徽州名媛略論. *Chizhou Xueyuan xuebao* 池州學院學報 25, no. 5 (2011): 80–82.

Yao Zhiwei 姚志偉. "Qingdai funü baogao tanxi" 清代婦女抱告探析. *Faxue zazhi* 法學雜誌 8 (2011): 63–66.

Yeh, Catherine Vance. "Reinventing Ritual: Late Qing Handbooks for Proper Customer Behavior in Shanghai Courtesan Houses." *Late Imperial China* 19, no. 2 (1998): 1–63.

———. *Shanghai Love: Courtesans, Intellectuals, and Entertainment Culture, 1850–1910*. Seattle: University of Washington Press, 2006.

Ying Zi 應紫. "Tanxi Qingdai Manzu nüciren Gu Taiqing de ci" 探析清代滿族女詞人顧太清的詞. *Dali Xueyuan xuebao* 大理學院學報 5 (2012): 22–25.

Yu Zhang. *Interfamily Tanci Writing in Nineteenth-Century China: Bonds and Boundaries*. Lanham, MD: Lexington Books, 2018.

Yuan Zhoufei 袁宙飛. "Ming Qing yilai nianhua zhong nüxing xingxiang de muti tanxi" 明清以來年畫中女性形象的母體探析. *Minsu yanjiu* 民俗研究 4 (2016): 114–20.

Zamperini, Paola. "Untamed Hearts: Eros and Suicide in Late Imperial Chinese Fiction." In *Passionate Women: Female Suicide in Late Imperial China*, edited by Paul S. Ropp et al., 77–104. Leiden: Brill, 2001.

Zarrow, Peter. "He Zhen and Anarcho-Feminism in China." *Journal of Asian Studies* 47, no. 4 (1988): 796–813.

Zeitlin, Judith T. "The Gift of Song: Courtesans and Patrons in Late Ming and Early Qing Cultural Production." *Hsiang Lectures on Chinese Poetry* 4 (2008): 1–46.

Zhan Yuehai 占躍海. "Qingdai 'Bai Miao tu' huigen zhong de 'nüguan'" 清代 "百苗圖" 繪本中的 "女官." *Yishu tansuo* 藝術探索 30, no. 5 (2016): 6–15.

Zhang Bangwei 張邦煒. *Songdai hunyin jiazu shilun* 宋代婚姻家族史論. Beijing: Renmin, 2003.

Zhang Benshun 張本順. "Songdai funü lianchan suoyouquan tanxi ji qi yiyi" 宋代婦女奩產所有權探析及其意義. *Fazhi yu shehui fazhan* 法制與社會發展 5 (2011): 79–95.

Zhang Boquan 張博泉. *Jinshi lungao* 金史論稿. Jilin: Jilin Wenshi, 1986.

Zhang Guogang 張國剛. *Jiating shihua* 家庭史話. Beijing: Shehui Kexue Wenxian, 2012.

Zhang Li 張麗. "Ming Qing funü shenghuo yu fojiao xinyang" 明清婦女生活與佛教信仰. *Hunan Renwen Keji Xueyuan xuebao* 湖南人文科技學院學報 3 (2012): 47–51.

Zhang Mengzhu 張孟珠. "'Mai mou shao tou zui': cong 'yi qi wei huo' xianxiang kuitan Taiwan diceng shehui de nengdongxing (cong Qingling dao rishi chuqi)" "賣某少頭嘴": 從 "以妻為貨" 現象窺探台灣底層社會的能動性 (從清領到日治初期). *Wenhua yanjiu* 文化研究 25 (2017): 81–130.

———. *Qingdai diceng shehui "yi qi duo fu" xianxiang zhi yanjiu* 清代底層社會一妻多夫現象之研究. Taipei: Guoli Zhenghi Daxue lishi, 2013.

———. "Renshen anquan zhi you: Qingdai zhenjie de kunjing" 人身安全之憂: 清代貞潔實踐的困境. *Zhengda shicui* 正大史粹 10 (2006): 89–130.

Zhang Tao 張濤. "Bei kending de fouding—cong Qingshi Gao Lienü zhuan zhong zisha xianxiang kan Qingdai funü jingyu" 被肯定的否定—從清史稿列女傳中的婦女自殺現象看清代婦女境遇. *Qingshi yanjiu* 清史研究 3 (2001): 40–49.

Zhang Tiansheng 張田生. "Nüxing bingzhe yu nanxing yijia—Qingdai lijiao wenhua zhong de nüxing yinji yingdui" 女性病者與男性醫家—清代禮教文化中的女性隱疾應對. *Ziran kexueshi yanjiu* 自然科學史研究 2 (2014): 188–200.

Zhang Wenlu 張文祿. "Ming Qing shiqi Wanbei nüzi xiaoxing yanjiu—yi Guangxu Shouzhou zhi, Suzhou zhi he Bozhou zhi wei kaocha duixiang" 明清時期皖北女子孝行研究—以光緒 "壽州志," "宿州志" 和 "亳州志" 為考察對象. *Liupanshui Shifan Xueyuan xuebao* 六盤水師範學院學報 30, no. 2 (2018): 61–65.

———. "Ming Qing Wanbei funü gegu liaoqin yuanyin tanlun" 明清皖北婦女割股料親原因探論. *Anhui Guangbo Dianshi Daxue xuebao* 安徽廣播電視大學學報 3 (2015): 105–8.

Zhang Xiaobei 張曉蓓. *Qingdai hunyin zhidu yanjiu* 清代婚姻制度研究. Chengdu: Sichuan Daxue Chubanshe, 2001.

Zhang Yuzhen 張育甄. "Gui zhong hanmo: Ming Qing Jiangnan cainü de cixiu wenhua" 閨中翰墨: 明清江南才女的刺繡文化. MA thesis, National Taiwan Normal University, 2011.

Zhang Zhijuan 張志娟. "Ming Qing Jin shang jiazu zhong de funü shenghuo kuitan" 明清晉商家族中的婦女生活窺探. *Heilongjiang shizhi* 黑龍江史志 10 (2013): 47–49.

Zhao Er 趙爾 et al. *Qingshi gao* 清史稿, annotated by Qi Gong 啟功 et al. Beijing: Zhonghua, 1976–1977.

Zhao Mingyang 趙明暘. "Tangdai hunyin fengsu de qianhouqi chayi" 唐代婚姻風俗的前後期差異. *Anqing Shifan Xueyuan xuebao* 安慶師範學院學報 35, no. 2 (2016): 55–58, 63.

Zheng Zhenyi 鄭真義. "Qianxi Jia Baoyu de shenjingzheng renge" 淺析賈寶玉的神經症人格. *Jiaying Daxue xuebao* 嘉應大學學報 35 (1995): 36–37.

Zhong Huiling 鍾慧玲. *Qingdai nüshiren yanjiu* 清代女詩人研究. Taipei: Liren shuju, 2000.

Zhong Jinlan 種晉蘭. "Kejia funü yu shenming chongbai—yi Ming Qing simiao beike jizai wei zhongxin de fenxi" 客家婦女與神明崇拜—以明清寺廟碑刻記載為中心的分析. *Jiaying Xueyuan xuebao* 嘉應學院學報 30, no. 4 (2012): 13–18.

Zhou Hong 周虹. *Manzu funü shenghuo yu minsu wenhua yanjiu* 满族婦女生活與民俗文化研究. Beijing: Zhongguo shehui kexue, 2005.

Zhou, Yiqun. *Festivals, Feasts, and Gender Relations in Ancient China and Greece*. Cambridge: Cambridge University Press, 2010.

Zhu Chun'e 祝春娥, Li Sifen 李四芬, Yao Juan 姚娟, and Long Juan 龍娟. "Tangdai funü xiaoxing tezheng: nü zhi xiao zhongyu fu zhi xiao" 唐代婦女孝行特徵: 女之孝重於婦之孝. *Hubei shehui kexue* 湖北社會科學 4 (2010): 112–14.

Zhu Huai 祝淮. *Xinxiu Xiangshan xianzhi* 新修香山縣誌. Taipei: Taiwan Xuesheng Shuju, 1968.

Zhu Ziyan 朱子彥. "Qingdai hougong zhidu lunshu" 清代後宮制度論述. In *Renwen yu shehui* 人文與社會, edited by Bao Zonghao 鮑宗豪 and Zhang Rongming 張榮明, vol. 2, 323–37. Shanghai: Shanghai Shehui Kexue Yuan Chubanshe, 2008.

Zito, Angela. "Secularizing the Pain of Footbinding in China: Missionary and Medical Stagings of the Universal Body." *Journal of the American Academy of Religion* 75, no. 1 (2007): 1–24.

Zurndorfer, Harriet T. "Cotton Textile Production in Jiangnan during the Ming-Qing Era and the Matter of Market Driven Growth." In *The Economy of Lower Yangzi Delta in Late Imperial China; Connecting Money, Markets, and Institutions*, edited by Billy K. L. So, 72–98. London: Routledge, 2013.

———. "Prostitutes and Courtesans in the Confucian Moral Universe of Late Ming China (1550–1644)." *International Review of Social History* 56 (2011): 197–216.

———. "Women in Chinese Learned Culture: Complexities, Exclusivities and Connecting Narratives." *Gender & History* 16, no. 1 (2014): 24–35.

Index

aborigine, xx, 137
abortion, 10–11, 113
actress, 60–61
adoption, 7
adultery, 26, 91, 95, 125
agency, xx–xxi, 34, 108, 116, 135
agriculture, x–xi, xvi, 45, 55–56
ancestor, xix, 10, 14–15, 18–19, 129
androgyny, 112–113
Anhui, 105
archery, 34

banner, xii, 2, 34, 40, 51
beauty, xiv, 17, 67, 69, 83, 111, 119, 122
Beijing, xiii, 37–39, 46, 92
betrothal gift, 3–4, 6, 8, 16, 31, 52, 54, 94–95, 138
blood, 114–115
body, 113–116
bondservant, xv, 32, 37, 44, 59, 62
bound feet. *See* footbinding
Boxer, 45–46, 48, 115, 132, 140
brideprice. *See* betrothal gift
Buddhism, 10, 18, 65, 71, 81, 83–87, 93, 102, 104, 113–114, 122, 131
Bumbutai, 34–36

Cai Runshi, 82
calligraphy, 65, 67, 71, 77
capitalism, 126, 139
Chai Jingyi, 33
Changzhou, 73
Chaoyi, 122
charity, xv, 19, 52, 131–132
Chen Susu, 91
cheongsam. *See qipao*
childbirth, 4, 12, 16, 114
Chongqing (empress dowager), 39
Christianity, xii, xviii, 11, 18–19, 124, 127, 129
Cixi, xxi, 38, 41–48, 128, 131, 140
clan. *See* lineage
clothing, 5, 24, 37, 40, 53, 57, 61, 62, 98, 115–116, 125, 134, 137
club, 78–79
concubine, 10, 15, 22, 27–32, 37–39, 52, 71, 77, 92–93, 113, 124–125, 138
contraception, 113
cooking, 25, 58, 65, 69
cotton, 56
courtesan, 18, 24, 59–63, 67, 73, 77, 98
cousin, 8

Dai, 137
dance, 61
Daoguang, xvii, 123
Daoism, 10, 18, 65, 83–85, 132
declension, ix, 124
disease, xii–xiv, 26–27, 44, 113
divination, 86
divorce, 26–27
Dong, 55
dowry, xx, 4–5, 10–11, 18–19, 25, 27, 32, 37, 40, 50–55, 77, 94, 137–138
Dream of the Red Chamber. *See Honglou meng*

embroidery. *See* textiles
empress, ix, xxi, 36–39, 41, 43–48
epitaph, 22, 24–25, 31, 66, 70
eunuch, 43–44
Europe, 61, 123–124, 130
exercise, 127, 139

faithful maiden, 102
famine, xii–xiii, xviii, 125
Fanhua meng, 113
feminism, ix, xx
filial piety, xv, 2–3, 10, 12, 18–19, 24, 26, 32, 39, 55, 71, 80, 103–105, 107, 109, 118, 129
footbinding, ix, xiii, xx, 29, 34, 46, 55–56, 66, 116–119, 124–125, 127
fox, 111
friend, 78
Fujian, 7, 18, 31, 54, 101, 106
funeral, 55, 103, 109
Fuqing, 106
Fuyang, 105

Gai Qi, 119–120
gambling, 50
Gaozu, 41
gazetteer, 65, 95–97, 103, 105–107
gentry, xv, 2, 4, 12, 15, 49, 62, 66–67, 69–70, 73, 77–78, 84, 89, 92, 97, 101–102, 136
ghost, 94
gift, 2
Gong (prince). *See* Yi Xin

gossip, 65
Great Britain, xi, xviii, 123, 131
Gu Chun, 80
Gu Taiqing, 80
Gu Yanwu, xiv
Gu Zhenli, 25, 121–122
Guangdong, 7–9, 15, 95
Guangxi, 79
Guangxu, 44–47
Guanyin, 84, 86, 113
Guizhou, 18
Gujin tushu jicheng, 95, 104–105
Gundai, 38

Hainan, 24
hair, xiii, 19, 61, 115–116, 122
Hakka, 56, 85, 116, 125
Hangzhou, 73, 79
Hao Yixing. *See* Langao
harem, 38–39
He Shuangqing, 25
He-Yin Zhen, 126
Hong Kong, xviii
Hong Taiji, 34
Hong Xiuquan, xviii, 125
Honglou meng, 72–73, 79, 112, 119
horse, 34, 37, 92, 122
Hua Mulan, 33
Huizhou, 19, 53, 67, 101, 106, 135
hunting, 34

incest, 1, 6
India, 86
infanticide, 11, 15, 27, 30, 32, 54
inheritance, ix, xx, 3, 14, 50–51, 77, 125, 138
insanity, 26

Japan, xix, 44–45, 47–48, 118, 128–129, 132, 138
jealousy, 22, 26–27, 29, 93
Jia Baoyu 112
Jiangnan, 56, 73, 83
Jiangsu, 62, 79
Jiaqing, xvii
Jimo, 96, 106
jinshi, 4–5, 31, 67, 79

Jurchen, xii, 6, 33–34, 37, 40, 58–59, 79, 92–93, 106, 108, 137

Kam, 55
Kang Youwei, 45, 126
Kangxi, x, xv–xvii, 36, 38, 41, 108–109
knight errant, 18, 33, 111

Langao, 24
lesbianism, 9–10
letter, 75–77
Lévi-Strauss, Claude, 135
levirate, 6, 54, 93, 137
Li Hongzhang, 44
Li Zicheng, xiii
Liang Hongyu, 33
Liang Qichao, 125–127
Lienü zhuan, 129
Lin Daiyu, 119, 121
Lin Yining, 103
lineage, xv, 12, 14–16, 51–52, 101, 136
Lingnan, 73
literacy, xvi, 28, 38, 65–66, 69–72, 75, 85, 127
Liu Xiang, 96
Longyu, 47
love, 24–25, 67, 83, 92, 108
Lü (empress), 41
Luo Qilan, 74

magazine, 129–130, 134, 139
magic, 46, 132
Marxism, 140
masculinity, 16
matchmaker, 58
matriarchy, 112
matricide, 38
matrilocal, 7
May Fourth Movement, 110
medical, 10, 58–59, 61, 85, 86, 90, 103–105, 113–114, 118
Meiji Restoration, 48
Mencius, 103
menstruation, 114–115
merchant, 22, 31, 49, 58, 62, 67, 89, 96, 124, 132, 135
Miao, 2, 55

Miaoshan, 86
missionary, xviii, 11, 18–19, 114, 117–118, 124, 127
Mongol, xii–xiii, 2, 6, 34, 40, 51, 54, 137
monogamy, xix, 6, 28
mother-in-law, 9
mourning, 21–22, 24, 27, 59, 103
Mulan, 33
murder, 11, 26, 38, 54, 82, 91, 106
music, 8, 30, 61–62, 71, 76, 81, 86, 91
mutilation, 10, 104–105, 116, 124

Naha, 42
Naitō Konan, ix
name, 1
Nanjing, xii, xviii
natal family, 27, 37, 103–104
natalocal, 8
Navarrete, Domingo, 92
Neo-Confucianism, x, xvi–xvii, xx, 2, 4, 21–22, 30, 51, 54, 73, 89, 112
Ningbo, 73
Nü lunyu, 71
Nü sishu, 71, 129
Nü Wa, 84
Nü xiaojing, 104
nun, 18, 73, 83, 86, 122
Nurhachi, 34, 38

opium, 131
Opium Wars, xi, xviii, 124, 131, 138
orphan, 7, 11, 19, 107, 127

painting, 19, 39, 65–67, 69, 71, 74, 76–77, 81, 118–119
palace, 37–39, 45
Pang Buyan, 24
patrilineal, 15, 51, 91, 97
patrilocal, 7
Pingpu, 137
poetry, xxi, 30, 33, 58–59, 62, 65–67, 69, 71–72, 74–82, 90, 108, 128, 130–131, 132
pollution, 114–115
polyandry, 27–29, 138
polygyny, 1, 26–27, 34, 37
pregnancy, 114–115

princess, 1, 39–40
property, 49–53, 59, 94–95, 101–102
prostitute, 2, 28–29, 32, 59–61, 92, 108, 115, 124–125, 138
Puyi, 47

Qian Fenglun, 72
qian kun, 111
Qianlong, x, xv–xvi, 39–40, 108
Qinghai, 106
Qingshi gao, 106, 109
Qingshui, 55
qipao, 115
Qiu Jin, 132–134

rape, xiii–xiv, 81, 91–92, 96, 101, 104, 106–107, 109
regent, 34, 36, 43
remarriage, xx, 6–7, 15, 22, 27, 52, 54, 93–94, 97, 99–101, 104, 106, 138
rites, xix, 12, 15, 21, 25, 27, 50, 52, 70, 89, 102, 137
romance. *See* love

Sanshui, 95
school, 127–128, 134, 139
seclusion, ix, 53, 55, 57–58, 66, 70, 72–74, 77, 83, 86–87, 89–92, 98, 101, 107, 115–117, 124
servant, 10, 31–32, 37, 59, 82, 92, 106, 125
sex, 16, 18, 26, 28, 36–37, 61, 63, 91–93, 95, 102, 107, 125
Shaanxi, 3
shaman, 58, 85, 114
shame, 15
Shandong, 96, 106
Shanghai, 62–63, 129
Shen Shanbao, 131
Shishuo xinyu, 112
shrew, 93
Shun dynasty, xiii
Shunzhi, xiii–xiv, 36
Sino-Japanese War, xix
spinning. *See* textiles
suicide, 26, 81, 101, 105–110, 124
Suzhou, 95

Taiping, xii, xviii–xix, 125, 138
Taiwan, xvi, xx, 7–8, 31, 44, 50, 54, 101, 118
tanci, 76–77
tenant, xv
textiles, ix, 9, 18–19, 25, 56–58, 65–66, 69, 81, 91, 98, 115–118, 128, 132
Tibet, xiii, 137
Tokyo, 129, 132
Tongren, 106–107
Tongzhi, 43–44
travel, 5, 39, 67, 74, 81, 83–84, 89, 130

Uighur, 137
United States, 130
uterine family, 9

vagina, 114
violence, 25, 27, 33, 125, 134, 138
virgin, 6, 18–19, 29, 46, 50, 85

Wang Duan, 78
Wang Duanshu, 75
Wang Xun, 98
Wang Yun, 91, 113
Wang Zhaoyuan, 24
warrior, 33–34, 46, 131, 134
weaving. *See* textiles
Wei Yizhen, 79
White Lotus, xviii, 85, 123, 138
widow, xx, 3, 6–7, 15, 22, 24, 46, 50–54, 77–78, 85, 93–102, 104, 106–109, 122, 124, 127, 131, 135–138
will, 50
work, ix, xix–xxi, 6, 8–9, 18–19, 25, 55, 58, 69, 90, 92, 98, 116–118, 122, 125–128, 132, 139
Wu Qi, 68–69
Wu Sangui, xiii
Wu Zetian, 36, 41–42
Wufeng, 31
Wushengmu, 84

Xi Peilan, 119, 121
Xia Jingqu, 130
Xianfeng, 43–44
Xiangshan, 95–96

Xiaojing, 71, 105
Xiaozhuangwen, 34–36
Xinjiang, xvi, 44
Xu Zihua, 118

Yangzhou, xiii–xiv, 91, 106
Yesou puyuan, 130
Yi, 39
Yi Xin, 43
Yijing, 72, 111
yin yang, 111, 114
Yingzhou, 105

Yongzheng, x, xv–xvi, 39, 59, 108–109
Yuan Mei, 79
Yuanduan, 86
Yunnan, xvi, 96

Zhang Xuecheng, 75
Zhejiang, 79
Zhen (empress), 43–44
Zhu Yuanzhang, 36
Zhu Xi, xvii, 21, 54, 73
Zhuang, 79

ASIAN VOICES
An Asia/Pacific/Perspectives Series
Series Editor: Mark Selden

Identity and Resistance in Okinawa
  by Matthew Allen
Tales of Tibet: Sky Burials, Prayer Wheels, and Wind Horses
  edited and translated by Herbert J. Batt, foreword by Tsering Shakya
Tiananmen Moon: Inside the Chinese Student Uprising of 1989, Twenty-fifth Anniversary Edition
  by Philip J. Cunningham
Voicing Concerns: Contemporary Chinese Critical Inquiry
  edited by Gloria Davies, conclusion by Geremie Barmé
The Subject of Gender: Daughters and Mothers in Urban China
  by Harriet Evans
Peasants, Rebels, Women, and Outcastes: The Underside of Modern Japan, Updated Second Edition
  by Mikiso Hane
Comfort Woman: A Filipina's Story of Prostitution and Slavery under the Japanese Military, Second Edition
  by Maria Rosa Henson, introduction by Yuki Tanaka, foreword by Cynthia Enloe
Women in Ancient China
  by Bret Hinsch
Women in Early Imperial China, Second Edition
  by Bret Hinsch
Women in Early Medieval China
  by Bret Hinsch
Women in Imperial China
  by Bret Hinsch
Women in Ming China
  by Bret Hinsch
Women in Song and Yuan China
  by Bret Hinsch
Women in Tang China
  by Bret Hinsch
Women in Qing China
  by Bret Hinsch
The Stories Clothes Tell: Voices of Working-Class Japan
  by Tatsuichi Horikiri, Translated by Rieko Wagoner
Japan's Past, Japan's Future: One Historian's Odyssey
  by Ienaga Saburō, translated and introduced by Richard H. Minear

I'm Married to Your Company! Everyday Voices of Japanese Women
    by Masako Itoh, edited by Nobuko Adachi and James Stanlaw
Sisters and Lovers: Women and Desire in Bali
    by Megan Jennaway
Moral Politics in a South Chinese Village: Responsibility, Reciprocity, and Resistance
    by Hok Bun Ku
Queer Japan from the Pacific War to the Internet Age
    by Mark McLelland
Behind the Silence: Chinese Voices on Abortion
    by Nie Jing-Bao
Rowing the Eternal Sea: The Life of a Minamata Fisherman
    by Oiwa Keibo, narrated by Ogata Masato, translated by Karen Colligan-Taylor
The Scars of War: Tokyo during World War II, Writings of Takeyama Michio
    edited and translated by Richard H. Minear
War and Conscience in Japan: Nambara Shigeru and the Asia-Pacific War
    edited and translated by Richard H. Minear
Growing Up Untouchable in India: A Dalit Autobiography
    by Vasant Moon, translated by Gail Omvedt, introduction by Eleanor Zelliot
Exodus to North Korea: Shadows from Japan's Cold War
    by Tessa Morris-Suzuki
Hiroshima: The Autobiography of Barefoot Gen
    by Nakazawa Keiji, edited and translated by Richard H. Minear
China Ink: The Changing Face of Chinese Journalism
    by Judy Polumbaum
Red Is Not the Only Color: Contemporary Chinese Fiction on Love and Sex between Women, Collected Stories
    edited by Patricia Sieber
Sweet and Sour: Life-Worlds of Taipei Women Entrepreneurs
    by Scott Simon
Dear General MacArthur: Letters from the Japanese during the American Occupation
    by Sodei Rinjirō, edited by John Junkerman, translated by Shizue Matsuda, foreword by John W. Dower
Unbroken Spirits: Nineteen Years in South Korea's Gulag
    by Suh Sung, translated by Jean Inglis, foreword by James Palais
Hidden Horrors: Japanese War Crimes in World War II, Second Edition
    by Yuki Tanaka
Zen Terror: The Death of Democracy in Prewar Japan
    by Brian A. Victoria

No Time for Dreams: Living in Burma under Military Rule
   by Carolyn Wakeman and San San Tin
A Thousand Miles of Dreams: The Journeys of Two Chinese Sisters
   by Sasha Su-Ling Welland
Dancing in Shadows: Sihanouk, the Khmer Rouge, and the United Nations in Cambodia
   by Benny Widyono
Voices Carry: Behind Bars and Backstage during China's Revolution and Reform
   by Ying Ruocheng and Claire Conceison

www.ingramcontent.com/pod-product-compliance
Lightning Source LLC
Chambersburg PA
CBHW051523230426
43668CB00012B/1712